GERMANY

LANGUAGE
SURVIVAL
GUIDE

HarperCollin

D0170445

HarperCollins Publishers
Westerhill Rd, Bishopbriggs, Glasgow, G64 2QT

www.**fire**and**water**.com

First published 2001

© HarperCollins Publishers, 2001

Reprint 10 9 8 7 6 5 4 3 2 1 0

ISBN 0 00 710162 7

Photography: Miroslav Imbrisevic/Brighteye Productions
    With additional photography/material from: Christine Bahr, Marianne
        Davidson & Gordon Noble, Hertie (Mainz), Hotel Dorint (Mainz),
        Opel-Bad (Wiesbaden)
        Artville (pp 89, 90, 91, 92, 93, 94, 95, 96, 97, 98, 99, 101, 102, 103)
        Anthony Blake (pp 75, 91[tl & mr], 92[tr], 93[mr], 95[br], 97[tr & br],
        98[bl], 99[tl], 101[tl], 102[tl, bl, mr] 103 [br], 105 [ml])
    Wine material: Andrea Gillies
    Map: Heather Moore
Layout: The Printer's Devil, Glasgow

Other titles in the Collins Language Survival Guide series:
    France (0 00 710161 9)
    Spain (0 00 710164 3)
    Italy (0 00 710163 5)
These titles are also published in a CD pack containing a 50-minute CD
and Language Survival Guide.

Printed in Italy by Amadeus SpA

CONTENTS

USEFUL WEBSITES

TOURIST INFORMATION SITES

Currency Converters
oanda.com
x-rates.com

Foreign Office Advice
fco.gov.uk/travel/countryadvice.asp

Passport Office
ukpa.gov.uk

Health Advice
thetraveldoctor.com
doh.gov.uk/traveladvice
doh.gov.uk/hat

Travel Insurance
insurance.org.uk

Pets
maff.gov.uk/animalh/quarantine

GERMAN SITES

Transport
bahn.de/ (National rail network)
thalys.com (Railways across Belgium, France, Holland & Germany)
www.mvv.de (Munich's integrated transport system)

Tourism
cyberwonders.com/germany.html (City profiles, travel guides, government & tourist resources)
germany-info.org
germany-tourism.de (German Tourist Board sites)
germany-tourism.net

www.berlin.de (All about Berlin)
www.koeln.de (All about Cologne)
www.muenchen.de (All about Munich)
www.hamburg.de (All about Hamburg)
mediaspec.com/castles/rhein (All about the Rhine castles)
era-ewv-ferp.org (Overview of walking possibilities)
bavaria.com (Information on Oktoberfest etc)
vacation-package.net/ (Rhine tours etc)

Hotels
urlaubstip.de/ (Accommodation by region, type)
eurohotel-online.de/hotels/ger
rhinecastles.com (Hotels in castles in Germany)

Shopping
buy-to-buy.de (German-language site)

Museums
icom.org/vlmp/germany.html (Official catalogue of the International Council of Museums for Germany)

Wine
wine.com
germanwine.de/english/

Internet cafes
netcafeguide.com
netcafes.com

INTRODUCTION

As technology sweeps across the world, travellers aren't just faced with the prospect of speaking a foreign language – they also have foreign machines to contend with. Machines for parking, for dispensing cash, for buying tickets and food. Often there is nobody about to ask how they work. *Collins Language Survival Guides* address this problem by showing photographically signs and situations you might come across.

The things that throw you are often the ones that look familiar – such as buses, trains or phones – but which operate slightly differently.

There are usually codes to how things operate and though you might not think you are aware of them, you are probably using them everyday: the colour-coding for roads (blue for motorways, green for major roads, yellow for temporary signs) or when buying milk (generally blue for whole milk, green for semi-skimmed and red for skimmed). It's when these familiar codes don't work in the same way, that you feel slightly at a loss and probably more unsure than you need be. By making a note of how these types of things work and knowing a few keywords, you will feel much more confident.

The unique combination of practical information, photos and phrases found in this book provides the key to hassle-free travel and the colour-coding below shows how information is presented and how to access it as quickly as possible.

General, practical information which will provide useful tips on getting the best out of your trip

keywords ◀

keywords	
rechts	these are words that are useful to know both
rekhts	when you see them written down or you
right	hear them spoken
links	
links	
left	

key talk ▶

short, simple phrases that you can change and adapt to suit your own situation

excuse me!	**can you help me**
entschuldigen Sie!	können Sie mir helfen?
entshool-di-gen zee	*kur'-nen zee meer hel-fen*
do you know where ...?	
wissen Sie, wo ...?	
vis-sen zee voh ...	

talking

The **Food Section** allows you to choose more easily from what is on offer both for snacks and at restaurants.

The practical 5000-word English–German, German–English **Dictionary** means that you will never be stuck for words.

SPEAKING GERMAN

We've tried to make the pronunciation under the phrases as clear as possible. We've split up words to make them easy to read, but don't pause too long between the syllables. German is not all that hard to pronounce and once you get the hang of unfamiliar letters or letter combinations, you should find yourself reading straight from the German phrases.

You'll notice some differences in the way the language is written. The most obvious is that all nouns begin with capital letters, eg table becomes **Tisch**. There is also a letter which doesn't exist in English – **ß** – as for instance in **Fuß** which is like **ss**.

Most letters are pronounced in much the same way as their English equivalents. However, when they appear at the end of a word **b** is pronounced like **p** (**halb** *halp*), **d** like **t** (**Hand** *hant*), and **g** like **k** (**Betrag** *be-trahk*); and in general **v** is pronounced like **f** (**Vogel** *foh-gel*), except in words of non-German origin, where **v** is pronounced like **v** in English (**Vase** *vah-ze*).

The German **w** is also pronounced like **v** in English (**Wasser** *vasser*). **S** is pronounced like **sh** in **shock** before **p** (**Spiel** *shpeel*) and **t** (**Stein** *shtine*) when they are at the beginning of a word, and when it is combined with **ch** (**Schule** *shoo-le*).

The umlaut ¨ often appears over German vowels, namely a (**Gaststätte** *gast-shte-te*), o (**Löffel** *lur'-fel*) and u (**süß** *zoos*), and makes a difference to the pronunciation. The two sounds, **ö** and **ü**, are rather different from anything in English. We show **ö** as *ur'* because the nearest sound to it is in English words like hurt, but don't roll the **r**! The sound of **ü** can be made if you purse your lips and try to say **ee**. We give this sound as **oo** in the pronunciation.

A final **e** is always pronounced, and sounds like **a** in sof**a** or **e** in Porsch**e**. So German **bitte** sounds like English bitter.

The syllable to be stressed is the one in *heavy type*.

Here are a few other rules to be aware of:

german	sounds like	example	pronunciation
au	*ow*	**Auto**	**ow**-*to*
äu	*oy*	**Säule**	**zoy**-*le*
ch	*kh*	**ich**	*ikh*
ei	*eye*	**ein**	*ine*
ie	*ee*	**sie**	*zee*
eu	*oy*	**neun**	*noyn*

EVERYDAY TALK

*There are two forms of address in German, formal (**Sie**) and informal (**du**). You should always stick with the formal until you are invited to use the informal. For the purposes of this book, we will use the formal.*

yes
ja
ya

no
nein
nine

ok/that's fine
okay
okay

please
bitte
bi-te

thank you
danke
dang-ke

thanks very much
danke vielmals
dang-ke feel-mals

don't mention it
bitte
bi-te

that's very kind
das ist sehr freundlich
das ist zehr froynt-likh

hello
guten Tag
gooten tahk

goodbye
auf Wiedersehen
owf vee-der-zayn

good evening
guten Abend
gooten ahbent

good night
gute Nacht
goo-te nakht

see you later
bis später
bis shpayter

excuse me!
entschuldigen Sie!
entshool-di-gen zee

sorry!
Entschuldigung!
entshool-di-goong

I am sorry
das tut mir Leid
das toot meer lite

I don't understand
ich verstehe nicht
ikh fer-shtay-e nikht

I don't know
ich weiß nicht
ikh vice nikht

Addressing people

When Germans meet they generally shake hands. The words for Mr and Mrs are **Herr** and **Frau**. Note that **Fräulein** is no longer used for Miss as it sounds rather patronising. Between young people, you will almost immediately be addressed in the informal form. As a rule, note how people address you and mirror their approach. You could, for instance, be addressed by your first name but still in the formal form. Here are some informal phrases.

hi, Michael
hallo, Michael
hal-loh mikha-el

bye, Christine
tschüss, Christine
tshoos kris-tee-ne

see you later
bis später
bis shpayter

how's life?
wie gehts?
vee gayts

what's up
was gibts?
vas gipts

*The simplest way to ask for something in a shop or bar is by naming what you want and adding **bitte**.*

keywords keywords keywords

1	**eins**
	ines
2	**zwei**
	tsvy
3	**drei**
	dry
4	**vier**
	feer
5	**fünf**
	foonf
6	**sechs**
	zekhs
7	**sieben**
	zeeben
8	**acht**
	akht
9	**neun**
	noyn
10	**zehn**
	tsayn

a ... please
einen/eine/ein ... bitte
*ine-en/ine-e/ine ... **bi**-te*

a coffee please
einen Kaffee bitte
*ine-en ka**fay bi**-te*

a beer please
ein Bier bitte
*ine beer **bi**-te*

a lemonade and 2 beers please
eine Limonade und zwei Bier bitte
*ine-e leemo-**nah**-de oont tsvy beer **bi**-te*

the ... please
der/die/das ... bitte
*der/dee/das ... **bi**-te*

the menu please
die Speisekarte bitte
*dee **shpy**-ze-kar-te **bi**-te*

the bill please
zahlen bitte
***tsah**-len **bi**-te*

another/more ...
noch/mehr ...
nokh/mehr ...

more money
mehr Gelt
mehr gelt

another beer
noch ein Bier
nokh ine beer

another tea
noch einen Tee
*nokh **i**ne-en tay*

2 more beers
noch zwei Bier
nokh tsvy beer

2 more coffees
noch zwei Kaffee
*nokh tsvy ka**fay***

3 tickets
drei Tickets
dry tickets

4 ice creams
vier Eis
feer ice

To catch someone's attention

In a shop or bar you would attract the attention of the assistant or waiter with ***bitte***. If you want to attract someone's attention in the street, for example, to ask directions, you would say *entschuldigen Sie!* When you ask the way to somewhere you use either *zum* (with *der/das* nouns), *zur* (with *die* nouns) or *nach* (with place names).

excuse me!
entschuldigen Sie!
*ent**shool**-di-gen zee*

can you help me?
können Sie mir helfen?
***kur'**-nen zee meer hel-fen*

do you know where ... is?
wissen Sie, wo ... ist?
***vis**-sen zee voh ... ist*

do you know how I get to... ?
wissen Sie, wie ich zum/zur/nach ... komme?
***vis**-sen zee vee ikh tsoom/tsoor/nakh ...**kom**me*

*By combining key words and phrases you can build up your
language and adapt the phrases to suit your own situation.*

haben Sie ...? **do you have ...?**	**do you have a map?** haben Sie eine Karte? *hah-ben zee ine-e kar-te*	**do you have a room?** haben Sie ein Zimmer? *hah-ben zee ine tsimmer*
was kostet es? **how much?**	**how much is the ticket?** was kostet das Ticket? *vas kostet das ticket*	**how much is the film?** was kostet der Film? *vas kostet der film*
ich möchte ... **I'd like ...**	**I'd like a red wine** ich möchte einen Rotwein *ikh mur'kh-te ine-en rohtvine*	**I'd like an ice-cream** ich möchte ein Eis *ikh mur'kh-te ine ice*
ich brauche ... **I need ...**	**I need a taxi** ich brauche ein Taxi *ikh brow-khe ine taxi*	**I need a receipt** ich brauche eine Quittung *ikh brow-khe ine-e kvi-toong*
wann? **when?**	**when does it open?** wann macht es auf? *van makht es owf*	**when does it close?** wann macht es zu? *van makht es tsoo*
	when does it leave? wann fährt es ab? *van fayrt es ap*	**when does it arrive?** wann kommt es an? *van komt es an*
wo? **where?**	**where is the bank?** wo ist die Bank? *voh ist dee bank*	**where is the hotel?** wo ist das Hotel? *voh ist das ho-tel*
gibt es? **is there?**	**is there a market?** gibt es einen Markt? *gipt es ine-en markt*	**where is there a market?** wo gibt es einen Markt? *voh gipt es ine-en markt*
es gibt kein ... **there is no ...**	**there is no bread** es gibt kein Brot *es gipt kine broht*	**is there no train?** gibt es keinen Zug? *gipt es kine-en tsook*
kann ich ...? **can I ...?**	**can I smoke?** kann ich rauchen? *kan ikh row-khen*	**can I go by train?** kann ich mit dem Zug fahren? *kan ikh mit dem tsook fah-ren*
	where can I buy milk? wo kann ich Milch kaufen? *voh kan ikh milkh kowfen*	**where can I hire...?** wo kann ich ... mieten? *voh kan ikh ... meeten?*
ist es ...? **is it ...?**	**is it near?** ist es nah? *ist es nah*	**is it far?** ist es weit? *ist es vite*
ich mag ... **I like ...**	**I like red wine** ich mag Rotwein *ikh mahk rohtvine*	**I don't like cheese** ich mag keinen Käse *ikh mahk kine-en kay-ze*

These are a selection of small but very useful words to know.

keywords keywords keywords keywords keywords

groß
grohs
large

klein
kline
small

ein bisschen
ine bis-khen
a little

genug
genook
enough

nächste
naykh-ste
nearest

weit
vite
far

zu teuer
tsoo toy-er
too expensive

und
oont
and

mit/ohne
mit/oh-ne
with/without

für
foor
for

mein
mine
my

das hier/das dort
das heer/das dort
this one/that one

sofort
zo-fort
straightaway

später
shpayter
later

a large car
ein großes Auto
ine groh-ses owto

a small portion
eine kleine Portion
ine kline-e port-syon

a little please
ein bisschen bitte
ine bis-khen bi-te

that's enough thanks
das ist genug danke
das ist genook dang-ke

where is the nearest chemist?
wo ist die nächste Drogerie?
voh ist die naykh-ste dro-ge-ree

it is too expensive
es ist zu teuer
es ist tsoo toy-er

it is too small
es ist zu klein
es ist tsoo kline

is it full?
ist es voll?
ist es foll

is it free?
ist es frei?
ist es fray

a tea and a coffee
einen Tee und einen Kaffee
ine-en tay oont ine-en kafay

with sugar
mit Zucker
mit tsoo-ker

with cream
mit Sahne
mit zah-ne

without sugar
ohne Zucker
oh-ne tsoo-ker

without cream
ohne Sahne
oh-ne zah-ne

for me
für mich
foor mikh

for her/for him
für sie/für ihn
foor zee/foor een

my passport
mein Pass
mine pass

my keys
meine Schlüssel
mine-e shloo-sel

I'd like this one
ich möchte das hier
ikh mur'kh-te das heer

I'd like that one
ich möchte das dort
ikh mu'rkh-te das dort

I need a taxi straightaway
ich brauche sofort ein Taxi
ikh brow-khe zo-fort ine taxi

is it far?
ist es weit?
ist es vite

I'll call you later
ich rufe Sie später an
ikh roo-fe zee shpayter an

It is always good to be able to say a few words about yourself to break the ice, even if you won't be able to tell your life story.

my name is ...
mein Name ist ...
*mine **nah**-me ist ...*

I am from ...
ich komme aus ...
*ikh **komm**e ows ...*

I am on holiday
ich bin im Urlaub
*ikh bin im **oor**-lowp*

I am on business
ich bin geschäftlich hier
*ikh bin ge-**sheft**-likh heer*

I am single
ich bin alleinstehend
*ikh bin al-**line**-shteh-ent*

I am married
ich bin verheiratet
*ikh bin fer-**hey**-ra-tet*

I have a partner *(male)*
ich habe einen Lebenspartner
*ikh **hah**-be ine-en **lay**-bens-partner*

I have a partner *(female)*
ich habe eine Lebenspartnerin
*ikh **hah**-be ine-e **lay**-bens-partnerin*

I am a widow
ich bin Witwe
*ikh bin **veet**-ve*

I am a widower
ich bin Witwer
*ikh bin **veet**-ver*

I am divorced
ich bin geschieden
*ikh bin ge-**shee**-den*

I am separated
ich lebe getrennt
*ikh **lay**-be ge-**trennt***

I have a child
ich habe ein Kind
*ikh **hah**-be ine kint*

I have ... children
ich habe ... Kinder
*ikh **hah**-be ... **kin**-der*

I work
ich arbeite
*ikh **ar**-by-te*

I am retired
ich bin im Ruhestand
*ikh bin im **roo**-he-shtant*

I am a student
ich bin Student
*ikh bin **shtoo**dent*

this is a beautiful country
diese Land ist sehr schön
***dee**-zes lant ist zehr shur'n*

I love your food
ich mag das Essen hier
*ikh makh das **es**-sen heer*

people are very kind
die Menschen sind sehr freundlich
*dee **men**-shen zint zehr **froynt**-likh*

I look forward to coming back
ich werde gern wieder kommen
*ikh **ver**-de gern **vee**-der **kom**men*

thank you very much for your kindness
vielen Dank, Sie waren sehr freundlich
***fee**-len dank zee **vah**-ren zehr **froynt**-likh*

I have enjoyed myself very much
es hat mir sehr gut gefallen
*es hat meer zehr goot ge-**fal**-len*

we will be back
wir werden wieder kommen
*veer **ver**-den **vee**-der **kom**men*

please keep in touch
bitte melden Sie sich mal
*bi-te **mel**-den zee zikh mal*

can I have your address?
kann ich ihre Adresse haben?
*kan ikh **ee**-re a-**dress**-e **hah**-ben*

Although problems are not something anyone wants, you might come across the odd difficulty, and it is best to be armed with a few phrases to cope with the situation.

excuse me!
entschuldigen Sie!
*ent**shool**-di-gen zee*

can you help me?
können Sie mir helfen?
***kur'**-nen zee meer **hel**-fen*

I don't speak ...
ich spreche kein ...
*ikh **shpre**-khe kine ...*

I am sorry, I did not know
Entschuldigung, das wusste ich nicht
*ent**shool**-di-goong das **voos**-te ikh nikht*

I am lost (in car)
ich habe mich verfahren
*ikh **hah**-be mikh fer-**fah**ren*

we are lost (on foot)
wir haben uns verlaufen
*veer **hah**-ben oons fer-**low**fen*

I have lost ...
ich habe ... verloren
*ikh **hah**-be ... fer-**loh**ren*

my money
mein Geld
mine gelt

my tickets
meine Tickets
mine-e tickets

my passport
meinen Pass
mine-en pass

I have left ...
ich habe ... vergessen
*ikh **hah**-be ... fer-**ges**sen*

in the restaurant
im Restaurant
*im restoh-**rong***

on the train
im Zug
im tsook

I have missed ...
ich habe ... verpasst
*ikh **hah**-be ... fer-**past***

my flight
meinen Flug
mine-en flook

the train
den Zug
den tsook

the coach
den Bus
den boos

I need to get to ...
ich muss nach ...
ikh moos nakh ...

how can I get there today?
wie komme ich heute noch dorthin?
*vee **kom**me ikh **hoy**-te nokh dort-**hin***

my luggage hasn't arrived
mein Gepäck ist nicht angekommen
*mine ge-**pek** ist nikht **an**-ge-kommen*

my case has been damaged
mein Koffer ist beschädigt worden
*mine **kof**-fer ist be-**shay**-dikht **vor**den*

my bag ...
meine Handtasche ...
*mine-e **hant**-ta-she ...*

my purse ...
mein Portemonnaie ...
*mine port-moh-**nay** ...*

my wallet ...
meine Brieftasche ...
*mine-e **breef**-ta-she ...*

... has been stolen
... ist gestohlen worden
*... ist ge-**shtoh**-len **vor**den*

please send my case to this address
bitte schicken Sie meinen Koffer an diese Adresse
*bi-te **shi**-ken zee mine-en **kof**-fer an **dee**-ze adres-se*

I need to go to hospital
ich muss ins Krankenhaus
*ikh moos ins **kran**ken-hows*

I have no money
ich habe kein Geld
*ikh **hah**-be kine gelt*

I can't find my child
ich kann mein Kind nicht finden
*ikh kan mine kint nikht **fin**-den*

go away!
hau ab!
how ap

that man is following me
dieser Mann folgt mir
***dee**-zer man folgt meer*

Germans expect to receive good service and quality. They will complain when things are not to their liking.

there is no ...
es gibt kein/keine ...
es gipt kine/kine-e ...

there is no soap
es gibt keine Seife
es gipt kine-e zay-fe

it is dirty
es ist schmutzig
es ist shmootsik

they are dirty
sie sind schmutzig
zee zint shmootsik

it is broken
es ist kaputt
es ist ka-putt

they are broken
sie sind kaputt
zee zint ka-putt

the ... does not work
der/die/das ... funktioniert nicht
der/dee/das ...foonk-tsyo-neert nikht

the ... do not work
die ... funktionieren nicht
dee ... foonk-tsyo-neeren nikht

the window doesn't open
das Fenster lässt sich nicht öffnen
das fens-ter lesst sikh nikht ur'f-nen

the window doesn't close
das Fenster lässt sich nicht schließen
das fens-ter lesst sikh nikht shlee-sen

the room is noisy
das Zimmer ist laut
das tsimmer ist lowt

the room is too small
das Zimmer ist zu klein
das tsimmer ist tsoo kline

the room is too hot
das Zimmer ist zu warm
das tsimmer ist tsoo varm

the room is too cold
das Zimmer ist zu kalt
das tsimmer ist tsoo kalt

it is too expensive
es ist zu teuer
es ist tsoo toy-er

you are charging too much
Sie verlangen zu viel
zee fer-langen tsoo veel

I want to complain
ich möchte mich beschweren
ikh mur'kh-te mikh be-shveh-ren

where is the manager?
wo ist der Manager?
voh ist der manager

we want to order
wir möchten bestellen
veer mur'kh-ten be-shtellen

the service is very bad
der Service ist sehr schlecht
der service ist zehr shlekht

this food is cold
das Essen ist kalt
das es-sen ist kalt

this coffee is cold
dieser Kaffee ist kalt
dee-zer kafay ist kalt

this isn't what I ordered
das habe ich nicht bestellt
das hah-be ikh nikht be-shtelt

please take it off the bill
bitte nehmen Sie das von der Rechnung
bi-te nay-men zee das fon der rekh-noong

there is a mistake
hier liegt ein Fehler vor
heer ligt ine fay-ler for

please check the bill
bitte überprüfen Sie die Rechnung
bi-te oober-proofen zee dee rekh-noong

The next four pages should give you an idea of the type of things you will come across in Germany.

◀ **OPEN**

CLOSED

PUSH

PULL

PRESS HERE FOR INFORMATION

Kasse→

CASH DESK/PAY HERE

OPENING ▶ HOURS

Geschäftszeiten:
Montag:	9.00 - 12.30	Uhr
Dienstag:	9.00 - 12.30	Uhr
Mittwoch:		Uhr
Donnerstag:	8.30-12.30	14.30-18.00 Uhr
Freitag:	8.30-12.30	14.30-18.00 Uhr
Samstag:	8.30-12.30	Uhr

Shops are open generally from 9 am–8 pm Mon–Fri and until 4 pm on Sat. Shops are shut on Sun except for tourist areas where they may open to sell holiday items. In smaller towns shops will close at 6 pm on weekdays and at 2 pm on Sat.

SNACK ▶ BAR

Germans are fond of snacks and there are numerous roadside stalls. There should be no worries over trying the food, as there are hygiene laws governing the operation of stalls.

LOTTERY TICKET ▶

There is one lottery draw on Sat night and two on Wed night. You have to mark 6 numbers out of 49. You can buy tickets where you see the sign *Lotto*.

do you have ...?	**stamps**	**phonecards**
haben Sie ...?	Briefmarken	Telefonkarten
hah-ben zee ...	***breef***-marken	taylay-***fon***-kar-ten
where can I get...?	**a travel card**	**a map**
wo kann ich ... bekommen?	Fahrscheine	eine Karte
voh kan ikh ... be-***kommen***	***fahr***-shy-ne	ine-e ***kar***-te

Ticket and paying ▶ machines are now more widespread.

PLEASE SELECT — Bitte wählen Sie

Kennzahl eingeben
ENTER CODE

zahlbar mit — **PAY WITH**
the panel shows coins and notes to use

Taste drücken **PRESS BUTTON**

CANCEL

Münzeinwurf — **INSERT COINS**
Storno

RECEIPT Quittung

◀ **CANCEL**
C is more common for cancel than Storno.
Korrektur

Postboxes are yellow. ▼

An airmail letter or postcard will usually arrive in Britain the third day after posting.

Automat gibt Rückgeld
CHANGE GIVEN

EINGANG
ENTRANCE
*(A vehicle entrance is marked **Einfahrt**)*

◀ **Ausgang**
EXIT
*(A vehicle exit is marked **Ausfahrt**)*

Außer Betrieb
OUT OF SERVICE

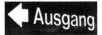

excuse me ...
entschuldigen Sie ...
*ent**shool**-di-gen zee ...*

what do I have to do?
was muss ich tun?
vas moos ikh toon?

how does this work?
wie funktioniert das?
*vee foonk-tsyo-**neert** das?*

what does this mean?
was bedeutet das?
*vas be-**doy**-tet das?*

talking

Alle Preise inkl. Bedienungsgeld und Mehrwertsteuer

ALL PRICES INCLUDE SERVICE AND VAT

Tipping in Germany is not compulsory and should be simply an appreciation of good service. You would tend to round your bill up to about 4 or 5 Marks more than the amount asked for.

Zutritt verboten

ENTRY PROHIBITED

Germans are generally very law- and rule-abiding. Jaywalking is frowned upon and you can even be fined for it. You will hardly see anybody dropping litter and people will not walk on lawns.

▶
Germans are very recycling-conscious and you must use the correct bin for your rubbish.

 ◀ Recycling symbol

biodegradable   paper   general   packaging
material   waste   carrying the
                                  recycling
                                  symbol (left)

NICHTRAUCHER-ZONE!
Bitte nehmen Sie Rücksicht auf die Nichtraucher
Danke für Ihr Verständnis

NO SMOKING ZONE

Smoking is not allowed in public buildings except in areas where ashtrays are provided. In most restaurants smoking will be allowed, only some have a dedicated non-smoking area.

t
a
l
k
i
n
g

can I smoke here?
kann ich hier rauchen?
*kan ikh heer **row**-khen*

I don't smoke
ich rauche nicht
*ikh **row**-khe nikht*

an ashtray please
einen Aschenbecher bitte
*ine-en **ash**en-**be**kher **bi**-te*

do you mind if I smoke?
stört es Sie, wenn ich rauche?
*shtur't es zee ven ikh **row**-khe*

please don't smoke
bitte rauchen Sie nicht
*bi-te **row**-khen zee nikht*

a non-smoking table please
einen Tisch in der Nichtraucherzone bitte
*ine-en tish in der **nikht**-rowkher-tsoh-ne **bi**-te*

There aren't very many public toilets around in Germany. Wherever you go, you will be expected to pay or at least leave a tip for the attendants. Check out shopping centres for toilets and some department stores will have them. In bigger cities, make for public buildings such as the railways station if you are looking for a toilet. You can also follow the city signpost system. In most petrol stations you will have to ask the attendant for the key to the toilet.

TREPPEN STAIRS TOILETTEN RESTROOMS

TOILETS

WC

Ladies and Gents are usually shown with a pictogram.

WC

GENTS ▶ **HERREN**

LADIES ▶ **DAMEN**

Heiß ◀ HOT

Kalt ◀ COLD

Trinkwasser

DRINKING WATER

Frei

FREE

Besetzt

OCCUPIED

excuse me! where is the toilet?
entschuldigen Sie! Wo ist die Toilette?
*ent**shool**-di-gen zee voh ist dee twa-**le**-te*

do you have the key for the toilet?
haben Sie den Schlüssel für die Toilette?
***hah**-ben zee den **shloo**-sel foor dee twa-**le**-te*

is there a disabled toilet?
gibt es hier eine Toilette für Behinderte?
*gipt es heer ine-e twa-**le**-te foor be-**hin**-derte*

is there a parent and child toilet?
gibt es hier eine Toilette für Mutter und Kind?
*gipt es heer ine-e twa-**le**-te foor **moot**-ter oont kint*

talking talking talking

 Newsagents, bookshops and kiosks sell **Stadtplan** – very handy street directories. You can ask for a free transport map when you buy your metro or bus tickets from stations or travel centres. Most cities will have maps of the centre displayed.

 townplan of Lübeck with surrounding area

Standort

YOU ARE HERE

4th edition
street index
with postcodes

RECHTS

RIGHT

LINKS

LEFT

Streetsigns are usually blue. They often have additional information on the person or even the event the street was named after.

talking talking talking

excuse me!
entschuldigen Sie!
ent**shool**-di-gen zee

do you know where ...?
wissen Sie, wo ...?
vis-sen zee voh ...

how do I get to ...?
wie komme ich zum/zur/nach ...
vee **kom**me ikh tsoom/tsoor/nakh ...

is this the right way to ...?
ist das hier richtig zum/zur/nach ...?
ist das heer **rikh**tikh tsoom/tsoor/nakh ...

do you have a map of the town?
haben Sie einen Stadtplan?
hah-ben zee ine-en **shtat**-plan

we're looking for ...
wir suchen ...
veer **zoo**khen ...

where is ...?
wo ist ...?
voh ist ...

is it far?
ist es weit?
ist es vite

a street directory
ein Straßenverzeichnis
ine **shtra**-sen-fer-tsykh-nis

can you show me on the map?
können Sie mir das auf der Karte zeigen?
kur'-nen zee meer das owf der **kar**-te **tsy**-gen

NO ENTRANCE *(on foot)*

NO EXIT *(on foot)*

Pedestrian city signs. Each city uses a different design and colour, and there is no set colour coding. ▼

St Stephan's with a window (Fenster) designed by Chagall —

old town —

cathedral —

Gutenberg museum —

boats on the Rhine —

weekly market Tue, Fri, Sat 7 am–2 pm —

On town road signs, local signs are in white
▼ and yellow signs are for out-of-town destinations.

out-of-town destination

town hall

police

pier

youth hostel

nach rechts
nakh rekhts
to the right

nach links
nakh links
to the left

geradeaus
grah-de-ows
straight ahead

gehen Sie
gay-en zee
go

biegen Sie ab
bee-gen zee ap
turn

Straße
shtra-se
road

Platz
plats
square

Ampel
am-pel
traffic lights

Kirche
kir-khe
church

erste
ers-te
first

zweite
tsvy-te
second

weit
vite
far

in der Nähe
in der nay-e
near

neben
ne-ben
next to

gegenüber
gay-gen-oober
opposite

bis
bis
until

keywords keywords keywords keywords

BANKS & MONEY

Germans use Eurocheque cards the way Switch cards are used in the UK and you will see the symbol at many cash dispensers. However, Eurocheque cards are now being withdrawn from the UK. If your bank card supports Maestro or Cirrus services, you will be able to use it in German cash dispensers. Otherwise most cash dispensers also accept credit cards. Credit cards are now becoming widely accepted and most purchases can be paid with them.

Öffnungszeiten

OPENING TIMES

Opening times may vary from bank to bank. Generally they resemble office hours rather than shop hours. Most banks open longer on Tuesdays and Thursdays.

Geldautomat

CASH DISPENSER

Most banks can be identified by the word *Bank* or *Sparkasse*. Among the big banks in Germany are *Sparkasse*, *Deutsche Bank* and *Dresdner Bank*.

Abbruch **CANCEL**

Korrektur **CORRECT/ERROR**

Bestätigung **ENTER**

Geldwechsel and *Reise Bank* both are **BUREAU DE CHANGE** ▼

Geldwechsel Change Cambio

Reise Bank

▼ Exchange rates

			Ankauf **WE BUY**	*Verkauf* **WE SELL**
			Ankauf	Verkauf
🇧🇪	Belgien	BEF	48.4838	48.4838
🏴	England	GBP	2.91	3.25
🇫🇷	Frankreich	FRF	29.8.164	29.8.164
🇬🇷	Griechenland	GRD	0.5	0.6508
🇮🇹	Italien	ITL	0.10.10.1	0.10.10.1

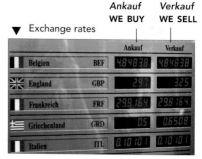

German money ▲
The German currency is the Mark (DM) which
breaks down into 100 Pfennigs (Pf).
Notes: 1,000, 500, 200, 100, 50, 20, 10 DM.
Coins: 1, 2, 5, 10, 50 Pf, 1, 2 & 5 DM
In January 2002 euro notes and coins (cents) will
come into circulation alongside DMs which will
then be withdrawn by the end of February 2002.

Gruppenaufenthalte		
Übernachtung / Frühstück	27,38 DM	**14,– €**
Halbpension	36,18 DM	**18,50 €**
Vollpension	42,05 DM	**21,50 €**

Price list showing DM and euros ▲
Note that the euros have been rounded (leaving the DM
price with odd figures). Generally a comma is used between
DM and Pf. A full point is used for thousands, i.e. 4.000,25.

where is there ...?
wo gibt es ...?
voh gipt es ...

a bank
eine Bank
ine-e bank

a bureau de change
eine Wechselstube
ine-e veksel-shtoo-be

where can I change money?
wo kann ich hier Geld wechseln?
voh kan ikh heer gelt vek-seln

I would like small notes
ich möchte kleine Scheine
ikh mur'kh-te kline-e shy-ne

where is the nearest cash dispenser?
wo ist der nächste Geldautomat?
voh ist der naykh-ste gelt-owto-maht

I want to change these travellers' cheques
ich möchte diese Reiseschecks einlösen
ikh mur'kh-te dee-ze ry-ze-sheks ine-lur'zen

the cash dispenser has swallowed my card
der Geldautomat hat meine Karte verschluckt
der gelt-owto-maht hat mine-e kar-te fer-shlookt

keywords keywords keywords

Kreditkarte
kre-deet-kar-te
credit card

Geldautomat
gelt-owto-maht
cash dispenser

PIN-Nummer
pin-noomer
pin number

Kleingeld
kline-gelt
change

einwerfen
ine-verfen
insert

Betrag eingeben
be-trahk ine-gay-ben
press amount

Banknoten
bank-no-ten
notes

Bargeld
bar-gelt
cash

Münze
moon-tse
coin

talking talking talking

WHEN IS...?

*The 24-hour clock is used in timetables. With the 24-hour clock, the words half (**halb**) and quarter (**Viertel**) are not used.*

keywords

Morgen
morgen
morning

Nachmittag
nakh-mitahk
afternoon

heute Abend
hoy-te ahbent
this evening

heute
hoy-te
today

morgen
morgen
tomorrow

gestern
gestern
yesterday

später
shpayter
later

sofort
zo-fort
straightaway

jetzt
yetst
now

um Viertel vor ...
*oom **feer**tel for ...*
at quarter to ...

um halb ...
oom halp ...
at half past ...

um null Uhr
oom nool oor

um dreiundzwanzig Uhr
*oom **dry**-oont-tsvan-tsikh oor*

um elf
oom elf

um zweiundzwanzig Uhr
*oom **tsvy**-oont-tsvan-tsikh oor*

um zehn
oom tsayn

um einundzwanzig Uhr
*oom **ine**-oont-tsvan-tsikh oor*

um neun
oom noyn

um zwanzig Uhr
*oom **tsvan**-tsikh oor*

um acht
oom akht

um neunzehn Uhr
*oom **noyn**-tsayn oor*

um sieben
*oom **zee**ben*

um achtzehn Uhr
*oom **akh**-tsayn oor*

um zwanzig vor ...
*oom **tsvan**-tsikh for ...*
at twenty to ...

talking

When is ...?	the next train	the next bus	the next boat
wann fährt ...?	der nächste Zug	der nächste Bus	das nächste Schiff
van fayrt ...	*der **naykh**-ste tsook*	*der **naykh**-ste boos*	*das **naykh**-ste shiff*

When is ...?	breakfast	lunch	dinner
wann ist ...?	Frühstück	Mittagessen	Abendessen
van ist ...	*froo-shtook*	*mitahk-es-sen*	*ahbent-es-sen*

When does it leave?
wann ist die Abfahrt?
*van ist dee **ap**-fahrt*

When does it arrive?
wann ist die Ankunft?
*van ist dee **an**-koonft*

When does it open?
wann wird geöffnet?
*van virt ge-**ur'f**net*

When does it close?
wann wird geschlossen?
*van virt ge-**shlos**-sen*

*Note that with **halb** Germans refer to the full hour to come not the past hour! For instance, **halb acht** actually means 7.30.*

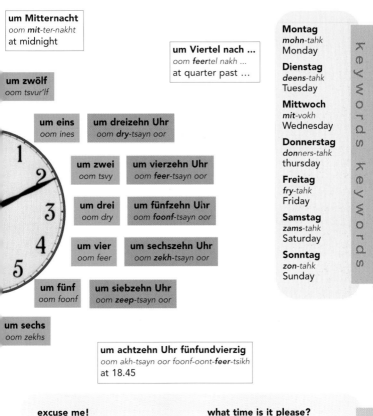

um Mitternacht
*oom **mit**-ter-nakht*
at midnight

um Viertel nach …
*oom **feer**tel nakh …*
at quarter past …

um zwölf
oom tsvur'lf

um eins
oom ines

um dreizehn Uhr
*oom **dry**-tsayn oor*

um zwei
oom tsvy

um vierzehn Uhr
*oom **feer**-tsayn oor*

um drei
oom dry

um fünfzehn Uhr
*oom **foonf**-tsayn oor*

um vier
oom feer

um sechszehn Uhr
*oom **zekh**-tsayn oor*

um fünf
oom foonf

um siebzehn Uhr
*oom **zeep**-tsayn oor*

um sechs
oom zekhs

um achtzehn Uhr fünfundvierzig
*oom **akh**-tsayn oor foonf-oont-**feer**-tsikh*
at 18.45

Montag
mohn-tahk
Monday

Dienstag
deens-tahk
Tuesday

Mittwoch
mit-vokh
Wednesday

Donnerstag
donners-tahk
thursday

Freitag
fry-tahk
Friday

Samstag
zams-tahk
Saturday

Sonntag
zon-tahk
Sunday

keywords keywords

excuse me!
entschuldigen Sie!
*ent**shool**-di-gen zee*

what time is it please?
wie spät ist es bitte?
*vee shpeht ist es **bi**-te*

what is the date?
der Wievielte ist heute?
*der vee-**feel**-te ist **hoy**-te*

it is the 8th May
heute ist der achte Mai
***hoy**-te ist der **akh**-te my*

16 September 2002
der sechzehnte September zweitausendzwei
*der **zekh**-tsayn-te sep-**tem**-ber **tsvy**-towzent-**tsvy***

which day?
welcher Tag?
***vel**-kher tahk*

which month?
welcher Monat?
***vel**-kher **moh**-nat*

talking

TIMETABLES

 Timetables use the 24-hour clock. Bus and train timetables usually change once a year in May. The German for timetable is **Fahrplan**.

Mo	*Mon*
Di	*Tues*
Mi	*Wed*
Do	*Thur*
Fr	*Fri*
Sa	*Sat*
So	*Sun*

TIMETABLE ▶
Make sure you are looking at the timetable for the right station, e.g. Frankfurt **Hbf** not Frankfurt **Flughafen** (airport – they are often shown next to each other).

Boat timetable ▼   *times & prices*

departure —
arrival —

Termine & Preise:
Abfahrt 19.30   Mainz-Fischtor
20.00   WI-Biebrich
Ankunft 23.00   WI-Biebrich
23.30   Mainz
Mi. 05. Juli, Mi 19. Juli,
Mi. 09. August und Mi. 30. August
DM 79,- inkl. 4-Gänge-Menü

— *79 DM incl. 4-course meal*

not a complete timetable (does not list all the trains on this route)

München Hbf
→ Chemnitz Hbf
Fahrplanauszug – Angaben ohne Gewähr –
Gültig von 28.05.2000 bis 09.06.2001

valid from   *until*

arrive at connecting station
departure   *change at*   *depart connecting station*
train   *arrive*
distance between points (tickets are calculated by km travelled)

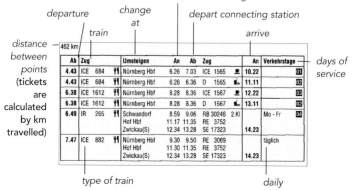

Ab	Zug		Umsteigen	An	Ab	Zug		An	Verkehrstage
			462 km						*days of service*
4.43	ICE	684 ¶¶	Nürnberg Hbf	6.26	7.03	ICE 1565	☎	10.22	01
4.43	ICE	684 ¶¶	Nürnberg Hbf	6.26	6.36	D 1565	🍴	11.11	02
6.38	ICE	1612 ¶¶	Nürnberg Hbf	8.28	8.36	ICE 1567	☎	12.22	03
6.38	ICE	1612 ¶¶	Nürnberg Hbf	8.28	8.36	D 1567	🍴	13.11	02
6.49	IR	265 ¶¶	Schwandorf	8.59	9.06	RB 30246 2.Kl			Mo - Fr 04
			Hof Hbf	11.17	11.35	RE 3752			
			Zwickau(S)	12.34	13.28	SE 17323		14.23	
7.47	ICE	882 ¶¶	Nürnberg Hbf	9.30	9.50	RE 3069			täglich
			Hof Hbf	11.30	11.35	RE 3752			
			Zwickau(S)	12.34	13.28	SE 17323		14.23	

type of train   *daily*

▼ Bus overhead-board

LINE   **DIRECTION**   *Abfahrt in Minuten*
departure in minutes

next services

Fahrplan
fahr-plan
timetable

Ab (Abfahrt)
ap-fahrt
departure

An (Ankunft)
an-koonft
arrival

umsteigen
oom-shtygen
change at

täglich
tehkh-likh
daily

nicht
nikht
no service

bis
bis
until

auch
owkh
also

gültig von
gooltikh fon
valid from

keywords keywords keywords

Detailed,
minute-by-
minute
timetables
like this are
usually found
at bus stops. ▶

Jan *Jan*
Feb *Feb*
März *March*
Apr *April*
Mai *May*
Jun *June*
Jul *July*
Aug *Aug*
Sep *Sep*
Okt *Oct*
Nov *Nov*
Dez *Dec*

do you have a timetable?
haben Sie einen Fahrplan?
hah-ben zee ine-en fahr-plan

can you explain the timetable?
können Sie mir den Fahrplan erklären?
kur'-nen zee meer den fahr-plan er-kleh-ren

talk

TICKETS

*Tickets for transport (bus, tram and train) are **Fahrkarten**. For entertainment or museum entry, etc, use simply **Karten** or **Tickets**.*

CHOOSE YOUR TICKET TYPE

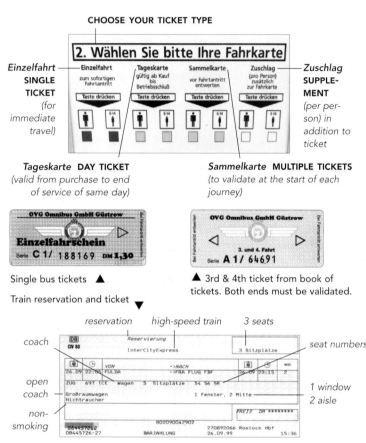

2. Wählen Sie bitte Ihre Fahrkarte

Einzelfahrt
SINGLE TICKET
(for immediate travel)

Einzelfahrt
zum sofortigen
Fahrtantritt
Taste drücken

Tageskarte
gültig ab Kauf
bis
Betriebsschluß
Taste drücken

Sammelkarte
vor Fahrtantritt
entwerten
Taste drücken

Zuschlag
(pro Person)
zusätzlich
zur Fahrkarte
Taste drücken

Zuschlag
SUPPLE-MENT
(per person) in addition to ticket

Tageskarte **DAY TICKET**
(valid from purchase to end of service of same day)

Sammelkarte **MULTIPLE TICKETS**
(to validate at the start of each journey)

OVG Omnibus GmbH Güstrow
Einzelfahrschein
Serie C 1/ 188169 DM 1,30

Single bus tickets ▲

OVG Omnibus GmbH Güstrow
◁ 3. und 4. Fahrt ▷
Serie A 1/ 64691

▲ 3rd & 4th ticket from book of tickets. Both ends must be validated.

Train reservation and ticket ▼

reservation   *high-speed train*   *3 seats*

coach

```
DB          Reservierung                        3 Sitzplätze
CIV 80      InterCityExpress
```
seat numbers

```
          VON          ->NACH
26.09 22:08 FULDA      ->FRA FLUG FBF      26.09 23:15  2
ZUG   697 ICE  Wagen  5  Sitzplätze  54 56 58
```

open coach

GroßraumWagen   1 Fenster, 2 Mitte
Nichtraucher

non-smoking

*1 window
2 aisle*

```
                       802090042902          PREIS DM ********
08445726
08445726-27   BARZAHLUNG    270892066 Rostock Hbf
                            26.09.99              15:36
```

single journey   *valid until*   *ticket*

```
DB EINFACHE FAHRT              FAHRSCHEIN    1  Erwachsene(r)
CIV 80  Gültig ab  Hinf.bis                 --  Kind(er)
        10.03.00   10.03.00
```

valid from

adult
child(ren)

```
          VON          ->NACH
          Rostock Hbf  ->Altefähr                     2
```

via

Über:
HST

class

price

```
Erm 50,0% BC(J)                           Preis DM ***10,10
          MWST D:  ***10,10 16,0% = ***1,39              12
4795451345                                               00
47554519-59   BARZAHLUNG    270892067 Rostock Hbf
                            10.03.00              19:49
```

reduction

*(reason)
Bahncard pass*

VAT

paid cash   *date*   *issuing station*

time issued

◀ The *Partner-Tageskarte* allows unlimited travel for a family or a group for a day.

unlimited travel in entire zone

valid from stamping until 6 am the following morning for 5 people. Two children (6–14 years old) count as one person

KARTEN HIER ERHÄLTLICH!

BUY YOUR TICKETS HERE!

Karten für die heutige Vorstellung

TICKETS FOR TODAY'S PERFORMANCE

Halber Preis für alle Senioren für Hin- und Rückfahrten bei Tagesfahrten am Montag und Mittwoch.

◀ Red text indicates that all seniors pay half price.

Red text indicates that children up to 5 go free, between 5 and 15, half-price. ▶

Junioren: bis 5 Jahre frei, bis 15 Jahre halber Preis, in den hessischen und rheinland-pfälzischen

Fahrkarte
fahr-kar-te
bus/metro ticket

Mehrfahrtenkarte
mehrfahrtenkar-te
book of tickets

Eintrittskarte
ine-tritts-kar-te
entry ticket

Pass
pass
travel card

einfach
ine-fakh
single

hin und zurück
hin oont tsoorook
return

Erwachsener
er-vak-se-ner
adult

Kind(er)
kind(er)
child(ren)

Student
shtoodent
student

Rentner
rent-ner
OAP

Behinderter
be-hin-der-ter
disabled

Familie
famee-lee-e
family

PUBLIC TRANSPORT

*Most German cities operate an integrated transport system which means that all the different kinds of transport are part of one network and you can use any of them with your ticket. You buy your ticket in advance (see **TICKETS**, p. 26). You validate your ticket in the validating machine when you get on board the bus or tram. With the **U-Bahn** and **S-Bahn** you validate your ticket on entering the station or platform. There are no ticket barriers. Most cities have a night service.*

Bus stop ▶
The ticket machine is located next to it.

Validator which you find on boarding the bus. ◀

▼ Bus tickets for sale

Fahrkarten **ESWE**

ESWE
Busfahrkarten

Bus stop ▶

(H)

bus stop location and zone

Memhardstraße   A

100 S+U-Bhf
     Zoolog. Garten

157 Mitte
     Bundeswehrkrkhs.

200 S+U Zool. Garten
     ü. Potsdamer Pl.

348 U-Bhf
     Breitenbachplatz

N58 S-Bhf
     Hackescher Markt

you can change onto **U-** or **S-Bahn**

DB

you can change onto long-distance rail network

N in front of a service number indicates it is a night service

Bus timetables are usually posted on the bus stop (see p. 25).

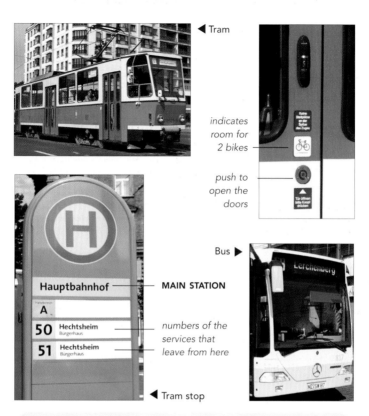

◀ Tram

indicates
room for
2 bikes

push to
open the
doors

Bus ▶

Hauptbahnhof — MAIN STATION

A

50 Hechtsheim
Burgerhaus

51 Hechtsheim
Burgerhaus

numbers of the
services that
leave from here

◀ Tram stop

where do I catch a bus to ...?
von wo fährt der Bus nach ...?
fon voh fayrt der boos nakh ...

which number goes to ...?
welche Linie fährt nach ...?
vel-khe lee-nee-e fayrt nakh ...

must I ring the bell to get off?
muss man das Aussteigen anmelden?
moos man das ows-shtygen an-mel-den

please tell me when to get off
bitte sagen Sie mir, wann ich aussteigen muss
bi-te zahgen zee meer van ikh ows-shtygen moos

excuse me, I'm getting off!
darf ich bitte vorbei?
darf ikh bi-te for-by

is there a bus to ...?
gibt es einen Bus nach ...?
gipt es ine-en boos nakh ...

does this bus go to ...?
fährt dieser Bus zum/zur/nach ...?
fayrt dee-zer boos tsoom/tsoor/nakh ...

which bus goes to the centre?
welcher Bus fährt ins Zentrum?
vel-kher boos fayrt ins tsentroom

what time is the next bus to ...?
wann fährt der nächste Bus nach ...?
van fayrt der naykh-ste boos nakh ...

talking talking talking

U is the sign for the metro (*U-Bahn*), *S* the sign for suburban trains (*S-Bahn*). Both are part of the integrated transport system of a city. Parts of the *U-Bahn* are overground. Lines can be identified by the *U* or *S* followed by the number.

indicates number of line and destination.

◀ Station sign showing that both *U-Bahn* and *S-Bahn* operate from there.

VALIDATE HERE

▶ Ticket validators are located at the entrance to stations.

▲ This sign shows which lines stop at the station. The lines are colour-coded.

If you are travelling to the ▶ airport, look out for this sign meaning airport transfer service.

STAND ON THE RIGHT, WALK ON THE LEFT ▼

Rechts stehen, Links gehen ◀

Overhead platform board ▼

hält in Frankfurt (M) Hbf
train stops at
Frankfurt Central Station

departure

*all of the
train is
going*
(the front
and rear
carriages
are not
separating)

The smaller board beside the main
destination board shows the train is going
via Mainz-Kastel and Frankfurt Airport.

*Offenbach Ost is
the final destination.*

a single
eine Einzelfahrkarte
*ine-e **ine**-tsel-fahr-kar-te*

a day ticket
eine Tageskarte
*ine-e **tah**ges-kar-te*

a group ticket
eine Gruppenkarte
*ine-e **groo**-pen-kar-te*

a book of tickets
eine Mehrfahrtenkarte
*ine-e **mehr**-fahrten-kar-te*

a weekly ticket
eine Wochenkarte
*ine-e **vo**-khen-kar-te*

a monthly ticket
eine Monatskarte
*ine-e **moh**-nats-kar-te*

have you a map of the U-Bahn?
haben Sie einen U-Bahn-Plan?
*hah-ben zee ine-en **oo**-bahn-plan*

where is the nearest U-Bahn station?
wo ist die nächste U-Bahn-Station?
*voh ist dee **naykh**-ste **oo**-bahn-shtah-**tsyohn***

I want to go to ...
Ich möchte zum/zur/nach ...
*ikh **mur'kh**-te tsoom/tsoor/nakh ...*

do I have to change?
muss ich umsteigen?
*moos ikh **oom**-shty-gen*

where?
wo?
voh

which line do I take?
welche Linie muss ich nehmen?
***vel**-khe **lee**-nee-e moos ikh **nay**-men*

in which direction?
in welche Richtung?
*in **vel**-khe **rikh**-toong*

which stop is it for ...?
wo ist die Haltestelle für ...?
*voh ist dee **hal**-te-shtel-le foor ...*

which station is it for ...?
welche Station muss ich für ... nehmen?
***vel**-khe shta-**tsyohn** moos ikh foor ... **nay**-men*

excuse me! I want to get off
entschuldigen Sie! Ich möchte aussteigen
*ent**shool**-di-gen zee ikh **mur'kh**-te **ows**-shty-gen*

talking talking talking talking

*Trains are an efficient way to get round the country and to cover long distances. You pay per kilometre, so getting a return fare doesn't reduce the price. Special reduced fares are available for children up to 11 years and young people up to 26 years. Children under 5 years travel free. There are special offers anybody can take advantage of, such as a special evening ticket, the **Guten-Abend-Ticket**, which allows you to travel as far as you can get between 7 pm and 3 am for a very cheap price. Another popular offer is the **Schönes-Wochenende-Ticket** where 5 people can travel for a whole day on one ticket (only valid at weekends and not valid on fast trains (**IR, IC, EC, ICE**). There are also saver and supersaver tickets, **Sparpreis** and **Supersparpreis**, for which special conditions and times of travel apply. Station staff will help you choose a ticket to meet your needs.*

ReiseZentrum

◀ Travel Centre for information and tickets. If you are not sure of what you want queue at the counter marked *Information*. If you know what you want go to the *Express-Schalter* where no information is given but service is faster.

TRAIN TICKETS
information
reservations
tickets for local transport

Fahrscheine
Information
Reservierungen
RMV-Fahrkarten

---

a single to ...
einmal einfach nach ...
ine-mal ine-fakh nakh ...

2 singles to ...
zweimal einfach nach ...
tsvy-mal ine-fakh nakh ...

a child's ticket
ein Kind
ine kint

first class
erste Klasse
er-ste kla-se

second class
zweite Klasse
tsvy-te kla-se

what special offers do you have?
was für Sonderangebote haben Sie?
vas foor zonder-an-ge-bo-te hah-ben zee

do I need a reservation?
muss ich eine Platzkarte kaufen?
moos ikh ine-e plats-kar-te kowfen

is there a supplement to pay?
muss man einen Zuschlag kaufen?
moos man ine-en tsoo-shlak kow-fen

do I have to change?
muss ich umsteigen?
moos ikh oom-shty-gen

I want to book...
ich möchte ... buchen
ikh mur'kh-te ... boo-khen

2 seats
zwei Sitzplätze
tsvy sits-plet-se

window seats
Fensterplätze
fenster-plet-se

a couchette
einen Liegewagenplatz
ine-en lee-ge-vah-gen-plats

smoking
Raucher
row-kher

non-smoking
Nichtraucher
nikht-row-kher

talking talking talking talking talking

type of train

Zuglauf
via

Hinweis
additional information

Zeit
time

Ziel
destination

Gleis
platform

▲ DEPARTURES

▲ TO THE TRAINS

GLEIS 2

▲ Platform number

You need a coin (1 or 2 DM) to operate the luggage trolley. ◀

Richtung ── DIRECTION

Heerstraße/Hausen

Information

Hinfahrt
hin-fahrt
single

Rückfahrt
rook-fahrt
return

Reservierung
ray-zer-vee-roong
reservation

Zuschlag
tsoo-shlak
supplement

besonderer Fahrpreis
be-zon-derer fahr-price
special rate

Ermäßigung
er-may-sigoong
reduction

Gang
gang
aisle

Fenster
fens-ter
window

Raucher
row-kher
smoking

Nichtraucher
nikht-row-kher
non-smoking

Schienenersatz-verkehr
sheenen-ersats-ferkehr
bus operates

the train to ...
der Zug nach ...
der tsook nakh ...

is this the train for ...?
ist das der Zug nach ...?
ist das der tsook nakh ...

which platform does it leave from?
von welchem Bahnsteig fährt er?
fon vel-khem bahn-shtike fayrt er ap

this is my seat
das ist mein Platz
das ist mine plats

talking

TAXI

i *There are dedicated taxi ranks at places such as stations.
You cannot hail a taxi in the street, you have to call a taxi
company. Numbers are displayed in phone boxes. You can tell
the taxi company your location by quoting the location of the
phone box which is written under the word* **Standort***.*

◄ Taxi sign in station

The number to call
for a taxi
▼

Taxi sign on car roof ▼

German taxis are beige.

where is the nearest taxi stand?
wo ist der nächste Taxistand?
*voh ist der **naykh**-ste **ta**xi-shtant*

to ... please
zum/zur/nach ... bitte
*tsoom/tsoor/nakh ... **bi**-te*

how much is it to ...?
wie viel kostet es zum/zur/nach ...?
*vee feel **kos**tet es tsoom/tsoor/nakh ...*

please order me a taxi
bitte bestellen Sie mir ein Taxi
***bi**-te be-**shtel**-len zee meer ine **ta**xi*

for now
für sofort
*foor zo-**fort***

for ...
für ...
foor ...

can I have a receipt
kann ich eine Quittung bekommen?
*kan ikh ine-e **kvi**-toong be-**kom**men*

keep the change
der Rest ist für Sie
der rest ist foor zee

is there a special rate for the airport?
gibt es einen besonderen Tarif zum Flughafen?
*gipt es ine-en be-**zon**-deren ta**reef** tsoom **flook**-hafen*

CAR HIRE

To hire a car in Germany you have to be over 18 years old and to have held a valid driving licence for at least 6 months. If you pay by credit card you won't have to leave a deposit (which is usually hefty). You can arrange car hire on the internet or through a UK branch of a car-hire company before your trip, so you will know exactly how much you have to pay. If you leave it until your arrival, there may be a more limited choice of cars available.

I want to hire a car
ich möchte ein Auto mieten
*ikh **mur'kh**-te ine **owto meeten***

for one day
für einen Tag
foor ine-en tahk

for ... days
für ... Tage
*foor ... **tah**-ge*

I want ...
ich möchte ...
*ikh **mur'kh**-te ...*

a small car
einen Kleinwagen
*ine-en **kline**-vahgen*

a large car
ein großes Auto
*ine **groh**-ses **owto***

a people carrier
einen Minivan
*ine-en **mini**-van*

an automatic
ein Auto mit Automatikgetriebe
*ine **owto** mit owto-**mah**-tik-ge-tree-be*

how much is it?
wie viel kostet es?
*vee feel **kos**tet es?*

is there a kilometre charge?
erheben Sie eine Kilometergebühr?
*er**hay**-ben zee ine-e keelo-**meh**ter-ge-**boor***

I am ... old
ich bin ... Jahre alt
*ikh bin ... **jah**-re alt*

here is my driving licence
hier ist mein Führerschein
*heer ist mine **fooh**-rer-shine*

what is included in the insurance?
was ist alles in der Versicherung inbegriffen?
*vas ist **al**-les in der fer-**zikh**eroong **in**-be-griffen*

how do the controls work?
wie funktionieren die Schalter?
*vee foonk-tsyo-**nee**-ren dee **shal**-ter*

where are the documents?
wo sind die Fahrzeugpapiere?
*voh zint dee fahr-tsoyk-pa**pee**-re*

what do we do if ...?
was tun wir bei ...?
vas toon veer by ...

we breakdown
einer Panne
*ine-er **pan**-ne*

have an accident
einem Unfall
*ine-em **oon**-fall*

can we hire a child-seat?
können wir einen Kindersitz mieten?
***kur'**-nen veer ine-en **kin**der-zits **mee**ten*

how is it fitted?
wie wird er montiert?
*vee virt er mon-**teert***

talking talking talking talking talking

German drivers stick to the rules but may not be too polite. Some driving rules are different and watch out for right of way from the right when no priority signs are displayed. Pedestrians always have the right of way, so take care when turning at traffic lights when you and the pedestrians can have a green light showing at the same time. Seatbelts are compulsory and you must carry in your car a first-aid kit, towing rope and warning triangle. Always carry your driving licence, car documents and passport when driving.

Speed restrictions

built up area	50 km/h
ordinary roads	100 km/h
motorway	no restriction,

but 130km/h is recommended and some sections will have speed restrictions

▲ German number plate
D on the blue panel is for *Deutschland*. The first 2 letters indicate which district the car is registered (WI = Wiesbaden).

▼ Colour-coded German road signs

München *motorways*

Germany has an extensive network of numbered motorways.

E 36 *European routes*

Green signs with E and a number indicate European routes.

Rostock *secondary roads*

Tourist and other information signs may also appear in yellow.

Rathaus *local destinations*

Where you see the sign below you must give way to the priority road. Drivers on the priority road must indicate when turning. Drivers on the top secondary road must yield to drivers on the bottom, as they are on their right.

Nord NORTH

WEST
West

Ost
EAST

SOUTH **Süd**

▲ Direction indicators

▼

DETOUR ▲

If no more detour signs are displayed, follow the priority road, as marked.

Restricted zone sign ▲
A 30km/h speed limit is in force. You only see the sign on entering the zone so you may be unaware that you are in a speed-restricted area. The enforcement ends at the end-of-zone sign. ▼

priority sign   The arrow indicates you can only go in this direction.

◀ **RED PHASE 5 MINS PLEASE TURN OFF ENGINES**

You should switch off your engine if you are stopped for some time (not at regular traffic lights, but at road works or level crossings). Watch what the people around you do.

we are going to ...
wir sind auf dem Weg nach ...
veer zint owf dem vehk nakh ...

which is the best route?
welche Route ist die beste?
vel-khe roo-te ist dee bes-te

is the road good?
ist die Straße gut?
ist dee shtra-se goot

can you show me on the map?
können Sie mir das auf der Karte zeigen?
kur'-nen zee meer das owf der kar-te tsy-gen

is the pass open?
ist der Pass geöffnet?
ist der pass ge-ur'fnet

do we need snow chains?
brauchen wir Schneeketten?
brow-khen veer shneh-ket-ten

talking

ONE-WAY STREET ▲

CITY CENTRE ▲

◀ German parking signs can be complicated. If in doubt, don't park!

the house numbers you find along this street

no waiting from this point onwards, i.e. to the left of this sign

no stopping from this point onwards, i.e. to the right of this sign

fire engine access

tourist-route sign

Yellow road signs are for out-of-town destinations ▶

is this the road to ... ?
ist das die Straße nach ...?
*ist das dee **shtra**-se nakh ...*

I am sorry, I did not know ...
Entschuldigung, ich wusste nicht, dass ...
*ent-**shool**-digoong ikh **voos**-te nikht, das ...*

this was a 30 km/h zone
das eine Zone 30 ist
*das ine-e **tsoh**-ne **dry**-sikh ist*

how do I get to ... ?
wie komme ich nach ...?
*vee **kom**-me ikh nakh ...*

this was a one-way street
das eine Einbahnstraße ist
*das ine-e **ine**-bahn-shtra-se ist*

I could not park here
das ich hier nicht parken kann
*das ikh heer nikht **par**-ken kan*

talking

*German motorways (**Autobahn**) are free. There is no speed
restriction, but 130 km/h is recommended, and some sections
have lower speed limits. There are usually two lanes (except in
areas of heavy traffic where there are three or more) which means you
have to watch out for fast upcoming cars before pulling out to overtake.*

▲ Sign directing to
motorway 66

Sign indicating the
motorway entrance
(The exit is *Ausfahrt*.)

Motorway
services sign ◀

▶ SOS box

48   Motorway
number

26   Motorway
exit
number

Unlike German
motorways, Austrian
and Swiss motorways
are not free. This sign
indicates Austrian
motorway stickers are
sold here.

If you break down on the motorway

If you break down on the motorway, first you should put on your
warning lights and place your warning triangle about 100 m behind the
car. Then make your way to the emergency phone. An arrow on the
distance indicator will show you which way the nearest phone is. It is
never more than 1 km away. The police will arrange for a recovery vehicle
to come to you.

my car's broken down
ich habe eine Panne
*ikh **hah**-be ine-e **pan**-ne*

what should I do?
was soll ich tun?
vas zoll ikh toon

my children are in the car
meine Kinder sind im Auto
*mine-e kin-der zint im **ow**to*

I am on my own
ich bin allein
*ikh bin al-**line***

it is a blue Fiat
es ist ein blauer Fiat
*es ist ein **blow**-er **fee**at*

registration number ...
Kennzeichen ...
***ken**-tsy-khen ...*

the car is ...
das Auto ist ...
*das **ow**to ist ...*

after junction ...
nach Abfahrt ...
*nakh **ap**-fahrt ...*

before junction ...
vor Abfahrt ...
*for **ap**-fahrt ...*

There are a number of different systems used for parking in Germany and you will have to pay in most city centres. Be warned – German traffic wardens are very efficient!

Sign indicates ▶ pay at this machine.

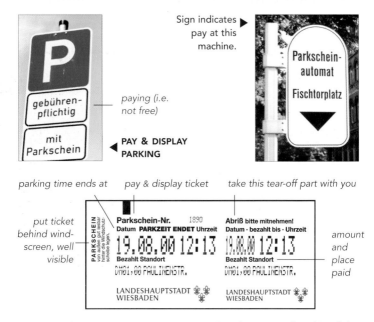

paying (i.e. not free)

◀ **PAY & DISPLAY PARKING**

Parkschein-automat
Fischtorplatz
▼

parking time ends at   *pay & display ticket*   *take this tear-off part with you*

put ticket behind wind-screen, well visible

Parkschein-Nr. 1890
Datum **PARKZEIT ENDET** Uhrzeit
19.08.00 12:13
Bezahlt Standort
DM01,00 PAULINENSTR.
LANDESHAUPTSTADT
WIESBADEN

Abriß bitte mitnehmen!
Datum · bezahlt bis · Uhrzeit
19.08.00 12:13
Bezahlt Standort
DM01,00 PAULINENSTR.
LANDESHAUPTSTADT
WIESBADEN

amount and place paid

PAY & DISPLAY TICKET

Petrol stations sell parking disks. Put the disk in sight on the dash-board. It works in 30-minute blocks: always rotate the arrow so it points to the next half hour or hour from your start time (i.e. if you arrive at 10.15, point the arrow to 10.30).
▼

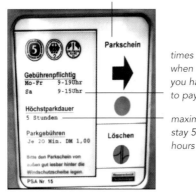

Parkschein

Gebührenpflichtig
Mo-Fr 9-19Uhr
Sa   9-15Uhr

Höchstparkdauer
5 Stunden

Parkgebühren
Je 20 Min. DM 1,00

Bitte den Parkschein von außen gut lesbar hinter die Windschutzscheibe legen.

PSA Nr. 15

Löschen

times when you have to pay

maximum stay 5 hours

ANKUNFTSZEIT
10 11
P

The picture of the parking disk on this sign ▶ indicates you must display a parking disk. You can park for 2 hours (**2 Std.**); this restriction applies weekdays 9 am–6 pm.

This tells you to park on the curb (see how the car is parked on the sign).

▲
Parkhaus is a multi-storey car park – note the roof over the P!

Parking system guiding you to car parks *(Don't be misled by Frei – it means spaces, not free of charge. Full is Belegt.)* ▶

▲ RING FOR ASSISTANCE

Instead of a ▶ paper ticket, you often get a *Parkchip*, a plastic token.

EXIT ──── ● Ausfahrt ●   ◑ ↓ Einfahrt ↓ ◐ ──── ENTRANCE
(note that Pedestrian Exit is Ausgang)   *(note that Pedestrian Entrance is Eingang)*

where is there a car park?
wo ist hier ein Parkplatz?
*voh ist heer ine **park**-plats*

can I park here?
kann ich hier parken?
*kan ikh heer **par**-ken*

where can I get a parking disk?
wo kann ich eine Parkscheibe kaufen?
*voh kan ikh ine-e **park**-shy-be **kow**fen*

where is the best place to park?
wo sollte ich am besten parken?
*voh **zoll**-te ikh am **bes**-ten **par**-ken*

how long for?
für wie lange?
*foor vee **lan**-ge*

the ticket machine doesn't work
der Automat funktioniert nicht
*der owto-**maht** foonk-tsyo-**neert** nikht*

talking

*Avoid filling at motorway service stations, unless you have to, as petrol is much more expensive. A cheaper alternative when you are on the motorway is an **Autohof** (a trucker stop) which you find just off the motorway.*

▲ Petrol pumps

Types and prices of petrol for sale. Leaded petrol is no longer sold. ▼

Diesel	**164⁹**
UNLEADED — **Benzin** bleifrei	**199⁹**
UNLEADED 4-STAR — **Super** bleifrei	**204⁹**
HIGH-PERFORMANCE UNLEADED 4-STAR — **Super** Plus	**209⁹**

▼ CAR WASH

Tanken Tag und Nacht
fill up day and night

Benzin

Betrag
amount
to be paid — **076,0 |**
Betrag   DM

Abgabe
how much — **038,80**
you put in   Abgabe   Liter

Preis je Liter — **195,9**
price per litre   Preis je Liter   Pf.

▲ Price display
on the petrol pump

WATER   AIR

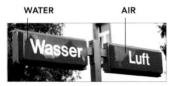

Wasser   **Luft**

where is the nearest petrol station?
wo ist die nächste Tankstelle?
*voh ist dee **naykh**-ste **tank**-shtel-le*

... worth of unleaded petrol
für ... Bleifrei
*foor ... **bly**-fry*

a token for wash number ...
einen Chip für Waschprogramm Nummer ...
*ine-en chip foor **wash**-pro-gram **noo**mer ...*

fill it up please
voll tanken bitte
*foll **tang**-ken **bi**-te*

pump number ...
Säule Nummer ...
*zoy-le **noo**mer ...*

how much is that?
wie viel macht das?
vee feel makht das

*Most repair shops are run by dealerships such as Audi, Ford, etc. However, there are some chains such as **Pit-Stop** which will do repairs while you wait.*

EXHAUST — Auspuff
BREMSEN — BRAKES
TYRES — Reifen
ÖLWECHSEL — OIL CHANGE
SHOCK ABSORBERS — Stoßdämpfer

I have broken down
ich habe eine Panne
*ikh **hah**-be ine-e **pan**-ne*

the car won't start
das Auto springt nicht an
*das **ow**to shpringt nikht an*

the battery is flat
die Batterie ist leer
*dee ba-te**ree** ist layr*

I have a flat tyre
ich habe einen Platten
*ikh **hah**-be ine-en **plat**-ten*

I need new tyres
ich brauche neue Reifen
*ikh **brow**-khe **noy**-e **ry**-fen*

I have run out of petrol
ich habe kein Benzin mehr
*ikh **hah**-be kayn ben**tseen** mehr*

where is the nearest garage?
wo ist die nächste Werkstatt?
*voh ist dee **naykh**-ste **verk**-shtat*

there is something wrong with ...
es stimmt etwas nicht mit ...
*es shtimt **et**-vas nikht mit ...*

the ... is not working
der/die/das ... funktioniert nicht
*der/dee/das ... foonk-tsyo-**neert** nikht*

the ... are not working
die ... funktionieren nicht
*dee ... foonk-tsyo-**nee**-ren nikht*

can you repair it?
können Sie es reparieren?
*kur'-nen zee es raypa-**ree**ren*

how long will it take?
wie lange wird das dauern?
*vee **lan**-ge virt das **dow**-ern*

when will it be ready?
wann ist es fertig?
*van ist es **fer**-tikh*

how much will it cost?
wie viel wird es kosten?
*vee feel virt es **kos**ten*

can you replace the windscreen?
können Sie die Windschutzscheibe ersetzen?
*kur'-nen zee dee **vint**-shoots-shy-be er-**ze**tsen*

please change ...	**the oil**	**the water**	**the tyres**
bitte wechseln Sie ...	das Öl	das Wasser	die Reifen
*bi-te **vek**-seln zee ...*	*das ur'l*	*das **vas**ser*	*dee **ry**-fen*

talking talking talking talking talking talking

SHOPPING

Shop opening hours are generally 8 am to 8 pm Monday to Friday and 8 am to 4 pm on Saturday. There is no Sunday opening (except in tourist areas where shops selling holiday items may be open). Petrol stations selling snacks, bread, drinks, etc, are open on Sundays. Baker's can also open on Sunday mornings.

keywords keywords keywords

Bäckerei
be-ke-rye
baker's

Metzgerei
mets-ge-rye
butcher's

Delikatessen
delicatessen
delicatessen

Lebensmittelladen
laybens-mittel-laden
grocer's

Konditorei
kon-dee-to-rye
cake shop

Supermarkt
sooper-markt
supermarket

Reformhaus
re-form-hows
health food

Drogerie
dro-ge-ree
drugstore

▲ Butcher's (*Metzgerei* is a southern German term for butcher; see below.)

Cake shop ▼

Baker's ▲

Netto is a brand of supermarket.

BUTCHER'S

BAKER'S

Lotto-Toto is a type of tobacconist's and newsagent's. They sell lottery tickets.

Traders' board at a shopping centre ▶

insurance office

Tele Service Nord is a phone company.

FRUIT & VEG

Werbung & Schrift is an advertising agency.

*Supermarkets are generally open from 8 am to 8 pm Monday to Friday and 8 am to 4 pm on Saturday. They are closed on Sundays. Most products are cheaper in supermarkets than in smaller shops; this includes film and tapes for camcorders. Supermarkets have a separate area for drinks and mineral waters, **Getränkemarkt**. Most bottles and carriers carry a deposit which you get back on returning them.*

You need a coin to release ▶ your trolley (mostly 1 DM, though some also take 2 DM). Watch out for kids wanting to offer you their trolley for 1 DM – they may have a plastic coin inside which means you won't get your money back.

Fruit and vegetables must be weighed and stickered in that department. It cannot be done at the checkout.

Lassen Sie bitte Ihre Taschen im Auto

LEAVE YOUR BAGS IN THE CAR
You are not allowed to take any bags (except handbags) in with you. If you need plastic carriers, you have to pay for them.

where can I buy ...?
wo kann ich ... kaufen?
*voh kan ikh ... **kow**fen*

do you have ...?
haben Sie ...?
***hah**-ben zee ...*

I am looking for ...
ich suche ...
*ikh **zoo**-khe ...*

is there a market?
gibt es hier einen Markt?
*gipt es heer **i**ne-en markt*

can I pay with this card?
kann ich mit dieser Karte bezahlen?
*kan ikh mit **dee**-zer **kar**-te be-**tsah**len*

batteries
Batterien
*ba-te**ree**-en*

how much is it?
wie viel kostet das?
*vee feel **kos**tet das*

a present
ein Geschenk
*ine ge-**shenk***

which day?
an welchem Tag?
*an **vel**-khem tahk*

a tin-opener
einen Dosenöffner
*ine-en **doh**zen-ur'fner*

a good wine
einen guten Wein
*ine-en **goo**ten vine*

talking talking talking

i Quantities are expressed in kilos and grams. A **Pfund** (meaning pound) is frequently used in markets and shops but it refers to half a kilo, or 500 g, rather than an Imperial pound. In everyday talk, **ein Pfund** and **ein halbes Pfund** are often preferred to 500 g (**fünfhundert Gramm**) and 250 g (**zweihundertfünfzig Gramm**). Just keep in mind that it is slightly more than our pound and half pound, and much easier to say than the metric equivalent.

◀ Sausages are sold either by the piece and weighed, for instance liversausage; in slices (for sliceable sausages); or in pairs (such as frankfurters).

▲ Cheese is sold either by the piece or by the packet.

Vegetables are sold by the kilo, individually (cauliflower) or by the ◀ bunch (radishes).

◀ Look out for the words *biologisch-dynamisch*, indicating organic.

— *artichokes grown on our own organic farm*

— *fresh and tender*

— *only 7.20 DM a kg*

Fruit is sold by the kilo, individually (e.g. kiwi, grapefruit) or by the punnet when in season (e.g. strawberries and cherries).

▼

▶

▲ *Graubrot*, one of the most popular of the many types of bread.

Kann Spuren von anderen Nüssen, Erdnüssen und Weizeneiweiß enthalten.

▲ *may contain traces of nuts, peanuts and wheat protein*

Nährwertangaben: 100 ml zubereitete Sächs. Kartoffel-suppe enthalten durchschnittlich:

nutritional info: 100 ml prepared product contains on average:

kjoules —	Kilojoule (kJ)	111
calories —	Kilokalorien (kcal)	26
protein —	Eiweiß	0,7g
carbohydrates —	Kohlenhydrate	5,6g
fat —	Fett	0,1g

Bio
◀ Indicates a product is organic. Also look out for *Öko.*

Glutenfreies Produkt
◀ *gluten-free product*

V
◀ Symbol for a vegetarian product.

Auch für Mikrowelle
◀ *also micro-waveable*

a piece of that cheese
ein Stück von diesem Käse
*ine shtook fon **dee**-zem **kay**-ze*

a little more
etwas mehr
et-vas mehr

a little less
etwas weniger
*et-vas **veh**-ni-ger*

that's fine thanks
das reicht danke
*das rykht **dang**-ke*

10 slices of ham
zehn Scheiben Schinken
*tsayn **shy**-ben **shin**-ken*

thick slices
dicke Scheiben
***dee**-ke **shy**-ben*

thin slices
dünne Scheiben
***doo**-ne **shy**-ben*

a carton of milk
einen Karton Milch
*ine-en kar-**ton** milkh*

a bottle of mineral water
eine Flasche Mineralwasser
*ine-e **fla**-she mineral-vasser*

still	**fizzy**
still	sprudelnd
shtill	***shproo**delnd*

a tin of ...	**a roll of ...**
eine Dose ...	eine Rolle ...
*ine-e **doh**-ze ...*	*ine-e **rol**-le ...*

a jar of ...	**a bottle of ...**
ein Glas ...	eine Flasche ...
ine glahs ...	*ine-e **fla**-she ...*

a packet of ...
ein Päckchen ...
*ine-**pek**-khen ...*

that is everything thanks
das ist alles danke
*das ist **al**-les **dang**-ke*

Everyday Foods Lebensmittel *lay*bens-mittel

biscuits	die Kekse *kayk*-se
bread	das Brot *broht*
bread roll	das Brötchen *brur't*-khen
bread *(sliced)*	das Brot in Scheiben *broht* in *shy*-ben
butter	die Butter *boo*-ter
cereal	die Cornflakes *corn*-flakes
cheese	der Käse *kay*-ze
chicken	das Hühnchen *hoohn*-khen
coffee	der Kaffee *kafay*
cream	die Sahne *zah*-ne
cream cheese	der Frischkäse *frish*-kay-ze
crisps	die Chips *chips*
eggs	die Eier *eye*-er
fish	der Fisch *fish*
flour	das Mehl *mehl*
ham *(cooked)*	der gekochte Schinken *ge-kokh*-te *shin*-ken
ham *(cured)*	der rohe Schinken *roh*-e *shin*-ken
herbal tea	der Kräutertee *kroy*-ter-tay
honey	der Honig *hoh*-nikh
jam	die Marmelade *mar-me-lah*-de
juice	der Saft *zaft*
margarine	die Margarine *margah-ree*-ne
marmalade	die Orangenmarmelade *oronjen-mar-me-lah*-de
meat	das Fleisch *flysh*
milk	die Milch *milkh*
mustard	der Senf *zenf*
oil	das Öl *ur'l*
orange juice	der Orangensaft *oronjen*-zaft
pasta	die Nudeln *noo*-deln
pepper	der Pfeffer *pfef*-fer
rice	der Reis *rice*
salt	das Salz *zalts*
sausage	die Wurst *woorst*
sugar	der Zucker *tsoo*-ker
stock cubes	die Brühwürfel *broo*-voor-fel
tea	der Tee *tay*
tomatoes *(tin)*	die Dosentomaten *doh*zen-tomah-ten
tuna	der Tunfisch *toon*fish
vinegar	der Essig *es*-sikh
yoghurt	der Jogurt *yo*-goort

Fruit	Obst *obst*
apples	die Äpfel *ep-fel*
apricots	die Aprikosen *apree-kohzen*
bananas	die Bananen *ba-nah-nen*
cherries	die Kirschen *kir-shen*
figs	die Feigen *fy-gen*
grapefruit	die Grapefruit *grape-fruit*
grapes	die Trauben *trow-ben*
lemon	die Zitrone *tsitroh-ne*
melon	die Melone *me-loh-ne*
nectarines	die Nektarinen *nekta-ree-nen*
oranges	die Orangen *oronjen*
peaches	die Pfirsiche *pfeer-zi-khe*
pears	die Birnen *bir-nen*
pineapple	die Ananas *ana-nas*
plums	die Pflaumen *pflow-men*
raspberries	die Himbeeren *him-beh-ren*
strawberries	die Erdbeeren *ert-beh-ren*
watermelon	die Wassermelone *vasser-me-loh-ne*

Vegetables	Gemüse *ge-moo-se*
artichokes	die Artischocken *arti-sho-ken*
aubergines	die Auberginen *ohber-jee-nen*
asparagus	der Spargel *shpar-gel*
carrots	die Möhren *mur'h-ren*
cauliflower	der Blumenkohl *bloo-men-kohl*
celery	der Sellerie *ze-le-ree*
courgettes	die Zucchini *tsoo-ki-ni*
cucumber	die Gurke *goor-ke*
french beans	die grünen Bohnen *groo-nen bohnen*
garlic	der Knoblauch *knohp-lowkh*
leeks	der Porree *po-ray*
lettuce	der Salat *za-laht*
mushrooms	die Pilze *pil-tse*
onions	die Zwiebeln *tswee-beln*
peas	die Erbsen *erp-sen*
peppers	die Paprika *pa-pri-ka*
potatoes	die Kartoffeln *kar-tof-feln*
radishes	die Radieschen *radees-khen*
spinach	der Spinat *shpi-naht*
spring onions	die Frühlingszwiebeln *froo-lings-tswee-beln*
tomatoes	die Tomaten *to-mah-ten*
turnip	die Rübchen *roop-khen*

*There are a number of good German department stores – such as **Kaufhof**, **Karstadt** and **Hertie**. Department stores are generally open from about 9 am to 8 pm Monday to Friday and 9 am to 4 pm on Saturday.*

keywords keywords

Kaufhaus
kowf-hows
department store

Untergeschoss
oonter-geshoss
basement

Erdgeschoss
ert-geshoss
ground floor

erste Etage
ers-te eta-zhe
first floor

Abteilung
ap-ty-loong
department

Elektrowaren
elektro-vahren
electrical goods

Schmuck
shmook
jewellery

Damen
dah-men
ladies'

Herren
her-ren
men's

Kinder
kin-der
children's

▲ Changing rooms

▼ Cash desk

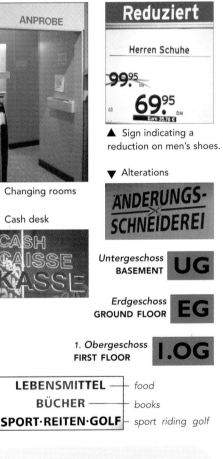

▲ Sign indicating a reduction on men's shoes.

▼ Alterations

ÄNDERUNGS-SCHNEIDEREI

Untergeschoss **UG**
BASEMENT

Erdgeschoss **EG**
GROUND FLOOR

1. Obergeschoss **I.OG**
FIRST FLOOR

LEBENSMITTEL — food
BÜCHER — books
SPORT·REITEN·GOLF – sport riding golf

talking

which floor is the ...?
auf welcher Etage ist ...?
owf vel-kher eta-zhe ist ...

lingerie
die Unterwäsche
dee oonter-ve-she

food department
die Lebensmittelabteilung
dee laybens-mittel-ap-ty-loong

shoe department
die Schuhabteilung
dee shoo-ap-ty-loong

Women's clothes sizes

UK/Australia	8	10	12	14	16	18	20	22
Europe	36	38	40	42	44	46	48	50
US/Canada	6	8	10	12	14	16	18	20

Men's clothes sizes (suits)

UK/US/Canada	36	38	40	42	44	46
Europe	46	48	50	52	54	56
Australia	92	97	102	107	112	117

Shoes

UK/Australia	2	3	4	5	6	7	8	9	10	11
Europe	35	36	37	38	39	41	42	43	45	46
US/Canada women	4	5	6	7	8	9	10	11	12	-
US/Canada men	3	4	5	6	7	8	9	10	11	12

Children's Shoes

UK/US/Canada	0	1	2	3	4	5	6	7	8	9	10	11
Europe	15	17	18	19	20	22	23	24	26	27	28	29

do you have size ...?
haben Sie Größe ...?
hah-ben zee grur'-se ...

shoe size ...
Schuhgröße ...
shoo-grur'-se ...

do you have this in my size?
haben Sie das in meiner Größe?
hah-ben zee das in mine-er grur'-se

I take size ...
ich habe Größe ...
ikh hah-be grur'-se ...

it is too big
es it zu groß
es ist tsoo grohs

it is too small
es ist zu klein
es ist tsoo kline

I need a smaller/larger size
ich brauche eine kleinere/größere Größe
ikh brow-khe ine-e kline-e-re/grur'-se-re grur'-se

do you have a smaller/larger size?
haben Sie eine kleinere/größere Größe?
hah-ben zee ine-e kline-e-re/grur'-se-re grur'-se

do you have this in ...?
haben Sie das in ...?
hah-ben zee das in ...

black/brown
schwarz/braun
shwarts/brown

other colours
anderen Farben
an-deren far-ben

talking talking talking

You can buy stamps at the post office counter or from the machines that are usually found there. Post office opening hours are 8 am to 6 pm Monday to Friday and 8 am to 2 pm on Saturday.

Post office logo
The word **Postbank** indicates there is a post office savings bank in the post office.

Postboxes are ▶ yellow. Collection times are marked. The red dot indicates a Sunday collection. The box should also list the nearest postbox (**nächster Briefkasten**) with different collection times.

◀ Stamp required for postcards within Europe (100 Pf)

▼ Slot for letters

BRIEFEINWURF

where is the post office?
wo ist die Post?
voh ist dee post

do you have stamps?
haben Sie Briefmarken?
hah-ben zee breef-marken

10 stamps please
zehn Briefmarken bitte
tsayn breef-marken bi-te

for postcards
für Postkarten
foor post-kar-ten

for letters
für Briefe
foor bree-fe

to Europe
nach Europa
nakh oy-ro-pa

to America
nach Amerika
nakh a-me-rika

to Australia
nach Australien
nakh owstra-lee-en

I want to send this registered ...
ich möchte das eingeschrieben schicken ...
ikh mur'kh-te das ine-ge-shreeben shi-ken ...

I want to send this parcel ...
ich möchte diese Paket schicken ...
ich mur'kh-te dee-zes pa-keht shi-ken ...

fast mail
per Express
per eks-press

surface mail
auf dem Landweg
owf dem lant-vehk

airmail
per Luftpost
per looft-post

talking talking

STAMPS

choose

pay

take your stamps

cancel

Film
film
film

Batterie
ba-teree
battery

matt
matt
mat

Hochglanz
hokh-glants
glossy

Dias
dee-as
slides

Camcorder
camcorder
camcorder

Verschluss
fer-shloos
shutter

Zoom
zoom
zoom

The drug-store is a cheaper place to get photos developed than a photographic shop.

where can I buy film?
wo kann ich einen Film kaufen?
voh kan ikh ine-en film kowfen

a colour film
einen Farbfilm
ine-en farp-film

a slide film
ein Diafilm
ine dee-a-film

can you develop this film?
können Sie diesen Film entwickeln?
kur'-nen zee dee-zen film ent-vikeln

can you take a picture of us?
können Sie ein Foto von uns machen?
kur'-nen zee ine foto fon oons makhen

tapes for this camcorder
Bänder für diesen Camcorder
ben-der foor dee-zen camcorder

with ... pictures
mit ... Bildern
mit ... bil-dern

24
vierundzwanzig
feer-oont-tsvan-tsikh

36
sechsunddreißig
zekhs-oont-dry-sikh

when will the photos be ready?
wann sind die Fotos fertig?
van zint dee fotos fer-tikh

can we film here?
können wir hier filmen?
kur'-nen veer heer fil-men

PHONES

i *Coin phones are not easily found. The majority of phone boxes operate with phonecards (**Telefonkarte**) which you can buy at the post office, newsagents' and telecommunications shops. There are numerous private phone companies operating each with their own cheap rates using a system of dialling prefixes.*

◀ Important numbers are displayed inside phone boxes and emergency calls are free.

Karten-telefon

▲ Card-phone symbol

Card-operated phone ▶

do you have phonecards?
haben Sie Telefonkarten?
*hah-ben zee taylay-**fon**-kar-ten*

a phonecard please
eine Telefonkarte bitte
*ine-e taylay-**fon**-kar-te **bi**-te*

Mr Meier please
Herrn Meier bitte
*hayrn **mei**-er **bi**-te*

can I speak to Paul?
kann ich bitte Paul sprechen?
*kan ikh **bi**-te paul **shpre**-khen*

12 DM
zwölf Mark
tsvur'lf mark

50 DM
fünfzig Mark
***foonf**tsikh mark*

extension ...
Apparat Nummer ...
*apa-**raht noo**mer ...*

this is Caroline
hier ist Caroline
heer ist Caroline

can I have an outside line please?
kann ich bitte einen Amtsleitung bekommen?
*kan ikh **bi**-te ine-e **amts**-ly-toong be-**kom**men*

I'd like to make a reverse charge call
ich möchte ein R-Gespräch anmelden
*ikh **mur'kh**-te ine **er**-ge-shpraykh **an**-mel-den*

what is you phone number?
wie ist Ihre Telefonnummer?
*vee ist **ee**-re taylay-**fon**-noomer*

my phone number is ...
meine Telefonnummer ist ...
***mine-**e taylay-**fon**-noomer ist ...*

Back of a phonecard; sold in units of 12 DM or 50 DM.
Like other items in Germany, phonecards are recycled. Dispose of used ones in a slot below the phone in call boxes; they are collected and the chips reused.

Freecall is the equivalent to the UK's Freephone and begins with 0800.

Telefonkarte
taylay-fon-kar-te
phonecard

Handy
handy
mobile

Vorwahl
for-vahl
code

Auskunft
ows-koonft
directory enquiries

Telefonbuch
phone book
taylay-fon-bookh

Gelbe Seiten
gel-be zye-ten
yellow pages

Vermittlung
fer-mitt-loong
operator

▲ Phone book

▼ Yellow pages

Coin-operated phones are becoming increasingly rare.

I will call back
ich rufe ... zurück
ikh roo-fe ... tsoorook

later
später
sphayter

tomorrow
morgen
morgen

do you have a mobile?
haben Sie ein Handy?
hah-ben zee ine handy

which network are you on?
bei welchem Netzbetreiber sind Sie?
by vel-khem nets-be-tryber zint zee

what is your mobile number?
wie ist Ihre Handynummer?
vee ist ee-re handy-noomer

my mobile number is ...
meine Handynummer ist ...
mine-e handy-noomer ist ...

*You will be able to find an internet café in most big cities. The most common internet service providers are T-Online and AOL. German websites end in .de for **Deutschland**.*

keywords keywords keywords

Abholen
ap-hoh-len
collect new mail

Versenden
fer-zen-den
send

Lesen
leh-zen
read

Weiterleiten
vy-ter-ly-ten
forward

Löschen
lur'-shen
delete

Antworten
ant-vor-ten
reply

Betreff
be-tref
subject

scanning
printing
copying
CD-burning
downloading

Some bookshops now have internet cafés. ▶

net(t)café GmbH

talking talking talking

what is your e-mail address?
wie ist Ihre E-Mail-Adresse?
vee ist ee-re ee-mail-adres-se

my e-mail address is ...
meine E-Mail-Adresse ist ...
mine-e ee-mail-adres-se ist ...

caroline.smith@anycompany.co.uk
caroline.smith@anycompany.co.uk
caroline poonkt smith at anycompany poonkt tsay oh poonkt oo kah

can I send an e-mail?
kann ich eine E-Mail schicken?
kan ikh ine-e ee-mail shi-ken

did you get my e-mail?
haben Sie meine E-Mail bekommen?
hah-ben zee mine-e ee-mail be-kommen

can I send and receive e-mail here?
kann ich hier E-Mails schicken und erhalten?
kan ikh heer ee-mails shi-ken oont er-halten

how much does an hour of netsurfing cost?
wie viel kostet eine Stunde Internet-Surfen?
vee feel kostet ine-e shtoon-de internet-surfen

pocket-money surfing

for pupils and students

5 DM per hour

National and local tourist and what's-on information can be accessed via the ▼ internet.

Schreiben
shry-ben
compose

Zurück
tsoo-rook
back

Vor
for
forward

Neu laden
noy lah-den
reload

Anfang
an-fang
home

Suchen
zoo-khen
search

Lesezeichen
lay-ze-tsy-khen
bookmark

Sicherheit
zikher-hite
security

keywords keywords keywords

I want to send a fax
ich möchte ein Fax schicken
*ikh **mur'kh**-te ine faks **shi**-ken*

can I send a fax from here?
kann ich von hier ein Fax schicken?
*kan ikh fon heer ine faks **shi**-ken*

how much is it to send a fax?
was kostet es, ein Fax zu schicken?
*vas **kost**et es ine faks tsoo **shi**-ken*

what is your fax number?
wie ist Ihre Faxnummer?
*vee ist **ee**-re **faks**-noomer*

I am trying to send a fax
ich versuche, ein Fax zu schicken
*ikh fer-**zoo**-khe ine faks tsoo **shi**-ken*

do you have a fax?
haben Sie ein Fax?
hah-ben zee ine faks

can I receive a fax here?
kann ich hier ein Fax erhalten?
*kan ikh heer ine faks er-**hal**-ten*

it has ... pages
es hat ... Seiten
*es hat ... **zye**-ten*

please confirm your number
bitte bestätigen Sie Ihre Nummer
*bi-te be-**shtay**-ti-gen zee **ee**-re **noo**mer*

did you get my fax?
haben Sie mein Fax bekommen?
*hah-ben zee mine faks be-**kom**men*

talking talking talking

OUT & ABOUT

*Monday is not a good day for sightseeing, as most places such as museums and art galleries are generally closed on Mondays. If you are going to a city with lots of tourist attractions, look out for tickets that allow you multiple entry. Tourist offices organise city walks (**Stadtrundgänge**) and there are also city bus tours (**Stadtrundfahrten**).*

▲ Tourist Offices are generally open 9 am–6 pm Mon–Fri and Sat mornings. In smaller places opening hours may be restricted.

Information ▶
about the
city walk
and bus
tour

BUY YOUR
TICKETS
HERE ▶

closed on Mondays

▲
Museum sign showing opening hours

Sign for
a listed
building ▶

▲ City sign

Ticket for the Munich Pinakothek Art Gallery ▼

▼ *Kunsthalle* Art Gallery

keywords keywords words

Stadthalle
civic hall
shtat-hal-le

Ausstellung
ows-shte-loong
exhibition

Wanderweg
van-der-vehk
trek, ramble

Weinprobe
vine-proh-be
wine tasting

Kirmes
kir-mes
funfair

Kirche
kir-khe
church

Dom
dome
cathedral

Schloss
shloss
castle

Rathaus
raht-hows
town hall

excuse me, where is the tourist office?
entschuldigen Sie, wo ist die Touristeninformation?
*ent**shool**-di-gen zee voh ist dee too**ris**ten-infor-ma-**tsyohn***

do you have ...?	**a map of the town**	**leaflets in English**
haben Sie ...?	einen Stadtplan	Broschüren in Englisch
hah-ben zee ...	*ine-en **shtat**-plan*	*bro-**shoo**-ren in **eng**-lish*

we want to visit ...
wir möchten ... besuchen
*veer **mur'kh**-ten ... be-**zoo**khen*

how do we get there?
wie kommen wir dorthin?
*vee **kom**men veer dort-**hin***

when can we visit the ...?
wann können wir ... besuchen?
*van **kur'**-nen veer ... be-**zoo**-khen*

when does it close?
wann ist es geschlossen?
*van ist es ge-**shlos**-sen*

is there a city walk?
gibt es einen Stadtrundgang?
*gipt es ine-en **shtat**-roont-gang*

is there a city bus tour?
gibt es eine Stadtrundfahrt?
*gipt es ine-e **shtat**-roont-fahrt*

talking talking talking

*There are many outdoor swimming pools open in the summer. Look out for the word **Freibad**. You can also swim in the many lakes. There are tourist resorts along the Baltic and North Sea. As in other areas of German life, there are a number of rules to observe.*

▼ A sign along the sand dunes

Textil means you must wear a costume (no nudist bathing)

no windsurfing

next crossing point this way is 16/6

this crossing point is number 4. It is suitable for wheelchairs.

emergency numbers

there are no lifeguards on this section of the beach

dogs are allowed on this beach

next crossing point this way is 3a/

PLEASE KEEP THE BEACH TIDY!

DO NOT WALK ON THE DUNES!

where can we ...?
wo können wir ...?
voh kur'-nen veer ...

how much is it ...?
was kostet es ...?
vas kostet es ...

per hour/day
pro Stunde/Tag
pro shtoon-de/tahk

is there a swimming pool?
gibt es hier ein Schwimmbad?
gipt es heer ine shwim-baht

where can we go ...?
wo können wir ...?
voh kur'-nen veer ...

play tennis
Tennis spielen
tennis shpee-len

to hire mountain bikes
Mountainbikes zu mieten
moun-tain-bikes tsoo meeten

can we hire equipment?
können wir die Ausrüstung mieten?
kur'-nen veer dee ows-roostoong meeten

is it dangerous to swim here?
ist das Baden hier gefährlich?
ist das bah-den heer ge-fayr-likh

windsurfing
surfen
surfen

play golf
Golf spielen
golf shpee-len

to go fishing
zu angeln
tsoo angeln

waterskiing
Wasserski fahren
vasser-shee fah-ren

how do we hire a beach hut?
wie können wir einen Strandkorb mieten?
vee kur'-nen veer ine-en shtrant-korb mee-ten

talking talking talking

You can hire a beach hut. You will be given a key with a number corresponding to the hut. The huts are good at keeping out a chill wind. ◀

▲ Sign indicating nudist bathing is allowed.

▼ Hiking-path sign

▶

Bike route following a wine theme through a wine-growing area.

Haupttribüne
main stand

Sitztribüne Nord
seating stand north

Plan of a football stadium ▶

▲ Poster advertising a football match

Stehtribüne Süd
standing stand south

Gegengerade
far stand

Gästeblock
guest area

---

we'd like to go to a football match
wir möchten ein Fußballspiel sehen
*veer **mur'kh**-ten ine **foos**ball-shpeel **zay**-en*

where can we get tickets?
wo können wir Tickets bekommen?
*voh **kur'**-nen veer **t**ickets be-**kom**men*

how do we get to the stadium?
wie kommen wir zum Stadion?
*vee **kom**men veer tsoom **shtah**-dee-ohn*

who is playing?
wer spielt?
ver shpeelt

how much are the tickets?
was kosten die Tickets?
*vas **kos**ten dee **t**ickets*

what time is the match?
wann fängt das Spiel an?
van fengt das shpeel an

talking

ACCOMMODATION

The German Tourist Office has brochures showing all private and hotel accommodation in their area. They will be able to advise and find the particular type of accommodation you are after.

▲ **Hotel Garni** This type of hotel is a bed-and-breakfast. Other hotels follow the star system.

▲ **Pension**
Similar to a *Hotel Garni*

► **Gasthof**
This is usually a pub or winebar with guestrooms. *Gasthofs* are usually a good-value option.

Booking in advance

The German Tourist Board in your country will be able to send you brochures about the area you want to visit, listing the different types of accommodation available. When you have chosen a place, you can either contact them direct or through the German Tourist Board.

I would like to book a room
ich möchte ein Zimmer buchen
*ikh **mur'kh**-te ine **tsim**mer **boo**-khen*

a single/a double
ein Einzelzimmer/Doppelzimmer
*ine **ine**-tsel-tsimmer/**dop**-pel-tsimmer*

for ... nights
für ... Nächte
*foor ... **nekh**-te*

from ... to ...
vom ... bis ...
fom ... bis ...

I will fax to confirm
ich schicke ein Fax zur Bestätigung
*ikh **shi**-ke ine faks tsoor be-**shtay**-tigoong*

my name is ...
mein Name ist ...
*mine **nah**-me ist ...*

my credit card number is ...
meine Kreditkartennummer ist ...
*mine-e kre-**deet**-kar-ten-noomer ist ...*

my phone number is ...
meine Telefonnummer ist ...
*mine-e taylay-**fon**-noomer ist ...*

◀ Hotel rates for different types of rooms

price list valid from 1 Jan 1998

Typ *grade*
Belegung *use of room*
Doppel *double*
Einzel *single*

DM pro Tag
DM per day
ohne Frühstück
without breakfast
mit Frühstück
with breakfast

Hotel Garni

Preisliste
gültig ab 01. Januar 1998

Typ	Belegung	DM pro Tag ohne Frühstück		DM pro Tag mit Frühstück	
A I	Doppel	DM	170.-	DM	200.-
	Einzel	DM	140.-	DM	155.-
A II	Doppel	DM	150.-	DM	180.-
	Einzel	DM	120.-	DM	135.-
B	Doppel	DM	135.-	DM	165.-
	Einzel	DM	110.-	DM	125.-
C	Doppel	DM	120.-	DM	150.-
	Einzel	DM	100.-	DM	120.-

do you have a room for tonight?
haben Sie ein Zimmer für heute Nacht?
hah-ben zee ine tsimmer foor hoy-te nakht

a single room
ein Einzelzimmer
ine ine-tsel-tsimmer

a double room
ein Doppelzimmer
ine dop-pel-tsimmer

a family room
ein Familienzimmer
ine famee-lee-en-tsimmer

with ensuite bath
mit Bad
mit baht

with shower
mit Dusche
mit doo-she

for tonight
für heute Nacht
foor hoy-te nakht

for one night
für eine Nacht
foor ine-e nakht

for... nights
für ... Nächte
foor ... nekh-te

how much is it?
wie viel kostet es?
vee feel kostet es

is breakfast included?
ist das Frühstück inbegriffen?
ist das froo-shtook in-be-grif-fen

how much is half board?
wie viel kostet Halbpension?
vee feel kostet halp-pensyon

how much is full board
wie viel kostet Vollpension?
vee feel kostet foll-pensyon

can I see the room?
kann ich das Zimmer ansehen?
kan ikh das tsimmer an-zay-en

what time should we check out?
wann sollen wir auschecken?
van zol-len veer ows-tshe-ken

talking talking talking talking

▲ HOLIDAY FLAT

The local tourist office will have a
brochure listing all private and
hotel accommodation in their area.

▲ RECEPTION

Where you see a
sign for holiday
accommodation
you can go in
and ask what is
available.

◀

**SELF-CATERING
HOLIDAY HOUSE**

vacancies

ROOMS

no vacancies

BED & BIKE This is a scheme run by the German Bicycle Club (ADFC)
▼ which can coordinate accommodation on cycling tours.

▼ ROOMS

▲ Symbol for German Youth Hostel
German youth hostels welcome everyone –
you don't have to be a member, though
members of the international youth hostel
association pay a reduced rate.

▲ Sign to a local youth hostel

Geschirrspülmittel
ge-shir-shpool-mittel
washing-up liquid

Waschmittel
vash-mit-tel
washing powder

Seife
zay-fe
soap

Dosenöffner
dohzen-ur'fner
tin-opener

Kerzen
ker-tsen
candles

Streichhölzer
shtraykh-hur'l-tser
matches

Gasbehälter
gas-be-hel-ter
gas cylinder

Sicherungen
zikh-eroon-gen
fuses

Wäscherei
ve-she-rye
laundry service

keywords keywords

there is/are no ...
es gibt kein/keine ...
es gipt kine/kine-e ...

can you show us how this works?
bitte zeigen Sie uns, wie das funktioniert
bi-te tsy-gen zee oons vee das foonk-tsyo-neert

how does ... work?
wie funktioniert ...?
vee foonk-tsyo-neert ...

the cooker
der Herd
der hert

the dishwasher
der Geschirrspüler
der ge-shir-shpoo-ler

the washing machine
die Waschmaschine
dee vash-ma-shee-ne

the microwave
die Mikrowelle
dee meekro-vel-le

who do I contact if there are problems?
an wen wende ich mich bei Problemen?
an ven ven-de ikh mikh by pro-bleh-men

when is the rubbish collected?
wann wird der Müll abgeholt?
van virt der mooll ap-geholt

where do we leave the rubbish?
wo tun wir den Müll hin?
voh toon veer den mooll hin

can you give us an extra set of keys?
können Sie uns noch ein Set Schlüssel geben?
kur'-nen zee oons nokh ine set shloo-sel gayben

talking talking talking

CAMPING

> If you are towing a caravan on German roads you must not
> exceed 50 km/h in built up areas and 80 km/h on other roads
> and motorways.

Road sign
for a
campsite ◀

Campsite
sign ▶

is there a campsite near here?
gibt es hier in der Nähe einen Campingplatz?
*gipt es heer in der **nay**-e ine-en **kam**ping-plats*

have you any vacancies?
haben Sie freie Plätze?
*hah-ben zee **fry**-e **plet**-se*

we want to stay for ... nights
wir möchten ... Nächte bleiben
*veer **mur'kh**-ten ... **nekh**-te **bly**-ben*

how much is it?
wie viel kostet es?
*vee feel **kos**tet es*

per tent
pro Zelt
pro tselt

per caravan
pro Wohnwagen
*pro **vohn**-vahgen*

where are ...?
wo sind ...?
voh zint ...

the showers
die Duschen
*dee **doo**-shen*

the toilets
die Toiletten
*dee twa-**le**-ten*

is there a restaurant on the campsite?
gibt es ein Restaurant auf dem Campingplatz?
*gipt es ine restoh-**rong** owf dem **kam**ping-plats*

can we have a more sheltered site?
können wir einen geschützteren Platz haben?
*kur'-nen veer ine-en ge**shoots**-te-ren plats **hah**-ben*

can we camp here overnight?
können wir hier über Nacht campen?
*kur'-nen veer heer **oo**ber nakht **kam**pen*

Launderette ▶
services

complete
dry-cleaning

household-
linen washing

carpet
cleaning

leather cleaning

we offer

shoe
repairs

alterations

carpet-
cleaner
rental

◀ Launderette

Collection point for
dry-cleaning and
▼ laundry service

where is the nearest launderette?
wo ist der nächste Waschsalon?
*voh ist der **naykh**-ste **vash**-salong*

where can I do some washing?
wo kann ich hier Wäsche waschen?
*voh kan ikh heer **ve**-she **va**shen*

can I have my laundry washed here?
kann ich hier Wäsche waschen lassen?
*kan ikh heer **ve**-she **va**shen **las**sen*

where is the nearest dry-cleaner?
wo ist die nächste Reinigung?
*voh ist dee **naykh**-ste **rye**-nee-goong*

how does this work?
wie funktioniert das?
*vee foonk-tsyo-**neert** das*

can I borrow an iron?
kann ich ein Bügeleisen borgen?
*kan ikh ine **boo**gel-eye-zen **bor**-gen*

when will my things be ready?
wann sind meine Sachen fertig?
*van zint **mine**-e **zakh**-en **fer**tikh*

talking

SPECIAL NEEDS

*Facilities are generally good for the disabled. There is wheelchair access almost everywhere. On the trains you can call 01805 512 512 to arrange in advance help with getting on and off trains and changing trains. At the station speak to the **Service Point**. They will arrange help for you. All long-distance trains have places and toilets for wheelchair-bound passengers.*

◀ Parking space for disabled

this symbol is generally used to show facilities for the disabled

▲ Button to press to have the floor of the bus or tram lowered.

Behinderten-Aufzug

◀ Lift for the disabled

Disabled seat symbol on public transport ▶

are there any disabled toilets?
gibt es hier Toiletten für Behinderte?
*gipt es heer twa-**le**-ten foor be-**hin**-der-te*

is there a wheelchair-accessible entrance?
gibt es einen Eingang für Rollstuhlfahrer?
*gipt es ine-en **ine**-gang foor **roll**-shtool-fahrer*

is it possible to visit ... with a wheelchair?
kann man ... im Rollstuhl besuchen?
*kan man ... im **roll**-shtool be-**zoo**khen*

is there a reduction for the disabled?
gibt es Ermäßigung für Behinderte?
*gipt es er-**may**-sigoong foor be-**hin**-der-te*

I need a bedroom on the ground floor
ich brauche ein Zimmer im Erdgeschoss
*ikh **brow**-khe ine **tsim**mer im **ert**-geshoss*

I use a wheelchair
ich sitze im Rollstuhl
*ikh **zit**-se im **roll**-shtool*

where is the lift?
wo ist der Aufzug?
*voh ist der **owf**-tsook*

WITH KIDS

School in Germany starts at 8 am so children go to bed quite early. Very young children (generally under 5) travel free on public transport and pay half price up to 14 (but check with the local operator). Children must use a booster seat in the car if under 12 and under 1.5 m in height. Children under 12 cannot travel in the front seat of the car.

Play park for children under 12 years ▶

SPIELPLATZ
für Kinder bis 12 Jahre.

Mother and child
▼ changing room

WICKELTISCH

Jeton's

für die Benutzung des Wickelraumes

erhalten Sie an der Kasse Kinderkonfektion oder "Le Buffet"

tokens for using this facility are available from the children's clothing cash desk or at 'Le Buffet'

is there a baby changing room?
gibt es hier einen Wickelraum?
gipt es heer ine-en vikel-rowm

where can I change the baby?
wo kann ich das Baby windeln?
voh kan ikh das baby vin-deln

do you have ...?
haben Sie ...?
hah-ben zee ...

a high chair
einen Kinderstuhl
ine-en kin-der-shtool

a cot
ein Kinderbett
ine kin-der-bett

do you sell nappies?
verkaufen Sie Windeln?
fer-kowfen zee vin-deln

baby wipes
Babytücher
baby-tookher

baby food
Babynahrung
baby-nahroong

is there a children's menu?
gibt es eine Karte für Kinder?
gipt es ine-e kar-te foor kin-der

a small portion
eine kleine Portion
ine-e kline-e port-syon

is there a play park near here?
gibt es hier in der Nähe einen Spielplatz?
gipt es heer in der nay-e ine-en shpeel-plats

talking talking talking

HEALTH

i

*You should fill in an E111 form before you leave. They are available from post offices and should be stamped by them. This form entitles you to free care from a doctor and dentist in an emergency. If you have to have treatment, take the form to any German health insurance office, **Krankenkasse**, to exchange for a treatment form **Abrechnungsschein** (for doctors) or **Erfassungsschein** (for dentists). Ask for a list of doctors or dentists you can visit. In an emergency you will be treated without having had to change the form – in that case, just present your E111. If you do have to pay a fee, make sure you have a receipt with an exact breakdown of the charges.*

Krankenkasse is a health insurance and **AOK** is one of the most common ones.
◄

Rota for the duty chemist shows which chemist is open.
◄ ►

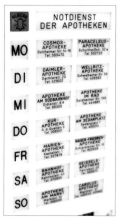

◄

Sign for the pharmacy
If you know roughly what is wrong with you, speak to a pharmacist. They can help with advising treatment

---

where is the nearest chemist?
wo ist die nächste Apotheke?
*voh ist dee **naykh**-ste apo-**teh**-ke*

have you something for ...?
haben Sie etwas gegen ...?
*hah-ben zee et-vas **gay**-gen ...*

an upset stomach
Magenverstimmung
mahgen-fer-shtimoong

sunburn	**diarrhoea**	**a headache**
Sonnenbrand	Durchfall	Kopfschmerzen
zonnen-brant	*doorkh-fall*	*kopf-shmert-sen*

I need painkillers
ich brauche Schmerztabletten
*ikh **brow**-khe **shmerts**-tab-le-ten*

I need antibiotics
ich brauche Antibiotika
*ikh **brow**-khe anti-bee-**o**-tika*

talking

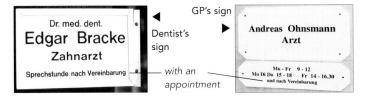

GP's sign

Dr. med. dent.
Edgar Bracke
Zahnarzt
Sprechstunde nach Vereinbarung

◀ Dentist's sign

▶

Andreas Ohnsmann
Arzt

Mo - Fr   9 - 12
Mo Di Do 15 - 18   Fr 14 - 16.30
und nach Vereinbarung

— with an appointment

I am not well
mir ist schlecht
meer ist shlekht

he/she is not well
ihm/ihr ist schlecht
eem/eer ist shlekht

I need to see a doctor
ich brauche einen Arzt
ikh brow-khe ine-en artst

we need a doctor to come out
wir brauchen einen Hausbesuch
veer brow-khen ine-en hows-be-zookh

please call the doctor
bitte rufen Sie einen Arzt
bi-te roo-fen zee ine-en artst

my child is ill
mein Kind ist krank
mine kint ist krank

I have a pain here
es tut hier weh
es toot heer veh

I am on this medication
ich nehme dieses Medikament
ikh nay-me dee-zes medeekament

I'm pregnant
ich bin schwanger
ikh bin shvanger

I am on the pill
ich nehme die Pille
ikh nay-me dee pil-le

I'm breastfeeding
ich stille mein Baby
ikh shti-le mine baby

I have cystitis
ich habe eine Blasenentzündung
ikh hah-be ine-e blahzen-entsoon-doong

I'm diabetic
ich bin Diabetiker
ikh bin dee-a-beh-tiker

I am allergic to ...
ich bin allergisch gegen ...
ikh bin a-ler-gish gay-gen ...

I have high blood pressure
ich habe zu hohen Blutdruck
ikh hah-be tsoo hoh-hen bloot-drook

my blood group is ...
meine Blutgruppe ist ...
mine-e bloot-groo-pe ist ...

I need a receipt for my insurance
ich brauche eine Quittung für meine Versicherung
ikh brow-khe ine-e kvi-toong foor mine-e fer-zikheroong

I need a dentist
ich brauche einen Zahnarzt
ikh brow-khe ine-en tsahnartst

I have toothache
ich habe Zahnschmerzen
ikh hah-be tsahn-shmer-tsen

my crown has come out
meine Krone ist herausgefallen
mine-e kroh-ne ist herows-ge-fal-len

can your repair my dentures?
können Sie mein Gebiss reparieren?
kur'-nen zee mine gebiss raypa-reeren

I need a temporary filling
ich brauche eine provisorische Füllung
ikh brow-khe ine-e provi-zori-she fooloong

I have an abscess
ich habe einen Abszess
ikh hah-be ine-en ap-sess

talking talking talking talking talking talking talking

*Hospital (**Krankenhaus**) visiting hours vary. If you are admitted you will be in a room with about three or four other people. You can hire a telephone and although it is expensive to make calls, it means you will also be able to receive them. You have to pay a daily hospital charge for the first 14 days of your stay. This is non-refundable.*

▲ Road sign for hospital;
  Klinik also means hospital.

▲ HOSPITAL

ACCIDENT & EMERGENCY ▼

If you need to go to hospital

will I/he/she have to go to hospital?
muss ich/er/sie ins Krankenhaus?
*moos ikh/er/zee ins **kran**ken-hows*

where is the hospital?
wo ist das Krankenhaus?
*voh ist das **kran**ken-hows*

where is the nearest A & E department?
wo ist das nächste Krankenhaus mit Notaufnahme?
*voh ist das **naykh**-ste **kran**ken-hows mit **noht**-owf-nah-me*

please take me to the nearest hospital
bitte bringen Sie mich zum nächsten Krankenhaus
*bi-te **brin**-gen zee mikh tsoom **naykh**-sten **kran**ken-hows*

I need to go to casualty
ich muss zur Notaufnahme
*ikh moos tsoor **noht**-owf-nah-me*

when are visiting hours?
wann ist die Besuchszeit?
*van ist dee be**zookhs**-tsite*

which ward?
welche Station?
vel**-khe shtah-**tsyohn

can you explain what is the matter?
können Sie mir erklären, was ich habe?
***kur'**-nen zee meer er-**kleh**-ren vas ikh **hah**-be*

EMERGENCY

The emergency number for the police is 110. You have to ring a local number for an ambulance (it is displayed in phone boxes), but if you need the ambulance urgently, you can ring the fire brigade. The emergency number is 112.

help!
Hilfe!
hil-fe

can you help me!
können Sie mir helfen?
kur'-nen zee meer hel-fen

please call ...
bitte rufen Sie ...
bi-te roo-fen zee ...

the police
die Polizei
dee poli-tsy

an ambulance
einen Krankenwagen
ine-en kran-ken-vahgen

help! Fire!
Hilfe! Feuer!
hil-fe! foy-er!

please call the fire brigade!
bitte rufen Sie die Feuerwehr
bi-te roo-fen zee dee foy-er-vehr

my ... has been stolen
mein/meine ... ist gestohlen worden
mine/mine-e ... ist geshtoh-len vorden

I want to report a theft
ich möchte einen Diebstahl melden
ikh mur'kh-te ine-en deep-shtahl mel-den

here are my insurance details
hier sind meine Versicherungsangaben
heer zint mine-e fer-zikheroongs-angaben

where is the police station/the hospital?
wo ist die Polizeistation/das Krankenhaus?
voh ist dee poli-tsy-shta-tsee-ohn/das kran-ken-hows

I would like to phone...
ich möchte ... anrufen
ikh mur'kh-te ... an-roofen

my car has been broken into
mein Auto ist gestohlen worden
mine owto ist geshtoh-len vorden

please give me your insurance details
bitte geben Sie mir Ihre Versicherungsangaben
bi-te gay-ben zee meer ee-re fer-zikheroongs-angaben

I need a report for my insurance
ich brauche einen Bericht für meine Versicherung
ikh brow-khe ine-en berikht foor mine-e fer-zikheroong

FOOD
AND
DRINK

GERMAN FOOD

The Germans take everything to do with food or drink with the utmost seriousness, and as a result all the products are handled very carefully in order to meet the highest standards of hygiene and quality control. Care and pride are taken in the preparation of meals. The food is hearty and warming and geared to satisfy large appetites. So be warned! Portions are large.

*In Germany the main meal of the day is usually **Mittagessen**, lunch. It starts with soup, followed by the main dish (meat with vegetables or salad and potato or rice, etc) and an optional dessert or fruit.*

*Dinner (**Abendessen**) consists of platters of cold meats and cheeses. On occasions Germans also have a hot meal, but not a heavy one.*

*Breakfast (**Frühstück**) generally consists of a variety of cold meats and cheeses, with different kinds of bread and jam and fresh coffee.*

▲ Sausage stall
Germany has a huge variety of sausages which are served at all times of the day. By law they are made with 100% meat.

In butcher's shops there is often an area for a quick meal (generally eaten standing) such as this dish: *Wiener Würstchen mit Kartoffelsalat* (boiled frankfurter with potato salad). ▼

▲ One of the unusual places where one can eat in Germany (and eat well) is the town hall (*Rathaus*), which normally has a restaurant open to the public (usually in the basement), called the *Ratskeller* (council's cellar). This one is a winebar which normally has a buffet.

durchgehend warme Küche

◀ **HOT MEALS SERVED ALL DAY**

◀
Beer garden
Beer is usually served with large Pretzels.

◀
A *Stehcafé* is a good place for a coffee and cake, generally standing only. They are often attached to a baker's and the 7 am opening means you can get breakfast.

where can we have a snack?
wo können wir einen Snack bekommen?
voh kur'-nen veer ine-en snack be-kommen

can you recommend a good local restaurant?
können Sie ein gutes Restaurant am Ort empfehlen?
kur'-nen zee ine gootes restoh-rong am ort em-faylen

are there any vegetarian restaurants?
gibt es hier vegetarische Restaurants?
gipt es heer vaygay-tarish-e restoh-rongs

do we need to book?
müssen wir einen Tisch reservieren?
moos-sen veer ine-en tish rayzer-veeren

what dishes should we try?
welche Gerichte sollten wir probieren?
vel-khe ge-rikh-te zoll-ten veer pro-bee-ren

how do we get to the restaurant?
wie kommen wir zu dem Restaurant?
vee kommen veer tsoo dem restoh-rong

talking talking talking

*Snacks can be bought at various **Imbiss** places. The local market or shopping area serve typical snacky food such as **Bratwurst** (fried sausage), **Bockwurst** (boiled sausage) and **Buletten** (thick hamburger). German standards of food hygiene are high.*

keywords

Bockwurst
boiled sausage
bok-voorst

Bratwurst
roast sausage
braht-voorst

Kartoffelsalat
potato salad
kartof-fel-zalaht

Bulette
thick hamburger
boo-le-te

Getränke
drinks
ge-tren-ke

◀ *Imbiss* stall
These serve cheap snacks: soup, hamburgers, sausages, barbecued chicken and chips. Most serve beer.

◀ *Bratwurst*

Wiener Würstchen ▶

talking talking talking

I'd like a ... please
ich möchte einen/eine/ein ... bitte
*ikh **mur'kh**-te ine-en/ine-e/ine ... **bi**-te*

a white coffee
einen Kaffee mit Milch
*ine-en ka**fay** mit milkh*

a large white coffee
ein Haferl mit Milch
*ine **haferl** mit milkh*

a decaff coffee
einen entkoffeinierten Kaffee
*ine-en ent-kof-fe-ee**neer**ten ka**fay***

a hot chocolate
eine heiße Schokolade
*ine-e **hay**-se shoko-**lah**-de*

a tea with milk
einen Tee mit Milch
ine-en tay mit milkh

a half lager
ein kleines Bier
*ine **kline**-es beer*

an orange juice
einen Orangensaft
*ine-en o**ron**jen-zaft*

an apple juice
einen Apfelsaft
*ine-en **ap**-fel-zaft*

a red wine
einen Rotwein
*ine-en **roht**vine*

a white wine
einen Weißwein
*ine-en **vice**vine*

a bottle of mineral water
eine Flasche Mineralwasser
*ine-e **fla**-she mine**ral**-vasser*

fizzy	**still**
sprudelnd	still
shproodelnt	shtill

◀ Snack board

sandwiches

bread roll with meat or cheese

soup

sweets

Pfefferminz
pfe-fer-mints
mint

Himbeere
him-beh-re
raspberry

Erdbeere
ert-beh-re
strawberry

Johannisbeere
yohanis-beh-re
blackcurrant

Zitrone
tsitroh-ne
lemon

Ananas
ana-nas
pineapple

Pfirsich
pfeer-zikh
peach

Pistazie
pis-ta-tsee-e
pistacchio

Haselnuss
hah-zel-noos
hazelnut

Weintraube
vine-trow-be
grape

keywords keywords keywords

▶
You can find a great variety of cakes at a *Café Konditorei.*

until
3 o'clock

lunch menu

can we eat here?
können wir hier essen?
kur'-nen veer heer es-sen

what can we eat?
was können wir essen?
vas kur'-nen veer es-sen

do you have a dish of the day?
haben Sie ein Tagesgericht?
hah-ben zee ine tah-ges-gerikht

what is the dish of the day?
was ist das Tagesgericht?
vas ist das tah-ges-gerikht

what sandwiches do you have?
was für Sandwiches haben Sie?
vas foor sandwiches hah-ben zee

what cakes do you have?
was für Kuchen haben Sie?
vas foor koo-khen hah-ben zee

I would like ice-cream
ich möchte Eis
ikh mur'kh-te ice

what flavours do you have?
was für Eissorten haben Sie?
vas foor ice-sor-ten hah-ben zee

talking

FOOD & DRINK ▶ MEALS

80

In smaller towns restaurants tend to shut one day (generally Mondays). As a rule, eating places (including restaurants) have a menu with prices outside, so you will be prepared for the cost before going in. Restaurants usually offer set-price meals.

price includes aperitif and parking

◀ Some hotels offer special deals. Check what is included in the price.

Restaurants usually offer set-price ▼ meals.

closed on Mondays

You will find a good variety of Chinese and Italian restaurants. Turkish food tends to be sold in snackbars rather than restaurants.

I would like to book a table
ich möchte einen Tisch reservieren
ikh mur'kh-te ine-en tish rayzer-veeren

for 4 people
für vier Personen
foor feer per-zohnen

for tonight
für heute Abend
foor hoy-te ahbent

for tomorrow night
für morgen Abend
foor morgen ahbent

for lunch
zum Mittagessen
tsoom mitahk-es-sen

at 12.30
um zwölf Uhr dreißig
oom tsvur'lf oor dry-sikh

at 7.30
um sieben Uhr dreißig
oom zeeben oor dry-sikh

at 8 o'clock
um acht Uhr
oom akht oor

smoking/non-smoking
Raucher/Nichtraucher
row-kher/nikht-row-kher

in the name of ...
auf den Namen ...
owf den nah-men ...

talking talking talking

◀ Look out for different restaurant offers.

post-theatre menu (from 10 pm)

Syrian and Lebanese dishes with pitta bread

vegetarian dishes on request

open from 12 noon to midnight

take-away and party catering

the menu please
die Speisekarte bitte
*dee **shpy**-ze-kar-te **bi**-te*

the wine list please
die Weinkarte bitte
*dee **vine**-kar-te **bi**-te*

do you have a children's menu?
haben Sie eine Kinderkarte?
*hah-ben zee ine-e **kin**-der-kar-te*

for a starter I will have ...
als Vorspeise nehme ich ...
*als **for**-shpy-ze **nay**-me ikh ...*

for a main dish I will have ...
als Hauptgericht nehme ich ...
*als **howpt**-gerikht **nay**-me ikh ...*

what vegetarian dishes do you have?
welche vegetarischen Gerichte haben Sie?
***vel**-khe vaygay-**ta**rish-en ge**rikh**-te **hah**-ben zee*

what desserts do you have?
welche Nachspeisen haben Sie?
***vel**-khe **nakh**-shpy-zen **hah**-ben zee*

some tap water please
etwas Leitungswasser bitte
***et**-vas **lye**-toongs-vasser **bi**-te*

some more bread please
noch etwas Brot bitte
*nokh **et**-vas broht **bi**-te*

the bill please
zahlen bitte
***tsah**len **bi**-te*

we would like to pay separately
wir möchten getrennt bezahlen
*veer **mur'kh**-ten ge-**trent** be-**tsah**len*

talking talking talking talking

*Service and VAT are included (**Alle Preise inklusive Bedienung und Mehrwertsteuer**). Tipping is optional.*

Snack menu
▼

chicken broth with egg and bread roll

chicken broth with bread roll

vol au vent filled with chicken in white sauce

vol au vent filled with meat sauce

ham open sandwich

salami open sandwich

cheese open sandwich

boiled sausage with bread

KLEINE SPEISEKARTE	DM
Hühnerbrühe mit Brötchen	4,20
Hühnerbrühe mit Ei und Brötchen	4,80
Köingspastete	9,50
Ragout fin	9,50
Schinkenbrot	7,20
Salamibrot	7,20
Käsebrot	7,20
Bockwurst mit Brot	4,50

Germany has a huge variety of bread. It is generally served at breakfast or with a light evening meal. Butter is usually served with bread. Note that German butter is unsalted. ▶

You will find a wonderful selection of mouth-watering cakes at **Café Konditorei**, generally served with cream (**mit Sahne**). ◀

Don't be overwhelmed by German words – they may be long, but they are made up of smaller bits of words. Try and work out what the item is by identifying what makes up the long word. So **Tomatencremesuppe** *is cream of tomato soup. You will also come across English terms such as* **Snacks** *and* **Fingerfood.** *There are also usually children's menus. Remember, German portions are quite large!*

SPEISEKARTE *menu*

FRÜHSTÜCK *breakfast*

SUPPEN *soups*

VORSPEISEN *starters*

EIERSPEISEN *egg dishes*

SALATE *salads*

HAUPTGERICHTE *main dishes*

NUDELGERICHTE *pasta dishes*

FISCH und MEERESFRÜCHTE *fish and seafood*

FLEISCHGERICHTE *meat dishes*

BEILAGEN *side dishes*

SPEZIALITÄTEN *special dishes*

GEMÜSE *vegetables*

NACHSPEISEN *sweet*

KUCHEN *cakes*

WARME GETRÄNKE *hot drinks*

ALKOHOLFREIE GETRÄNKE *alcohol-free drinks*

FRUCHTSÄFTE *fruit juice*

BEER

*If you are a beer lover, Germany is the place to be. There are over 1,000 breweries with more than half of them in Bavaria. Many cities have at least one brewpub. Wheat beers are a speciality of Bavaria along with smoked beer. It is best to sample the local beer in the place it has been brewed. In Cologne you should try the pale refreshing **Kölsch** and in Düsseldorf sample the darkish malty **Altbier**.*

▲ *Pilsner*
A typical lager available all over Germany

▲ *Hefe-Weißbier*
A speciality beer from Bavaria with a fruity, slightly smoked aroma.

▲ *Kölsch*
A pale-coloured, light-textured, fruity-flavoured beer brewed in Cologne. Best drunk in a brewpub.

▲ *Weißbier*
The Bavarians also brew dark versions of their wheat beers. These may contain some malted wheat that has been darkened by roasting. *Dunkel* means dark.

Pilsner
pils-ner
pils lager

Weißbier
vice-beer
wheat beer

Fassbier
fass-beer
draught

Rauchbier
rowkh-beer
smoked beer

Radler
rad-ler
lager shandy

Helles
hel-les
lager

Dunkles
doonk-les
ale

ein Großes
ine groh-ses
large

ein Kleines
ine kline-es
small

what beers do you have?
was für Biere haben Sie?
*vas foor **bee**-re **hah**-ben zee*

can you recommend a local beer?
können Sie ein Bier aus dieser Gegend empfehlen?
***kur'**-nen zee ine beer ows **dee**zer **gay**gent em-**fay**len*

I would like to try a speciality beer
ich möchte eine Bierspezialität probieren
*ikh **mur'kh**-te ine-e **beer**-sphay-tsya-litayt pro-**bee**-ren*

do you have alcohol-free beers?
haben Sie alkoholfreie Biere?
***hah**-ben zee alko-**hol**-fry-e **bee**-re*

a large beer
ein großes Bier
*ine **groh**-ses beer*

a small beer
ein kleines Bier
*ine **kli**ne-es beer*

a litre glass of beer
eine Maß Bier
ine-e mahs beer

what bottled beer do you have?
was für Flaschenbiere haben Sie?
*vas foor **fla**shen-bee-re **hah**-ben zee*

*Wines are usually categorised according to three criteria: the overall growing area, the village or even the vineyard where they are produced, and the type of grape they are made from. Major grape varieties include **Riesling**, **Edelzwicker**, **Gewürztraminer** and **Müller-Thurgau**. The names of the villages and vineyards producing wines are innumerable. The name of the wine is often the name of the village (e.g. **Nierstein**) plus the name of the particular vineyard (e.g. **Gutes Domtal**) which combined become **Niersteiner Gutes Domtal**.*

Qualitätsweine mit Prädikat
This is the mark of the highest quality wine. If you want a good German wine, choose this rather than *Tafelwein*, *Landwein* or *QbA* (wine from a specified region).

Meßmer

1996
SCHEUREBE
KABINETT
Burrweiler Altenforst
Gutsabfüllung

bottled at source

Weingut
Herbert Meßmer D-76835 Burrweiler
Qualitätswein mit Prädikat A.P.Nr. 50160952597

750 ml   PFALZ   alc. 11.0%vol

Qualitätswein b. A.
This indicates that the grapes are from one region; in this case, Rheinhessen.

1993 er

Bereich Nierstein

RHEINHESSEN

Qualitätswein b. A.
L - A. P. Nr. 4 342 352 018 94

Produce of Germany

BOTTLED FOR ODDBINS BY RP 342352 IN D 87339005

9.5% vol

75cle

Note this wine's lower alcoholic content. In general drier wines benefit from some bottle age, and lower alcohol or sweeter wines are good for instant drinking.

Weingut
KÜNSTLER

RHEINGAU

1997

Riesling
Kabinett halbtrocken
Qualitätswein mit Prädikat
A.P.Nr. 40 060 012 98

11,0% Alc.
by Vol.

Erzeugerabfüllung Rheingau
PRODUCE OF GERMANY

750 ml e

Halbtrocken **MEDIUM DRY**

◀ German *Riesling* is one of the best, most rewarding wines in the world. The finest examples contrive to be tangy, steely, minerally, densely fruity and bone-dry all at once. It is worth trying those from *Rheinhessen*, *Pfalz*, *Nahe* or *Rheingau* regions.

This is a good medium dry wine. If you are choosing a wine from a cool area like the *Mosel*, select a *Riesling Kabinett* that is only moderate in alcohol, say 8 or 9%, so that the fruit sweetness remains to counter the cool-climate acidity. Other *Rieslings* are better at 12% alcohol upwards.

keywords keywords keywords

Weisswein
vice-vine
white wine

Roséwein
rohzay-vine
rosé wine

Rotweine
rohtvine
red wine

Sekt
zekt
sparkling wine

trocken
tro-ken
dry

halbtrocken
halp-tro-ken
medium dry

lieblich
leeb-likh
sweet

Tafelwein
tahfel-vine
table wine

the wine list please
die Weinkarte bitte
dee vinekar-te bi-te

what wines do you have?
was für Weine haben Sie?
vas foor vine-e hah-ben zee

is there a local wine?
gibt es einen Wein aus dieser Gegend?
gipt es ine-en vine ows dee-zer gaygent

can you recommend a good wine?
können Sie mir einen guten Wein empfehlen?
kur'-nen zee mee ine-en goo-ten vine em-fay-len

a glass of red wine please
ein Glas Rotwein bitte
ine glahs roht-vine bi-te

a glass of white wine please
ein Glas Weisswein bitte
ine glahs vice-vine bi-te

a bottle of wine
eine Flasche Wein
ine-e fla-she vine

red wine
Rotwein
roht-vine

white wine
Weisswein
vice-vine

a carafe of house wine
eine Karaffe Hauswein
ine-e kara-fe hows-vine

a glass of wine
ein Glas Wein
ine glahs vine

talking talking talking

Krabben
*fresh shrimps served along the
North Sea coast*
Friesischer Tee
*tea served in Frisia with its
tradition of tea trading*
Grünkohl mit Speck und Pinkel
curly kale with bacon & sausage

Saure Rippchen
sweet and sour pork ribs
Sauerfleisch
marinated sour meat
Rübenmalheur
turnip stew
Lübecker Marzipan
marzipan, a specialty of Lübeck

DÄNE

Potthucke
potato fritters with soft smoked sausage
Kölsch
*top-fermented speciality beer
from Cologne*
Westfälische Bohnensuppe
bean soup

K
SCH
HO

NIEDERLANDE

Hamb

• Bremer

NIEDERSACHS
H

Schwälm
dumplings with sour cream salad
Rotweinbraten
braised beef in red wine
Rehbraten
roast venison

• Dortmund
• Essen
BELGIEN   • Duisburg
• Köln
NORDRHEIN-
WESTFALEN

RHEINLAND-
PFALZ   Frankfurt

Saumagen
stuffed pig's stomach from the Palatinate
Wein
try some of the excellent local white wine
Forelle
trout is often on the menu in this region

LUXEMBURG   SAARLAND

Stuttg

FRANKREICH

BAD
WÜRTTE

Viez
apple wine from the region
Budeng mit Gellenewemutsch
*hot black pudding served with mash
of carrots and potatoes*
Dibbelabbes
potato soufflé with bacon

SCHWE

Schwarzwälder Schinken
smoked Black Forest ham
Schwarzwälder Kirschtorte
Black Forest gateau
Spätzle
special noodles

Himmel und Erde
stew made with apples and potato
Grützwurst
sausage similar to black pudding
Mecklenburger Rippenbraten
*rib roast best served with potatoes
and red cabbage*
Tollatschen
sweet and sour meat

Currywurst
*roast sausage served in a
spicy sauce*
Spreewälder Gurken
*pickled cucumbers from the
Spreewald region*
Zinnaer Klosterbruder
a dark herb liqueur

Arme Ritter
*'poor knights': white bread steeped
in egg and fried*
Baumkuchen
*'tree cake':cake made up of many
layers with filling inbetween*
Nordhäuser Doppelkorn
local rye schnapps

Quarkkeulchen
curd cheese dough fried and sliced
Sauerbraten
*marinated beef roast often served
with dumplings and red cabbage*
Rinderrouladen
beef olives

Thüringer Bratwurst
*the famous Thuringian roasted
sausage*
Thüringer Klöße
*Thuringian dumplings, among the
most famous in Germany*
Rotkäppchen-Sekt
a locally produced sparkling wine

Weißwurst
veal sausage
Brez'n
large pretzel
Leberkäse
*fine meat loaf, served warm in a
bread roll at snackbars*

There are times when you cannot eat some things. It is as well warning the waiter before making your choice.

I'm vegetarian
ich bin Vegetarier
*ikh bin vaygay-**ta**ree-er*

I don't eat meat/pork
ich esse kein Fleisch/Schweinefleisch
*ikh **es**-se kayn flysh/**shvy**-ne-flysh*

I don't eat fish/shellfish
ich esse keinen Fisch/Meeresfrüchte
*ikh **es**-se **kay**-nen fish/**meh**res-frur'kh-te*

I'm allergic to shellfish
ich bin allergisch gegen Meeresfrüchte
*ikh bin a-**ler**-gish **gay**-gen **meh**res-frur'kh-te*

I am allergic to peanuts
ich bin allergisch gegen Erdnüsse
*ikh bin a-**ler**-gish **gay**-gen **ert**-noos-se*

I can't eat raw eggs
ich kann kein rohes Ei essen
*ikh kan kayn **roh**-es eye **es**-sen*

I can't eat liver
ich kann keine Leber essen
*ikh kan **kay**-ne **lay**-ber **es**-sen*

I am on a diet
ich bin auf Diät
*ikh bin owf dee-**ayt***

I don't drink alcohol
ich trinke keinen Alkohol
*ikh **trin**-ke **kay**-nen **al**ko-hol*

what is in this?
was ist darin enthalten?
*vas ist da-**rin** ent-**hal**ten*

is it raw?
ist das roh?
ist das roh

is it made with unpasteurised milk?
ist das mit nicht pasteurisierter Milch gemacht?
*ist das mit nikht pastur'-ree-**zeer**-ter milkh ge**makht***

gebraten
*ge-**brah**-ten*
fried

gekocht
*ge-**kokht***
boiled

gedämpft
*ge-**dempft***
steamed

geröstet
*ge-**rur's**-tet*
roast

am Spieß
am shpees
kebab

gefüllt
*ge-**foolt***
stuffed

gegrillt
*ge-**grilt***
grilled

geräuchert
*ge-**roy**-khert*
smoked

geschmort
*ge-**shmohrt***
stewed/braised

mariniert
*maree-**neert***
marinated

eingelegt
*ine-ge-**lehgt***
pickled

pochiert
*po-**kheert***
poached

gezuckert
*ge-**tsoo**-kert*
sugared

gesalzen
*ge-**zalt**-sen*
salted

MENU READER

A

Apfelstrudel

Aal eel
  Aalsuppe eel soup
Allgäuer Emmentaler whole-milk hard cheese from the Allgäu
Allgäuer Käsespätzle cheese noodles from the Allgäu
Alpzirler cow's milk cheese from Austria
Alsterwasser lager shandy
Altbier top-fermented beer from the lower Rhine
Ananas pineapple
Apfel apple
  Apfelkorn apple brandy
  Apfelkuchen apple cake
  Apfelsaft apple juice
  Apfelsalami salami with apple
  Apfelstrudel flaky pastry filled with apples and spices
  Apfelwein cider (apple wine)

Aprikose

Aprikose apricot
Art style or fashion of
Artischocken artichokes
Aubergine aubergine
Auflauf baked dish, can be sweet or savoury
Aufschnitt sliced cold meats
Austern oysters

Aufschnitt

B

Bäckerofen 'baker's oven', pork and lamb bake from Saarland
Backpflaumen prunes
Banane banana
Bandnudeln ribbon pasta
Barack apricot brandy
Barsch perch
Bauernfrühstück scrambled eggs, bacon, cooked diced potatoes, onions, tomatoes
Baunzerl little bread roll with distinctive cut on top
Bayrisch Kraut shredded cabbage cooked with sliced apples, wine and sugar
Beilage side dish
Bereich Bernkastel area along the Moselle producing crisp white wines

Bergkäse cheese from the Alps

Berliner doughnut filled with jam

Berliner Weiße fizzy beer with fruit syrup added

Berner Erbsensuppe soup made of dried peas with pig's trotters

Bienenstich type of cake, baked on a tray with a coating of almonds and sugar

Bierschinken beer sausage with ham

Bierwurst beer sausage

Birchermüsli muesli

Birne pear
  Birnenmost pear wine
  Birnensekt sparkling pear wine

Birne

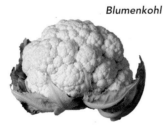

Blattsalat green salad

blau rare (meat); poached (fish)

Blauschimmelkäse blue cheese

Blumenkohl cauliflower

Blumenkohl

Blunz'm black pudding

Blutwurst black pudding

Bockbier strong beer (light or dark), drunk especially in Bavaria

Bockwurst

Bockwurst boiled sausage. A popular snack served with a bread roll

Böhmische Knödel sliced dumpling

Bohnen beans
  Bohnensalat bean salad
  Bohnensuppe thick bean and bacon soup

Bosniakerl wholemeal roll with caraway seeds

Brathähnchen roast chicken

Brathering fried herring (eaten cold)

Bratkartoffeln fried potatoes

Bratwurst fried sausage. A popular snack served with a bread roll

Brauner strong black coffee with a little milk

Bremer Kükenragout Bremen chicken fricassée

Broiler spit-roasted chicken

Brombeeren blackberries

Bröselknödel soup with little dumplings prepared with bone marrow and breadcrumbs

Brot bread

Brötchen bread roll

Brühwurst thick frankfurter

B'soffene pudding soaked in mulled wine

Buletten thick hamburgers
  Buletten mit Kartoffelsalat

thick hamburgers with potato salad

Bündnerfleisch raw beef smoked and dried, served thinly sliced

Burgenländische Krautsuppe thickened cabbage and vegetable soup

Butter butter
   Butterbrot open sandwich
   Butterkäse high-fat cheese

C

Cervelat fine beef and pork salami

Chindbettering ring of bread

Cremeschnitten cream slices

Champignons button mushrooms

Currywurst sausage served with a spicy sauce. A popular snack originally from Berlin.

D

Damenkäse mild buttery cheese

Dampfnudeln hot yeast dumplings with vanilla sauce

Danziger Goldwasser schnapps containing tiny bits of gold leaf

Datteln dates

Deutsches Beefsteak thick hamburger

dicke Bohnen broad beans

Doppelbockbier like *Bockbier*, but still stronger

Dorsch cod

Dresdner Suppentopf Dresden vegetable soup with dumplings

Dunkles dark beer

E

Ei egg
   Eier im Glas soft boiled eggs served in a glass

Eierkuchen pancakes

Eierschwammerln chanterelles

Eierspeispfandl special Viennese omelette

eingelegt pickled

Einmachsuppe chicken or veal broth with cream and egg

Einspänner coffee with whipped cream served in a glass

Eintopf stew

Eis ice cream

Eisbecher knickerbocker glory

Eisbein boiled pork knuckle often served with sauerkraut

Eisbein mit Bockwurst und Sauerkraut

Eiskaffee iced coffee served with vanilla ice cream

Eiswein a rich, naturally sweet, white wine made from grapes which are harvested only after a period of frost

Emmentaler Swiss Emmental, whole-milk hard cheese

Ennstaler blue cheese from mixed milk

Ente duck

Erbach area producing scented white wines mainly from Riesling grape

Erbsen

Erbsen peas
  Erbsenpüree green pea purée
  Erbsensuppe pea soup

Erdäpfel potatoes
  Erdäpfelgulasch spicy sausage and potato stew
  Erdäpfelknödel potato and semolina dumplings
  Erdäpfelkren relish with potato and horseradish
  Erdäpfelnudeln fried, boiled potato balls tossed in fried breadcrumbs

Erdbeeren strawberries

Fenchel

Fenchel fennel

fettarm low in fat

Fisch fish
  Fischfilet fish fillet
  Fischgerichte fish and seafood
  Fischklöße fish dumplings
  Fischsuppe fish soup

flambiert flambé

Fledermaus boiled beef in horseradish cream browned in the oven

Fleisch meat
  Fleischgerichte meat dishes
  Fleischklößchen meatballs
  Fleischlaberln highly seasoned meat cake
  Fleischpflanzerl meatballs, a Bavarian speciality
  Fleischsalat sausage salad with onions
  Fleischsuppe meat soup served with dumplings

Flunder flounder

Fondue melted cheese with wine and bread for dipping

Erdbeeren

erster Gang first course

Essig vinegar

Export Bier premium beer

F

Feigen

Falscher Hase baked mince meatloaf

Fasan pheasant

Feigen figs

Forelle trout
  Forelle blau steamed trout with potatoes and vegetables
  Forelle Müllerin trout fried in batter with almonds
  Forelle Steiermark trout fillet with bacon in white sauce

Frikadelle thick hamburger

frisch fresh

Fritattensuppe beef broth with strips of pancake

Froschschenkel frogs' legs

Frucht fresh fruit

Früchtetee fruit tea

Fruchtsaft fruit juice

Fünfkernbrot wholemeal bread made with five different cereals

G

Gang course

Gans goose
   Gänseleber foie gras
   Gänseleberpastete goose liver pâté

Gebäck pastries

gebacken baked

gebackene Leber liver fried in breadcrumbs

Gebildebroten ornamented bread loaf

gebraten roasted/fried

gedämpft steamed

Geflügel poultry

gefüllt stuffed/filled
   gefüllte Kalbsbrust stuffed breast of veal
   gefüllte Paprika peppers filled with mince

gegrillt grilled
   gegrillter Lachs grilled salmon

Gehacktes mince

gekocht boiled
   gekochtes Rindfleisch mit grüner Soße boiled beef with green sauce

gemischter Salat mixed salad

Gemüse vegetables
   Gemüse und Klöße vegetables and dumplings
   Gemüselasagne vegetable lasagne
   Gemüseplatte mixed vegetables
   Gemüsesuppe vegetable soup

geräuchert smoked

Gericht dish

geschmort braised

Geschnetzeltes thinly sliced

grüne Bohnen

meat in sauce served with potatoes or rice

Geselchtes smoked meats

Gespritzter spritzer, white wine and soda water

Gewürzgurken gherkins

Gitziprägel baked rabbit in batter (a Swiss dish)

Glühwein mulled wine

Goldbarsch redfish

Graf Görz Austrian soft cheese

Grammeln croissant stuffed with bacon

Grießklößchensuppe soup with semolina dumplings

Grießtaler gnocchi

Grog hot rum

grüne Bohnen green beans

grüne Veltlinersuppe green wine soup

grüner Salat green salad

Gulasch

Gurke

Gruyère gruyère cheese

Güggeli roast chicken with onions and mushrooms in white wine sauce

Gulasch stewed diced beef and pork with paprika served with dumplings and red cabbage

Gulaschsuppe spicy meat soup with paprika

Gulyas beef stew with paprika

Gumpoldskirchner spicy white wine from Austria

Gurke cucumber
  Gurkensalat cucumber salad

gutbürgerliche Küche traditional German cooking

Gyros kebab

H

Hackbraten mincemeat roast

Hackepeter auf Schrippen mit Zwiebeln spiced minced pork on rolls, with onions

Hackfleisch mince

Hähnchen chicken
  Hähnchenbrust chicken breast

halbtrocken medium-dry

Hamburger Rundstück Hamburg meat roll

Hammel mutton

Hartkäse hard cheese

Hase hare

Hasenbraten roast hare

Hauptgericht main course

Hausbrauerei house beer (own brewery)

hausgemacht home-made

Hausmannskost good traditional home cooking

Hecht pike

Hefe-Weizen wheat beer

Heidschnuckenragout lamb stew

heiß hot

Helles light beer

Hering herring
  Heringsschmaus herring in creamy sauce

Herz heart

Heuriger new wine

Himbeeren raspberries
  Himbeergeist raspberry brandy

Himbeeren

Hirn brain

Hirsch venison

Hockheim strong white wines from the Rheingau region

Honig honey

Hühnchen chicken

Hühnerfrikasse chicken fricassée

Hühnerschenkel chicken drumsticks

Hühnerleber chicken liver

Hummer lobster

I

Ingwer ginger

J

Jägerschnitzel cutlet served with mushrooms and wine sauce

Joghurt yoghurt

Johannisbeeren redcurrants

Jura Omelette bacon, potato and onion omelette

Karotten

Kartoffelsuppe

K

Kabeljau cod

Kaffee coffee
  Kaffee komplett coffee with milk and sugar
  Kaffee mit Milch coffee with milk

Kaisermelange black coffee with an egg yolk

Kaiserschmarren strips of pancake served with raisins, sugar and cinnamon

Kakao cocoa

Kalb veal
  Kalbsbraten roast veal
  Kalbshaxe knuckle of veal
  Kalbskoteletts veal cutlets
  Kalbsleber calf's liver
  Kalbsschnitzel veal escalope

kalt cold
  kalte Platte cold meat platter

Kaninchen rabbit

Kapuziner Austrian equivalent to a cappuccino which is black coffee with a drop of milk

Karotten carrots

Karpfen carp
  Karpfen blau poached carp
  Karpfen in Bier carp poached in beer with herbs

Kartoffeln potatoes
  Kartoffelklöße potato dumplings
  Kartoffelpuffer potato pancakes. A popular snack

Kartoffelpüree mashed potatoes
Kartoffelsalat potato salad
Kartoffelsuppe potato soup

Käse cheese
  Käsebrötchen roll with small bacon pieces in the dough and melted cheese on top
  Käsefondue dish made from melted cheese and flavoured with wine and kirsch into which you dip bread
  Käsekuchen cheesecake
  Käsenudeln noodles served with cheese
  Käseplatte cheese platter with various cheeses
  Käsesuppe cheese soup

Kasseler smoked pork
  Kasseler Rippe mit Sauerkraut smoked pork rib with sauerkraut

Kastanienroulade roulade with chestnut filling

Kassler mit Rotkohl und Spätzle

Kirschen

Katenspeck streaky bacon

Kaviar caviar

Kekse biscuits

Kirschen cherries

Kirschwasser cherry schnapps

Kirtagssuppe soup with caraway seed thickened with potato

Klops rissole

Klöße dumplings

Knackwurst hot spicy sausage. A popular snack served with bread

Knoblauch garlic

Knödel dumpling
  Knödelbeignets fruit dumplings

Knöderl dumplings

Kohl cabbage

Kohlsprossen Brussels sprouts

Kölsch top-fermented beer from Cologne

Knödelbeignets mit Pflaumenkompott

Kompott stewed fruit

Königsberger Klopse meatballs served in thick white sauce with capers

Kopfsalat lettuce salad

Korn rye spirit

Kotelett pork chop/cutlet dipped in breadcrumbs and deep fried

Krabben prawns
  Krabbencocktail prawn cocktail

Kraftbrot wheatgerm bread

Kraftfleisch corned beef

Kraftsuppe consommé

Krapfen doughnut

Kräutertee herbal tea

Krautwickerl stuffed cabbage

Kren horseradish

Kristall-Weizen a kind of sparkling beer

Kroketten croquettes

Kürbis pumpkin

L

Labskaus cured pork, herring and potato stew

Lachs salmon
  Lachsbrot smoked salmon with bread

Lamm lamb

Lammkeule leg of lamb

Lasagne lasagne

Lauch leeks

Leber liver

Leberkäse pork liver meatloaf

Leberknödelsuppe light soup with chicken liver dumplings

Leberpastete liver paté

Leberwurst liver sausage

Leinsamenbrot wholemeal bread with linseed

Leipziger Allerlei vegetable dish made from peas, carrots, cauliflower and cabbage

Likör liqueur

Lammkeule mit Rotkohl und Klößen

Limburger strong cheese flavoured with herbs

Limonade lemonade

Linsen lentils
  Linsenspecksalat lentil salad with bacon
  Linsensuppe lentil and sausage soup

Linzer Torte latticed tart with jam topping

Liptauer Quark cream cheese with paprika and herbs

Lunge lungs

M

Mais sweetcorn

Maiskolben corn on the cob

Makrele mackerel

Malzbier dark malt beer (unfermented)

Mandarine tangerine

Maiskolben

Marillenknödel apricot dumplings

Marmelade jam

Maronitorte chestnut tart

Märzenbier beer made for the Oktoberfest, the famous Munich Beer Festival

Mastochsenhaxe knuckle of beef (with sauce) from Sachsen-Anhalt

Matjes herring

Maultaschen ravioli-like pasta filled with pork, veal and spinach mixture

Meeresfrüchte seafood

Mehrkornbrötchen rolls made with several kinds of wholemeal flour

Melange milky coffee

Melone melon

Mettenden sausage with a filling similar to mince

Milch milk
  Milchrahmstrudel strudel filled with egg custard and soft cheese
  Milchshake milk shake

Mineralwasser mineral water

Mirabellen small yellow plums

Mischbrot grey bread made with rye and wheat flour

Mohn poppy seed
  Mohnnudeln noodles with poppy seeds, cinnamon, sugar and butter
  Mohntorte gâteau with poppy seeds

Möhren carrots
  Möhrensalat carrot salad

Mohr im Hemd chocolate pudding

Most fruit juice; (in the south) fruit wine

Münchener a kind of dark lager from Munich

Muscheln mussels

N

Nachspeisen desserts

Nieren kidneys

Nierstein village on the Rhine producing medium to sweet white Rheinwein

Nockerln small dumplings

Nudeln noodles
Nudelsuppe noodle soup

Nüsse nuts
Nusskuchen nut cake
Nusstorte nut gâteau

O

Obst fruit
Obstkuchen fruit cake
Obstsalat fruit salad

Ochsenschwanz oxtail
Ochsenschwanzsuppe oxtail soup

Öl oil

Oppenheim village on the Rhine producing fine white wines

Orange orange

Orangensaft orange juce

P

Paprika

Palatschinken pancakes filled with curd mixture or jam or ice cream

Pampelmuse grapefruit

paniert coated with breadcrumbs

Paprika peppers

Pellkartoffeln small jacket potatoes served with their skins, often accompanied by Quark

Pfannkuchen pancakes

Pfeffer pepper
Pfefferkäse mit Schinken ham and pepper cheese log

Pfirsich peach

Pflaume

Pflaumen plums
Pflaumenkuchen plum tart

Pilsner a strong, slightly bitter lager

Pilze mushrooms

Pilzsuppe mushroom soup

Pommes frites chips

Powidltascherl ravioli-like pasta filled with plum jam

Pumpernickel very dark bread made with wholemeal coarse rye flour

Punschpudding pudding containing alcohol

Pute turkey
Putenschnitzel turkey breast in breadcrumbs

Pilze

Rinderbraten

Q

Quark curd cheese

R

Raclette melted cheese and potatoes

Ragout stew

Rahm sour cream

Rahmschnitzel cutlet with a creamy sauce

Rahmsuppe creamy soup

Räucherkäse mit Schinken smoked cheese with bacon pieces in it

Räucherkäse mit Walnüssen smoked cheese with pieces of walnut in it

Räucherlachs smoked salmon

Räucherspeck smoked bacon

Reh venison
  Rehrücken roast saddle of venison

Reibekuchen potato cakes

Reis rice

Riesling Riesling wine
  Rieslingsuppe wine soup made with Riesling

Rind(fleisch) beef
  Rinderbraten roast beef
  Rinderrouladen rolled beef (beef olives)

Rippenbraten roast spare ribs

Risi lisi, Risipisi rice with peas

Rollmops marinated herring fillets rolled up with small pieces of onion, gherkins and white peppercorns

Rosenkohl Brussels sprouts

Roséwein rosé wine

Rosinen raisins

Rösti fried diced potatoes, onions and bacon

Rotbarsch rosefish

rote Bete beetroot

rote Grütze raspberry, red currant and wine jelly served with fresh cream

rote Rübe beetroot

Rotkohl red cabbage

Rotkohl

Rotwein red wine

Roulade beef olive

Rübe turnip

Rührei scrambled eggs

S

Sachertorte rich chocolate gâteau

Saft juice

Sahne cream

Salat salad

Salz salt

Salzkartoffeln boiled potatoes

Sardellen anchovies

Sardinen sardines

Sauerbraten braised pickled beef served with dumplings and vegetables

Sauerbraten mit Rotkohl und Klößen

Sauerkraut shredded pickled white cabbage

saure Lunge pickled lungs

Scampi scampi

Schafskäse ewe's milk cheese

Schaschlik shish kebab

Schellfisch haddock

Schnaps strong spirit

Schinken ham
  Schinkenkipferl ham-filled croissant
  Schinkenwurst ham sausage

Schlachtplatte mixture of cold sausages and meat

Schmelzkäse cheese spread

Schmorgurken hotpot with cucumber and meat

Schnecke snail

Sauerkraut mit Bockwurst

Schnittlauch chives
  Schnittlauchbrot chives on bread

Schnitzel escalope served with potatoes and vegetables

Schokolade chocolate

Schokoladentorte chocolate gateaux

Scholle plaice

Schwäbischer Apfelkuchen apple cake from Swabia

Schwammerlgulasch mushroom stew

Schwarzbrot wholemeal rye bread

schwarze Johannisbeeren blackcurrants

schwarzer Tee black tea

Schwarzwälder Kirschtorte

Schwarzwälder Kirschtorte Black Forest gâteau

Schwarzwälder Schinken Black Forest ham

Schwarzwälder Torte fruit compote flan with cream

Schwein pork
  Schweinebraten roast pork
  Schweinefleisch pork
  Schweinehaxe knuckle of pork
  Schweinekotelett pork chop
  Schweinsrostbraten roast pork

Schwertfisch swordfish

Seezunge sole

Spargel

Sekt sparkling wine like champagne

Selters(wasser) sparkling mineral water

Semmelknödel whole roll dumpling

Senf mustard

Sesam sesame

Skampi scampi

Slivovitz plum schnapps

Sonnenblumenbrot wholemeal bread with sunflower seeds

Soße sauce

Spanferkel suckling pig

Spargel asparagus
　Spargelcremesuppe cream of asparagus soup
　Spargelsalat asparagus salad

Spätzle home-made noodles

Speck bacon (fat)

Spiegelei fried egg, sunny side up

Spieß kebab style

Spinat spinach

Spinat

Sprudel sparkling mineral water

Stachelbeeren gooseberries

Stachelbeertorte gooseberry tart

Stangl croissant covered with cheese

Starkbier strong beer

Steinbutt turbot

Steinpilze wild mushroom found in the woods

Steirischer Selchkäse ewe's milk cheese

Steirisches Lammkarree mit Basilikum lamb baked with basil

Sterz Austrian polenta

Stollen spiced loaf with candied peel traditionally eaten at Christmas

Stollen

Strudel strudel

Sulz/Sülze meat in aspic

Suppen soups

süß sweet

süßsauer sweet-and-sour

T

Tafelspitz boiled beef of various cuts

Tafelspitzsulz beef in aspic

Tagesgericht dish of the day

Tee tea
  Tee mit Milch tea with milk
  Tee mit Zitrone tea with lemon

Thunfisch tuna fish

Thüringer Rostbratwurst sausages from Thuringia, grilled or fried

Tilsiter savoury cheese with sharpish taste

Tintenfisch squid

Tomaten

Tomaten tomatoes
  Tomatensaft tomato juice
  Tomatensoße tomato sauce

Topf stew

Topfen curd cheese (Austria)
  Topfenknödel curd cheese dumplings
  Topfennudeln pasta with cheese
  Topfenstrudel flaky pastry strudel with curd-cheese filling

Torte gateau

Trauben grapes
  Traubensaft grape juice

Truthahn turkey

Türkischer Turkish coffee

U

überbacken baked in the oven with a layer of cheese on top

Trauben

V

Vollkorn- wholemeal

Vollkornbrot wholemeal bread

Vorspeisen starters

W

Wacholder juniper

Waldpilze wild mushrooms

Walnüsse walnuts

warm warm
  warmer Krautsalat salad with warm cabbage and crunchy bacon

Wasser water

Weichkäse cream cheese

Wein vine

Weinbrand brandy

Weinkarte wine list

Weißbrot wheat bread

Weiße golden wheat beer

Weißkohl white cabbage

Weißwein white wine

Weißwurst white sausage (veal and pork with herbs)

Weizenbier wheat beer (light or dark)

Wels catfish

Westfälischer Schinken Westphalian ham

Wiener frankfurters

Wiener Backhendl roast chicken covered in breadcrumbs

Wiener Fischfilets fish fillets baked in sour cream sauce

Wiener Hofburgtorte chocolate gâteau

Wiener Kartoffelsuppe potato soup with mushrooms

Wiener Schertorte Viennese chocolate cake

Wiener Schnitzel veal escalope fried in breadcrumbs

Wiener Würstchen frankfurter

Wild game
  Wildbraten roast venison
  Wildgulasch game stew

Wildschwein wild boar

Wirsingkohl Savoy cabbage

Zitrone

Wurst

Wurst sausage

Würstchen frankfurter

Würzfleisch strips of meat roasted in a spicy sauce

Z

Zander pike-perch

Ziegenkäse goat's milk cheese

Ziegett mixed milk cheese

Zigeunerschnitzel cutlet in paprika sauce

Zillertaler cow's cheese from the Zillertal

Zitrone lemon
  Zitronentee lemon tea

Zopf braided bread loaf

Zucchini courgette

Zucker sugar

Zuger Köteli baked dace with herbs and wine

Zunge tongue

Zwetschgen plums
  Zwetschgendatschi damson tart
  Zwetschgenknödel plum dumplings

Zwiebeln onions
  Zwiebelkuchen onion flan
  Zwiebelrostbraten large steak with onions
  Zwiebelsalami salami with onion
  Zwiebelsuppe onion soup

Zwiebeln

DICTIONARY

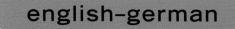

english–german

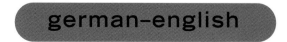

german–english

A

a *(with der words)* ein
  (with die words) eine
  (with das words) ein
abbey die Abtei
able: to be able können
abortion die Abtreibung
about *(concerning)* über
  about 4 o'clock ungefähr vier Uhr
above *(overhead)* oben
  (higher than) über
abroad im Ausland
abscess der Abszess
accelerator das Gaspedal
accent *(pronunciation)* der Akzent
to accept akzeptieren
accident der Unfall
accident and emergency department
  die Notaufnahme
accommodation die Unterkunft
to accompany begleiten
account *(bill)* die Rechnung
  (in bank) das Konto
account number die Kontonummer
to ache: it aches es tut weh
acid die Säure
actor der Schauspieler
adaptor der Zwischenstecker
address die Adresse
  what is the address? wie ist die
  Adresse?
address book das Adressbuch
adhesive tape das Klebeband
admission fee der Eintrittspreis
to admit *(to hospital)* einweisen
adult der/die Erwachsene
  for adults für Erwachsene
advance: in advance im Voraus
advertisement *(in paper)* die Anzeige
to advise raten
A&E die Notaufnahme
aeroplane das Flugzeug
aerosol die Spraydose
afraid: to be afraid of Angst haben
  vor
after *(afterwards)* danach
  after lunch nach dem Mittagessen
afternoon der Nachmittag
  this afternoon heute Nachmittag
  tomorrow afternoon morgen
  Nachmittag

in the afternoon am Nachmittag
aftershave das Rasierwasser
again wieder
against gegen
age das Alter
agency die Agentur
ago: *a week ago* vor einer Woche
to agree vereinbaren
agreement die Vereinbarung
AIDS das Aids
airbag der Airbag
airbed die Luftmatratze
air conditioning die Klimaanlage
air freshener der Lufterfrischer
airline die Fluggesellschaft
air mail: *by air mail* per Luftpost
airplane das Flugzeug
airport der Flughafen
airport bus der Flughafenbus
air ticket das Flugticket
aisle *(theatre, plane)* der Gang
alarm die Alarmanlage
alarm call der Weckruf
alarm clock der Wecker
alcohol der Alkohol
alcohol-free alkoholfrei
alcoholic alkoholisch
all alle
allergic: to be allergic to allergisch
  sein gegen
  I'm allergic to... ich bin allergisch
  gegen...
allergy die Allergie
to allow erlauben
  to be allowed dürfen
all right *(agreed)* in Ordnung
  are you all right? geht es Ihnen gut?
almost fast
alone allein
Alps die Alpen
already schon
also auch
altar der Altar
aluminium foil die Alufolie
always immer
a.m. vormittags
am: *I am* ich bin
amber *(traffic lights)* das Gelb
ambulance der Krankenwagen
America Amerika
American *adj* amerikanisch
  m/f der/die Amerikaner(in)
amount: *total amount* die
  Gesamtsumme

109 anaesthetic die Narkose
local anaesthetic die örtliche Betäubung
general anaesthetic die Vollnarkose
anchor der Anker
and und
angina die Angina
angry zornig
animal das Tier
ankle der Knöchel
anniversary der Jahrestag
to announce bekannt geben
announcement die Bekanntmachung
annual jährlich
another *(additional)* noch ein/noch eine/noch ein
(different) ein anderer/eine andere/ein anderes
another beer please noch ein Bier bitte
answer die Antwort
to answer antworten
answerphone der Anrufbeantworter
antacid das säurebindende Mittel
antibiotic das Antibiotikum
antifreeze das Frostschutzmittel
antihistamine das Antihistamin
anti-inflammatory das entzündungshemmende Mittel
antiques die Antiquitäten
antique shop der Antiquitätenladen
antiseptic das Antiseptikum
any jegliche(r/s)
have you any apples? haben Sie Äpfel?
anybody jeder
anything irgendetwas
anywhere irgendwo
apartment das Appartement
appendicitis die Blinddarmentzündung
apple der Apfel
appointment der Termin
I have an appointment ich habe einen Termin
approximately ungefähr
April der April
apron die Schürze
architect der/die Architekt(in)
architecture die Architektur
are sind ; seid ; bin
arm der Arm
armbands *(to swim)* die Schwimmflügel
armchair der Sessel
to arrange vereinbaren
to arrest verhaften

arrival die Ankunft
to arrive ankommen
art die Kunst
art gallery die Kunsthalle
arthritis die Arthritis
artificial künstlich
artist der/die Künstler(in)
ashtray der Aschenbecher
to ask *(question)* fragen
(for something) bitten um
asleep: to be asleep schlafen
to fall asleep einschlafen
aspirin das Aspirin
asthma das Asthma
I have asthma ich habe Asthma
at: at the hotel im Hotel
at home zu Hause
at 8 o'clock um acht Uhr
at once sofort
at night am Abend
to attack angreifen
attractive attraktiv
auction die Auktion
audience das Publikum
August der August
aunt die Tante
au pair das Au-pair-Mädchen
Australia Australien
Australian *adj* australisch
m/f der/die Australier(in)
Austria Österreich
Austrian *adj* österreichisch
m/f der/die Österreicher(in)
author der/die Autor(in)
automatic automatisch
automatic car das Automatikauto
auto-teller der Geldautomat
autumn der Herbst
available erhältlich
avalanche die Lawine
avenue die Allee
average der Durchschnitt
to avoid *(obstacle)* ausweichen
(person) meiden
awake wach
away weg
awful schrecklich
axe die Axt
axle *(car)* die Achse

B

baby das Baby
baby food die Babynahrung
baby milk die Babymilch
baby's bottle die Babyflasche
baby seat (in car) der Kindersitz
babysitter der/die Babysitter(in)
baby wipes die Babytücher
back (of body, hand) der Rücken
backpack der Rucksack
bacon der Speck
bad (weather, news) schlecht
  (fruit, vegetables) verdorben
badminton das Federballspiel
bag die Tasche
baggage das Gepäck
baggage allowance das Freigepäck
baggage reclaim die Gepäckausgabe
bait (for fishing) der Köder
baked gebacken
baker's die Bäckerei
balcony der Balkon
ball der Ball
ballet das Ballett
balloon der Ballon
Baltic Sea die Ostsee
banana die Banane
band (musical) die Band
bandage der Verband
bank die Bank
  (river) das Ufer
bank account das Bankkonto
banknote der Geldschein
bar die Bar
bar of chocolate der Schokoriegel
barbecue der Grill
  to have a barbecue eine Grillparty
  geben
barber der Herrenfriseur
to bark bellen
barn die Scheune
barrel (wine/beer) das Fass
basement das Souterrain
basket der Korb
basketball der Basketball
Basle Basel
bat (for baseball, etc) der Schläger
bath das Bad
  to have a bath ein Bad nehmen

bathing cap die Badekappe
bathroom das Badezimmer
  with bathroom mit Bad
battery die Batterie
bay (along coast) die Bucht
B&B Übernachtung mit Frühstück
to be sein
beach der Strand
  private beach der Privatstrand
  sandy beach der Sandstrand
  nudist beach der FKK-Strand
beach hut der Strandkorb
beans die Bohnen
beard der Bart
beautiful schön
beauty salon der Kosmetiksalon
because weil
to become werden
bed das Bett
  double bed das Doppelbett
  single bed das Einzelbett
  twin beds zwei Einzelbetten
bed and breakfast Übernachtung mit
  Frühstück
bedclothes die Bettwäsche
bedroom das Schlafzimmer
bee die Biene
beef das Rindfleisch
beer das Bier
before vor
  before breakfast vor dem Frühstück
to begin beginnen
behind hinter
beige beige
to believe glauben
bell (church) die Glocke
  (door) die Klingel
to belong to gehören zu
below unterhalb
belt der Gürtel
bend (in road) die Kurve
berth (train, ship) die Kabine
beside (next to) neben
best: the best der/die/das beste
bet die Wette
to bet on wetten auf
better besser
  better than besser als
between zwischen
bib (baby's) das Lätzchen
bicycle das Fahrrad
  by bicycle mit dem Fahrrad
bicycle repair kit das Fahrradflickzeug
big groß
  bigger than größer als

11 **bike** *(push bike)* das Fahrrad
(motorbike) das Motorrad
bike lock das Fahrradschloss
bikini der Bikini
bill *(account)* die Rechnung
bin *(dustbin)* der Mülleimer
bin liner der Müllbeutel
binoculars das Fernglas
bird der Vogel
biro der Kugelschreiber
birth die Geburt
birth certificate die Geburtsurkunde
birthday der Geburtstag
happy birthday! alles Gute zum
Geburtstag!
my birthday is on... ich habe am ...
Geburtstag
birthday card die Geburtstagskarte
birthday present das Geburtstagsgeschenk
biscuits die Kekse
bit *(piece)* das Stück
a bit (a little) ein bisschen
bite *(by insect)* der Biss
(of food) der Bissen
to bite beißen
(insect) stechen
bitten *(by insect)* gestochen
I've been bitten ich bin gestochen
worden
bitter *(taste)* bitter
black schwarz
black ice das Glatteis
blanket die Decke
bleach das Bleichmittel
to bleed bluten
blender der Mixer
blind *(person)* blind
blind *(for window)* das Rollo
blister die Blase
blocked *(pipe, road)* verstopft
blond *(person)* blond
blood das Blut
blood group die Blutgruppe
blood pressure der Blutdruck
blood test der Bluttest
blouse die Bluse
to blow-dry föhnen
blue blau
dark blue dunkelblau
light blue hellblau
blunt *(knife, blade)* stumpf
boar das Wildschwein
to board *(plane, train, etc)* einsteigen
boarding card/pass die Bordkarte

boarding house die Pension
boat *(large)* das Schiff
(small) das Boot
boat trip die Bootsfahrt
body der Körper
(dead) die Leiche
to boil kochen
boiled gekocht
boiler der Boiler
bomb die Bombe
bone der Knochen
fish bone die Gräte
bonfire das Feuerwerk
bonnet *(car)* die Motorhaube
book das Buch
book of tickets die Mehrfahrtenkarte
to book buchen
booking *(in hotel, train, etc)* die
Reservierung
booking office *(train)* der Fahrkartenschalter
bookshop die Buchhandlung
boot *(car)* der Kofferraum
boots *(long)* die Stiefel
(ankle) die Schnürschuhe
border *(of country)* die Grenze
boring langweilig
born: I was born in 1960 ich bin neun-
zehnhundertsechzig geboren
to borrow borgen
boss der/die Chef(in)
both beide
bottle die Flasche
a bottle of wine eine Flasche Wein
a half-bottle eine kleine Flasche
bottle opener der Flaschenöffner
bowl *(for soup, etc)* die Schüssel
bow tie die Fliege
box *(of wood)* die Kiste
(of cardboard) der Karton
box office die Kasse
boy der Junge
boyfriend der Freund
bra der BH
bracelet das Armband
to brake bremsen
brake fluid die Bremsflüssigkeit
brake light das Bremslicht
brake pads die Bremsbeläge
brakes die Bremsen
branch *(of tree)* der Ast
(of bank, etc) die Filiale

brand *(make)* die Marke
brass das Messing
brave mutig
bread das Brot
  brown bread das Schwarzbrot
  French bread das Baguette
  sliced bread geschnittenes Brot
  white bread das Weißbrot
bread roll das Brötchen
to break *(object)* kaputtmachen
breakable zerbrechlich
breakdown *(car)* die Panne
  (nervous) der Nervenzusammenbruch
breakdown van die Pannenhilfe
breakfast das Frühstück
  when is breakfast? wann gibt es Frühstück?
breast die Brust
to breast-feed stillen
to breathe atmen
brick der Ziegel
bride die Braut
bridegroom der Bräutigam
bridge die Brücke
briefcase die Aktentasche
Brillo pad der Scheuerschwamm
to bring bringen
Britain Großbritannien
British britisch
brochure die Broschüre
broken gebrochen
broken down *(car, etc)* kaputt
bronchitis die Bronchitis
bronze die Bronze
brooch die Brosche
broom der Besen
brother der Bruder
brother-in-law der Schwager
brown braun
bruise der Bluterguss
brush die Bürste
  (for sweeping floor) der Besen
bubble bath das Schaumbad
bucket der Eimer
buffet car der Speisewagen
to build bauen
building das Gebäude
bulb *(electric)* die Glühbirne
bumbag die Gürteltasche
bumper *(on car)* die Stoßstange
bunch *(flowers)* der Blumenstrauß

  (grapes) die Weintraube
bureau de change die Wechselstube
burger der Hamburger
burglar der/die Einbrecher(in)
burn *(on skin)* die Brandwunde
to burn verbrennen
bus der Bus
bus station der Busbahnhof
bus stop die Bushaltestelle
bus ticket der Busfahrschein
bus tour die Busfahrt
business das Geschäft
  on business geschäftlich
business address die Geschäftsadresse
business card die Visitenkarte
business class die Business-Class
businessman/woman der Geschäftsmann/ die Geschäftsfrau
business trip die Dienstreise
busy beschäftigt
but aber
butcher's die Fleischerei
butter die Butter
button der Knopf
to buy kaufen
by *(beside)* bei
  (via) über
  by bus mit dem Bus
  by car mit dem Auto
  by ship mit dem Schiff
  by train mit dem Zug
bypass die Umgehungsstraße

C

cab *(taxi)* das Taxi
cabaret das Varieté
cabin *(on ship)* die Kabine
cabin crew die Besatzung
cable car die Seilbahn
café das Café
  internet café das Internet-Café
cake der Kuchen
cake shop die Konditorei
calculator der Taschenrechner
calendar der Kalender
call *(on phone)* der Anruf
  long-distance call das Ferngespräch
to call *(on phone)* anrufen
calm *(person)* ruhig
  (weather) windstill
camcorder der Camcorder
camera die Kamera
camera case die Kameratasche

camera shop das Fotogeschäft
to camp campen
camping gas das Campinggas
camping stove der Campingkocher
campsite der Campingplatz
can die Dose
can opener der Dosenöffner
can (to be able) können
  I can/we can ich kann/wir können
  can I...? kann ich...?
  I cannot... ich kann nicht...
  can we...? können wir...?
  we cannot... wir können nicht...
Canada Kanada
Canadian *adj* kanadisch
  m/f der/die Kanadier(in)
canal der Kanal
to cancel (ticket, etc) stornieren
cancellation die Stornierung
cancer der Krebs
candle die Kerze
canoe das Kanu
canoeing das Kanufahren
cap (hat) die Mütze
  (diaphragm) das Pessar
capital (city) die Hauptstadt
car das Auto
car alarm die Autoalarmanlage
car ferry die Autofähre
car hire die Autovermietung
car insurance die Kfz-Versicherung
car keys die Autoschlüssel
car park der Parkplatz
car parts die Ersatzteile
car radio das Autoradio
car seat (children's) der Kindersitz
car wash die Waschanlage
caravan der Wohnwagen
carburettor der Vergaser
card (greetings) die (Glückwunsch)karte
  (playing) die Spielkarte
cardboard die Pappe
cardigan die Strickjacke
careful vorsichtig
  be careful! passen Sie auf!
carpet der Teppich
carriage (railway) der Wagen
carrot die Karotte
to carry tragen
carton der Karton
case (suitcase) der Koffer
cash das Bargeld
to cash (cheque) einlösen
cash desk die Kasse**

cash dispenser der Geldautomat
cashier der/die Kassierer(in)
cashpoint der Geldautomat
casino das Kasino
casserole dish die Kasserolle
cassette die Kassette
cassette player der Kassettenrekorder
castle das Schloss
  (medieval fortress) die Burg
casualty department die Unfallstation
cat die Katze
cat food das Katzenfutter
catalogue der Katalog
to catch (bus, train) nehmen
cathedral der Dom
Catholic katholisch
cave die Höhle
cavity (in tooth) das Loch
CD die CD
CD player der CD-Spieler
ceiling die Decke
cellar der Keller
cellphone das Handy
cemetery der Friedhof
centimetre der Zentimeter
central zentral
central heating die Zentralheizung
central locking (car) die Zentralverriegelung
centre das Zentrum
century das Jahrhundert
ceramic die Keramik
cereal (breakfast) die Cornflakes
certain (sure) sicher
certificate die Bescheinigung
chain die Kette
chair der Stuhl
chairlift der Sessellift
chalet das Chalet
chambermaid das Zimmermädchen
champagne der Champagner
change (money) das Wechselgeld
to change (to alter) ändern
  (on bus, train, etc) umsteigen
  to change money Geld wechseln
  to change clothes sich umziehen
changing room die Umkleidekabine
Channel (English) der Kanal
chapel die Kapelle
charcoal die Holzkohle
charge (fee) die Gebühr

to charge berechnen
  please charge it to my account bitte setzen Sie es auf meine Rechnung
charger *(for battery, etc)* das Ladegerät
charter flight der Charterflug
cheap billig
cheaper billiger
cheap rate *(phone)* der Billigtarif
check *(to examine)* überprüfen
  (passports, tickets) kontrollieren
to check in *(at airport)* einchecken
  (at hotel) sich an der Rezeption anmelden
check-in der Check-in
cheers! *(toast)* Prost!
cheese der Käse
chef der Koch/die Köchin
chemical toilet die chemische Toilette
chemist's die Drogerie
  (for medicines) die Apotheke
cheque der Scheck
cheque book das Scheckheft
cheque card die Scheckkarte
chest *(body)* die Brust
chewing gum der Kaugummi
chicken das Hühnchen
chickenpox die Windpocken
child das Kind
children die Kinder
  for children für Kinder
chimney der Schornstein
chin das Kinn
china das Porzellan
chips *(french fries)* die Pommes frites
chocolate die Schokolade
chocolates die Pralinen
choir der Chor
to choose auswählen
chopping board das Küchenbrett
Christian name der Vorname
Christmas Weihnachten
  merry Christmas! frohe Weihnachten!
Christmas card die Weihnachtskarte
Christmas Eve Heiligabend
church die Kirche
cigar die Zigarre
cigarette die Zigarette
cigarette lighter das Feuerzeug
cigarette papers das Zigarettenpapier
cinema das Kino
circle *(theatre)* der Rang

circuit breaker der Unterbrecher
circus der Zirkus
cistern *(of toilet)* der Spülkasten
city die Stadt
city centre das Stadtzentrum
class: first class erste Klasse
  second class zweite Klasse
clean sauber
to clean säubern
cleaner *(woman)* die Reinemachfrau
cleanser *(facial)* das Gesichtswasser
clear klar
client der Kunde/die Kundin
cliff *(along coast)* die Klippe
  (in mountains) der Felsen
to climb *(mountains)* klettern
climbing boots die Bergschuhe
clingfilm® die Frischhaltefolie
clinic die Klinik
cloakroom die Garderobe
clock die Uhr
to close schließen
closed *(shop, etc)* geschlossen
cloth *(rag)* der Lappen
  (fabric) der Stoff
clothes die Kleider
clothes line die Wäscheleine
clothes peg die Wäscheklammer
clothes shop das Bekleidungsgeschäft
cloudy bewölkt
club der Club
clutch *(car)* die Kupplung
coach *(bus)* der Bus
coach station der Busbahnhof
coach trip die Busreise
coal die Kohle
coast die Küste
coastguard die Küstenwache
coat der Mantel
coat hanger der Kleiderbügel
cockroach die Kakerlake
cocoa der Kakao
code der Kode
coffee der Kaffee
  black coffee schwarzer Kaffee
  white coffee Kaffee mit Milch
  decaffeinated coffee koffeinfreier Kaffee
coil *(IUD)* die Spirale
coin die Münze
Coke® die Cola
colander das Sieb
cold kalt
  I'm cold mir ist kalt
  it's cold es ist kalt

15 cold (illness) die Erkältung
I have a cold ich habe mich erkältet
cold sore der Ausschlag
collar der Kragen
collar bone das Schlüsselbein
colleague der Kollege/die Kollegin
to collect (someone) abholen
(something) (etwas) sammeln
collection die Sammlung
Cologne Köln
colour die Farbe
colour-blind farbenblind
colour film der Farbfilm
comb der Kamm
to come kommen
(to arrive) ankommen
to come back zurückkommen
to come in hereinkommen
come in! herein!
comedy die Komödie
comfortable bequem
company (firm) die Firma
compartment (in train) das Abteil
compass der Kompass
to complain sich beschweren
complaint die Klage
complete vollständig
to complete vervollständigen
compulsory obligatorisch
computer der Computer
computer disk (floppy) die Diskette
computer game das Computerspiel
computer program das Computerprogramm
concert das Konzert
concert hall die Konzerthalle
concession die Ermäßigung
concussion die Gehirnerschütterung
conditioner (hair) der Conditioner
condom das Kondom
conductor der Schaffner/die Schaffnerin
conference die Konferenz
to confirm bestätigen
please confirm bitte bestätigen Sie
confirmation (flight, etc) die Bestätigung
confused verwirrt
congratulations! herzlichen
Glückwünsch!
connection (train, etc) die Verbindung
constipated verstopft
consulate das Konsulat
to contact kontaktieren
contact lens cleaner der Kontaktlinsenreiniger

contact lenses die Kontaktlinsen
to continue weitermachen
contraceptive das Verhütungsmittel
contract der Vertrag
convenient: *is it convenient?* passt
es so?
convulsions die Krämpfe
to cook kochen
cooked gekocht
cooker der Herd
cookies die Kekse
cool kühl
cool-box (for picnic) die Kühlbox
copy (duplicate) die Kopie
to copy kopieren
cork der Korken
corkscrew der Korkenzieher
corner die Ecke
cornflakes die Cornflakes
corridor der Flur
cosmetics die Kosmetikartikel
cost (price) die Kosten
to cost kosten
how much does it cost? wie viel
kostet es?
costume (swimming) der Badeanzug
cot das Kinderbett
cottage das Ferienhäuschen
cotton die Baumwolle
cotton bud der Wattebausch
cotton wool die Watte
couchette der Liegewagen
cough der Husten
to cough husten
cough mixture der Hustensaft
cough sweets die Hustenbonbons
counter (in shop, bar) die Theke
country das Land
countryside die Landschaft
couple (two people) das Paar
a couple of... ein paar...
courier service der Kurierdienst
course (of study) der Kurs
(of meal) der Gang
cousin der Cousin/die Cousine
cover charge (in restaurant) die
Gedeckkosten
cow die Kuh
crafts die Kunstgewerbearbeiten
craftsperson der Handwerker/die
Handwerkerin

cramps die Krämpfe
crash (collision) der Zusammenstoß
to crash einen Unfall haben
crash helmet der Sturzhelm
cream (lotion) die Creme
  (on milk) die Sahne
  soured cream saure Sahne
  whipped cream Schlagsahne
credit card die Kreditkarte
crime das Verbrechen
crisps die Chips
to cross (road) überqueren
cross-channel ferry die Kanalfähre
cross-country skiing der Skilanglauf
crossing (sea) die Überfahrt
crossroads die Kreuzung
crossword puzzle das Kreuzworträtsel
crowd die Menge
crowded (train, shop) überfüllt
crown die Krone
cruise die Kreuzfahrt
crutches die Krücken
to cry (weep) weinen
crystal das Kristall
cucumber die Gurke
cufflinks die Manschettenknöpfe
cul-de-sac die Sackgasse
cup die Tasse
cupboard der Schrank
curlers die Lockenwickler
currency die Währung
current (electric) der Strom
  (water) die Strömung
curtains die Vorhänge
cushion das Kissen
custom (tradition) der Brauch
customer der Kunde/die Kundin
customs (duty) der Zoll
cut die Schnittwunde
to cut schneiden
cutlery das Besteck
cutlet das Schnitzel
to cycle Rad fahren
cycle track der Radweg
cycling das Radfahren
cyst die Zyste
cystitis die Blasenentzündung

daily (each day) täglich
dairy products die Milchprodukte
dam der Damm
damage der Schaden
damp feucht
dance der Tanz
to dance tanzen
danger die Gefahr
dangerous gefährlich
dark dunkel
  after dark nach Einbruch der
  Dunkelheit
date das Datum
date of birth das Geburtsdatum
daughter die Tochter
daughter-in-law die Schwiegertochter
dawn die Morgendämmerung
day der Tag
  every day jeden Tag
  per day pro Tag
dead tot
deaf taub
dear (in letter) liebe(r/s)
  (expensive) teuer
debts die Schulden
decaffeinated coffee der koffeinfreie
  Kaffee
December der Dezember
deckchair der Liegestuhl
to declare erklären
  nothing to declare nichts zu verzollen
deep tief
deep freeze die Tiefkühltruhe
deer das Reh
to defrost entfrosten
to de-ice enteisen
delay die Verspätung
  how long is the delay? wie viel
  beträgt die Verspätung?
delayed verspätet
delicatessen das Feinkostgeschäft
delicious köstlich
demonstration die Demonstration
dental floss die Zahnseide
dentist der Zahnarzt/die Zahnärztin
dentures das Gebiss
deodorant das Deo
to depart abfahren
department die Abteilung
department store das Kaufhaus

17 **departure** *(train, bus)* die Abfahrt
(plane) der Abflug
departure lounge die Abflughalle
deposit die Anzahlung
to describe beschreiben
description die Beschreibung
desk der Schreibtisch
dessert der Nachtisch
details die Details
detergent das Waschmittel
detour der Umweg
to develop *(photos)* entwickeln
diabetes der Diabetes
diabetic person der Diabetiker/die
Diabetikerin
to dial wählen
dialling code die Vorwahl
dialling tone der Wählton
diamond der Diamant
diarrhoea der Durchfall
diapers die Windeln
diaphragm *(in body)* das Zwerchfell
(contraception) das Pessar
diary der Terminkalender
dice der Würfel
dictionary das Wörterbuch
to die sterben
diesel der Diesel
diet die Diät
I'm on a diet ich muss eine Diät
einhalten
special diet spezielle Diät
different verschieden
difficult schwierig
to dilute verdünnen
dinghy *(rubber)* das Schlauchboot
dining room das Esszimmer
dinner *(evening meal)* das Abendessen
to have dinner zu Abend essen
diplomat derDiplomat/die Diplomatin
direct *(route)* direkt
(train, bus, etc) durchgehend
directions: to ask for directions nach
dem Weg fragen
directory *(phone)* das Telefonbuch
directory enquiries die Auskunft
dirty schmutzig
disability die Behinderung
disabled *(person)* behindert
to disagree nicht zustimmen
to disappear verschwinden
disco die Disko
discount der Rabatt
to discover entdecken

disease die Krankheit
dish die Schale
(food) das Gericht
dishtowel das Geschirrtuch
dishwasher die Geschirrspülmaschine
disinfectant das Desinfektionsmittel
disk *(floppy disk)* die Diskette
to dislocate *(joint)* auskugeln
disposable wegwerfbar
distance die Entfernung
distilled water das destillierte Wasser
district der Bezirk
to disturb stören
to dive tauchen
diversion die Umleitung
diving das Tauchen
divorced geschieden
DIY shop der Baumarkt
dizzy schwindelig
to do machen
doctor der Arzt/die Ärztin
documents die Dokumente
dog der Hund
dog food das Hundefutter
dog lead die Hundeleine
doll die Puppe
dollar der Dollar
domestic *(flight, etc)* Inlands-
donor card der Organspenderausweis
door die Tür
doorbell die Klingel
double Doppel-
double bed das Doppelbett
double room das Doppelzimmer
doughnut der Berliner
down: to go down nach unten gehen
downstairs unten
drain der Abfluss
draught *(of air)* der Durchzug
there's a draught hier zieht es
draught lager das Fassbier
drawer die Schublade
drawing die Zeichnung
dress das Kleid
to dress *(get dressed)* sich anziehen
dressing *(for food)* die Soße
(for wound) das Verbandsmaterial
dressing gown der Morgenmantel
drill *(tool)* der Bohrer
drink das Getränk

to drink trinken
drinking water das Trinkwasser
to drive fahren
driver *(of car)* der Fahrer/die Fahrerin
driving licence der Führerschein
to drown ertrinken
drug *(medicine)* das Medikament
(narcotic) die Droge
drunk betrunken
dry trocken
to dry trocknen
dry cleaner's die Reinigung
dryer der Wäschetrockner
due: *when's it due?* *(train, bus)* wann
soll er ankommen?
dummy *(for baby)* der Schnuller
during während
dust der Staub
duster das Staubtuch
dustpan and brush Schaufel und
Handfeger
duty-free zollfrei
duvet die Bettdecke
duvet cover der Bettbezug
to dye färben
dynamo die Lichtmaschine

E

each jede(r/s)
ear das Ohr
earache die Ohrenschmerzen
I have earache ich habe
Ohrenschmerzen
earlier früher
early früh
to earn verdienen
earphones die Kopfhörer
earrings die Ohrringe
earth die Erde
earthquake das Erdbeben
east der Osten
Easter Ostern
Happy Easter! fröhliche Ostern!
easy leicht
to eat essen
economy die Wirtschaft
economy class die Touristenklasse
egg das Ei
fried egg das Spiegelei
hard-boiled egg das hart gekochte Ei

scrambled egg das Rührei
soft-boiled egg das weich gekochte Ei
either ... or entweder ... oder
elastic band das Gummiband
Elastoplast® das Pflaster
elbow der Ellbogen
electric elektrisch
electric blanket die Wärmedecke
electric razor der Elektrorasierer
electric shock der elektrische Schlag
electrician der Elektriker
electricity die Elektrizität
electricity meter der Stromzähler
elevator der Fahrstuhl
e-mail die E-Mail
to e-mail e-mailen
e-mail address die E-Mail-Adresse
embassy die Botschaft
emergency der Notfall
emergency exit der Notausgang
emery board die Nagelfeile
empty leer
end das Ende
engaged *(to be married)* verlobt
(toilet, telephone) besetzt
engine der Motor
engineer der Ingenieur/die Ingenieurin
England England
English *adj* englisch
Englishman/woman der Engländer/die
Engländerin
to enjoy *(to like)* mögen
I enjoy dancing ich tanze gern
enjoy your meal! guten Appetit!
enough genug
that's enough das reicht
enquiry desk die Auskunft
to enter eintreten
entertainment das Entertainment
entrance der Eingang
entrance fee der Eintrittpreis
envelope der Umschlag
epileptic der Epileptiker/die
Epileptikerin
epileptic fit der epileptische Anfall
equal gleich
equipment die Ausrüstung
eraser der Radiergummi
error der Fehler
escalator die Rolltreppe
to escape entkommen
essential wesentlich
estate agent's der Grundstücksmakler

19 **euro** der Euro

eurocheque der Euroscheck

Europe Europa

European europäisch

European Union die Europäische Union

evening der Abend
this evening heute Abend
tomorrow evening morgen Abend
in the evening am Abend

evening dress das Abendkleid

evening meal das Abendessen

every *(each)* jede(r/s)

everyone jeder

everything alles

everywhere überall

examination *(medical)* die Untersuchung
(school) die Prüfung

example: for example zum Beispiel

excellent ausgezeichnet

except außer

excess baggage das Übergewicht

exchange der Austausch

to exchange tauschen
(money) wechseln

exchange rate der Wechselkurs

exciting aufregend

excursion der Ausflug

excuse me! *(sorry)* Entschuldigung!
(when passing) entschuldigen Sie bitte!

exhaust der Auspuff

exhibition die Ausstellung

exit der Ausgang

expense Account das Spesenkonto

expenses die Spesen

expensive teuer

expert der Experte/die Expertin

to expire *(ticket, etc)* ungültig werden

to explain erklären

explanation die Erklärung

explosion die Explosion

export der Export

to export exportieren

express *(train)* der Schnellzug

express *(parcel, etc)* per Express

extension lead das Verlängerungskabel

extra *(spare)* übrig
(more) noch ein(e)
an extra towel ein zusätzliches Handtuch

eye das Auge

eyebrows die Augenbrauen

eye drops die Augentropfen

eye liner der Eyeliner

eye shadow der Lidschatten

F

fabric der Stoff

face das Gesicht

face cloth der Waschlappen

facial die Gesichtspflege

facilities die Einrichtungen

factory die Fabrik

to faint ohnmächtig werden

fainted ohnmächtig

fair *(hair)* blond
(just) gerecht

fair *(trade fair)* die Messe
(funfair) die Kirmes

fake unecht

fall *(autumn)* der Herbst

to fall fallen
I have fallen ich bin hingefallen

false teeth das Gebiss

family die Familie

famous berühmt

fan *(electric)* der Ventilator
(football, music) der Fan

fan belt der Keilriemen

fancy dress die Verkleidung

far weit
how far is it? wie weit ist es?

fare *(train, bus, etc)* der Fahrpreis

farm der Bauernhof

farmer der Bauer/die Bäuerin

farmhouse das Bauernhaus

fashionable modern

fast schnell
too fast zu schnell

to fasten: to fasten the seatbelt sich anschnallen

fat *(big)* dick

fat das Fett
saturated fat gesättigte Fettsäuren
unsaturated fat ungesättigte Fettsäuren

father der Vater

father-in-law der Schwiegervater

fault *(defect)* der Fehler
it wasn't my fault das war nicht meine Schuld

favour der Gefallen

favourite Lieblings-

fax das Fax
by fax per Fax

to fax faxen

fax number die Faxnummer
February der Februar
to feed füttern
feeding bottle die Babyflasche
to feel fühlen
  I don't feel well ich fühle mich nicht wohl
  I feel sick mir ist schlecht
feet die Füße
female weiblich
ferry die Fähre
festival das Fest
to fetch *(bring)* holen
fever das Fieber
few: *a few* ein paar
fiancé(e) der/die Verlobte
field das Feld
to fight kämpfen
file *(nail)* die Feile
  (computer) die Datei
  (for papers) der Ordner
to fill füllen
to fill in *(form)* ausfüllen
to fill up *(tank)* voll tanken
fillet das Filet
filling *(in tooth)* die Plombe
film der Film
Filofax® der Terminkalender
filter der Filter
to find finden
fine *(to be paid)* die Geldstrafe
finger der Finger
to finish beenden
fire das Feuer
fire alarm der Feuermelder
fire brigade die Feuerwehr
fire engine das Feuerwehrauto
fire escape die Feuertreppe
fire exit der Notausgang
fire extinguisher der Feuerlöscher
fireplace der Kamin
fireworks das Feuerwerk
firm *(company)* die Firma
first erste(r/s)
first aid die erste Hilfe
first aid kit der Verbandskasten
first class *(travel)* erste Klasse
first name der Vorname
fish der Fisch
to fish angeln

fishing permit der Angelschein
fishing rod die Angel
fishmonger's die Fischhandlung
fit *(seizure)* der Anfall
to fit passen
  it doesn't fit es passt nicht
to fix reparieren
  can you fix it? können Sie es reparieren?
fizzy sprudelnd
flag die Fahne
flames die Flammen
flash *(for camera)* das Blitzlicht
flashlight die Taschenlampe
flask *(thermos)* die Thermosflasche
flat *(level)* flach
flat *(apartment)* die Wohnung
flat battery die leere Batterie
flat tyre die Reifenpanne
flavour der Geschmack
  what flavour? welchen Geschmack?
flaw der Mangel
fleas die Flöhe
flesh das Fleisch
flex die Verlängerungsschnur
flight der Flug
flip-flops die Badelatschen
flippers die Schwimmflossen
flood die Flut
  flash flood die Überschwemmung
floor *(of building)* die Etage
  (of room) der Boden
  which floor? auf welcher Etage?
  on the ground floor im Erdgeschoss
  on the first floor in der ersten Etage
floorcloth der Scheuerlappen
florist's shop der Blumenladen
flour das Mehl
flowers die Blumen
flu die Grippe
fly die Fliege
to fly fliegen
fly sheet das Überzelt
fog der Nebel
foggy neblig
foil die Folie
to fold falten
to follow folgen
food das Essen
food poisoning die Lebensmittelvergiftung
foot der Fuß
  on foot zu Fuß
football der Fußball

21 **football match** das Fußballspiel
football pitch der Fußballplatz
football player der Fußballer
footpath der Fußweg
for für
  for me für mich
  for him/her für ihn/sie
  for us für uns
  for you für Sie/dich
forbidden verboten
forehead die Stirn
foreign ausländisch
foreigner der Ausländer/die Ausländerin
forest der Wald
forever für immer
to forget vergessen
fork *(for eating)* die Gabel
  (in road) die Gabelung
form *(document)* das Formular
fortnight zwei Wochen
forward vorwärts
fountain der Brunnen
four wheel drive der Allradantrieb
fox der Fuchs
fracture der Bruch
fragile zerbrechlich
fragrance das Parfüm
frame *(picture)* der Rahmen
France Frankreich
free *(not occupied)* frei
  (costing nothing) umsonst
freezer die Tiefkühltruhe
French *adj* französisch
French fries die Pommes frites
Frenchman/woman der Franzose/die Französin
frequent häufig
fresh frisch
fresh water das frische Wasser
Friday der Freitag
fridge der Kühlschrank
fried gebraten
friend der Freund/die Freundin
friendly freundlich
frog der Frosch
from von
  from Scotland aus Schottland
  from England aus England
front die Vorderseite
  in front of vor
front door die Eingangstür
frost der Frost
frozen gefroren
fruit das Obst
  dried fruit das Trockenobst

fruit juice der Fruchtsaft
to fry braten
frying pan die Bratpfanne
fuel *(petrol)* der Treibstoff
fuel gauge die Tankanzeige
fuel pump *(in car)* die Benzinpumpe
  (at petrol station) die Zapfsäule
fuel tank der Tank
full voll
  (occupied) besetzt
full board die Vollpension
fumes die Abgase
fun der Spaß
funeral die Beerdigung
funfair die Kirmes
funny *(amusing)* komisch
fur der Pelz
furnished möbliert
furniture die Möbel
fuse die Sicherung
fuse box der Sicherungskasten
future die Zukunft

G

gallery die Galerie
game das Spiel
  (meat) das Wild
garage *(private)* die Garage
  (for repairs) die Werkstatt
  (petrol station) die Tankstelle
garden der Garten
garlic der Knoblauch
gas das Gas
gas cooker der Gasherd
gas cylinder die Gasflasche
gastritis die Gastritis
gate *(airport)* das Gate
gay *(person)* der/die Homosexuelle
gearbox das Getriebe
gears das Getriebe
  first gear der erste Gang
  second gear der zweite Gang
  third gear der dritte Gang
  fourth gear der vierte Gang
  neutral der Leerlauf
  reverse der Rückwärtsgang
generous großzügig
gents' *(toilet)* die Herrentoilette
genuine echt
German *adj* deutsch
  m/f der/die Deutsche

German measles die Röteln
Germany Deutschland
to get (to obtain) bekommen
  (to fetch) holen
to get in(to) (bus, etc) einsteigen
to get off (bus, etc) aussteigen
gift das Geschenk
gift shop der Geschenkeladen
girl das Mädchen
girlfriend die Freundin
to give geben
to give back zurückgeben
glacier der Gletscher
glass das Glas
  a glass of water ein Glas Wasser
glasses (spectacles) die Brille
glasses case das Brillenetui
gloves die Handschuhe
glue der Klebstoff
to go (on foot) gehen
  (in car) fahren
  I'm going to... ich fahre nach...
  we're going to... wir fahren nach...
  to go home nach Hause fahren
  to go on foot zu Fuß gehen
to go back zurückgehen
to go in hineingehen
to go out ausgehen
God Gott
goggles (swimming) die Taucherbrille
  (skiing) die Schneebrille
gold das Gold
golf das Golf
golf ball der Golfball
golf clubs die Golfschläger
golf course der Golfplatz
good gut
  (pleasant) schön
good afternoon guten Tag
goodbye auf Wiedersehen
good day guten Tag
good evening guten Abend
good morning guten Morgen
good night gute Nacht
goose die Gans
grandchild das Enkelkind
granddaughter die Enkelin
grandfather der Großvater
grandmother die Großmutter
grandparents die Großeltern

grandson der Enkel
grapes die Trauben
grass das Gras
grated (cheese) gerieben
gram das Gramm
grater die Reibe
great (big) groß
  (wonderful) großartig
Great Britain Großbritannien
green grün
green card (car insurance) die grüne
  Versicherungskarte
greengrocer's der Gemüseladen
greetings card die Grußkarte
grey grau
grill der Grill
to grill grillen
grilled gegrillt
grocer's der Lebensmittelladen
ground der Boden
ground floor das Erdgeschoss
  on the ground floor im Erdgeschoss
groundsheet der Zeltboden
group die Gruppe
guarantee die Garantie
guard m/f (on train) der Schaffner/die
  Schaffnerin
guest der Gast
guesthouse die Pension
guide m/f (tour guide) der Fremdenführer/
  die Fremdenführerin
guidebook der Reiseführer
guided tour die Führung
guitar die Gitarre
gun die Waffe
gym das Fitnesscenter
gym shoes die Turnschuhe

H

haemorrhoids die Hämorrhoiden
hail der Hagel
hair die Haare
hairbrush die Haarbürste
haircut der Haarschnitt
hairdresser der Friseur
hairdryer der Föhn
hair dye die Tönung
hair gel das Haargel
hairgrip die Haarklemme
hair mousse der Schaumfestiger
hair spray das Haarspray

23 half halb
  a half bottle eine kleine Flasche
  half an hour eine halbe Stunde
half board die Halbpension
half fare der halbe Fahrpreis
half price der halbe Preis
ham der Schinken
  (cooked) Kochschinken
  (cured) geräucherter Schinken
hamburger der Hamburger
hammer der Hammer
hand die Hand
handbag die Handtasche
hand-made handgearbeitet
handicapped behindert
handkerchief das Taschentuch
handle der Griff
handlebars der Lenker
hand luggage das Handgepäck
hands-free phone das Telefon mit
  Freisprechanlage
handsome gut aussehend
hanger *(coat hanger)* der Bügel
hang gliding das Drachenfliegen
hangover der Kater
to hang up *(phone)* auflegen
to happen passieren
  what happened? was ist passiert?
happy glücklich
  happy birthday! alles Gute zum
  Geburtstag!
harbour der Hafen
hard *(difficult)* schwierig
  (not soft) hart
hardware shop die Eisenwarenhandlung
to harm schädigen
harvest die Ernte
hat der Hut
to have haben
  I have... ich habe...
  we have... wir haben...
  do you have...? haben Sie...?
to have to müssen
hay fever der Heuschnupfen
he er
head der Kopf
headache die Kopfschmerzen
  I have a headache ich habe
  Kopfschmerzen
headlights die Scheinwerfer
headphones die Kopfhörer
health die Gesundheit
health food shop das Reformhaus
healthy gesund
to hear hören

hearing aid das Hörgerät
heart das Herz
heart attack der Herzanfall
heartburn das Sodbrennen
to heat up *(food, milk)* aufwärmen
heater das Heizgerät
heating die Heizung
heavy schwer
heel der Absatz
heel bar die Absatzbar
height die Höhe
helicopter der Helikopter
hello hallo
helmet *(for bike)* der Schutzhelm
help! Hilfe!
to help helfen
  can you help me? können Sie mir
  helfen?
hem der Saum
hepatitis die Hepatitis
her *(with der words)* ihr
  (with das words) ihr
  (with die words) ihre
  to her zu ihr
herbal tea der Kräutertee
herbs die Kräuter
here hier
  here is... hier ist...
hernia der Eingeweidebruch
hi! hallo!
to hide verstecken
high hoch
  (number, speed) groß
high blood pressure der hohe Blutdruck
high chair der Kinderstuhl
high tide die Flut
hill der Hügel
hill-walking das Bergwandern
him ihm
hip die Hüfte
hip replacement die künstliche Hüfte
hire die Vermietung
  car hire die Autovermietung
  bike hire die Fahrradvermietung
  boat hire der Bootsverleih
  ski hire der Skiverleih
to hire mieten
hire car das Mietauto
his *(with der words)* sein
  (with das words) sein
  (with die words) seine
historic historisch

history die Geschichte
to hit schlagen
to hitchhike trampen
hobby das Hobby
to hold halten
(to contain) enthalten
hold-up *(traffic jam)* der Stau
hole das Loch
holiday der Feiertag
holidays der Urlaub
on holiday in den Ferien
public holiday der gesetzliche Feiertag
home das Zuhause
at home zu Hause
homesick *(to be)* Heimweh haben
I'm homesick ich habe Heimweh
homosexual homosexuell
honest ehrlich
honey der Honig
honeymoon die Flitterwochen
hood *(of jacket)* die Kapuze
hook der Haken
to hope hoffen
I hope so hoffentlich
I hope not hoffentlich nicht
horn *(car)* die Hupe
hors d'œuvre die Vorspeise
horse das Pferd
horse racing das Pferderennen
to horse ride reiten
hosepipe der Schlauch
hospital das Krankenhaus
hostel das Wohnheim
hot heiß
I'm hot mir ist heiß
it's hot (weather) es ist heiß
hot-water bottle die Wärmflasche
hotel das Hotel
hour die Stunde
1 hour eine Stunde
2 hours zwei Stunden
half an hour eine halbe Stunde
house das Haus
housewife/husband die Hausfrau/der Hausmann
house wine der Hauswein
housework die Hausarbeit
how wie
how much? wie viel?
how many? wie viele?
how are you? wie geht es Ihnen?
hungry *(to be)* hungrig
to hunt jagen

hunting permit die Jagderlaubnis
hurry: *I'm in a hurry* ich habe es eilig
to hurt *(be painful)* weh tun
my back hurts mir tut der Rücken weh
that hurts das tut weh
husband der Mann
hut *(beach)* der Strandkorb
(mountain) die Hütte
hypodermic needle die Spritze

I

I ich
ice das Eis
with/without ice mit/ohne Eis
ice box die Kühlbox
ice cream das Eis
ice cube der Eiswürfel
ice rink die Eisbahn
to ice-skate Schlittschuh laufen
ice skates die Schlittschuhe
iced: *iced coffee* der Eiskaffee
iced tea der Eistee
idea die Idee
identity card der Personalausweis
if wenn
ignition die Zündung
ignition key der Zündschlüssel
ill krank
I'm ill ich bin krank
illness die Krankheit
immediately sofort
immersion heater der Boiler
immunisation die Immunisierung
to import importieren
important wichtig
impossible unmöglich
to improve verbessern
in in
in 2 hours in zwei Stunden
in Vienna in Wien
in front of vor
included inbegriffen
inconvenient unpassend
to increase vergrößern
indicator *(in car)* der Blinker
indigestion die Magenverstimmung
indigestion tablets die Magentabletten
indoors drinnen
infection die Infektion
infectious ansteckend
information die Auskunft
information desk der Informationsschalter
information office das Informationsbüro

25

ingredients die Zutaten
inhaler *(for medication)* der Inhalationsapparat
injection die Spritze
to injure verletzen
injured *(person)* verletzt
injury die Verletzung
ink die Tinte
inn das Gasthaus
inner tube der Schlauch
inquiries die Auskunft
inquiry desk der Auskunftsschalter
insect das Insekt
insect bite der Insektenstich
insect repellent das Insektenschutzmittel
inside in
instant coffee der Pulverkaffee
instead of anstelle von
instructor der Lehrer/die Lehrerin
(ski) der Skilehrer/die Skilehrerin
insulin das Insulin
insurance die Versicherung
insurance certificate die Versicherungsbescheinigung
to insure versichern
insured versichert
to intend to vorhaben
interesting interessant
international international
(arrivals, departures) Ausland
internet das Internet
internet café das Internet-Café
interpreter der Dolmetscher/die Dolmetscherin
interval die Pause
into in
into town in die Stadt
into the centre ins Zentrum
to introduce vorstellen
invitation die Einladung
to invite einladen
invoice die Rechnung
Ireland Irland
Irish *adj* irisch
Irishman/woman der Ire/die Irin
iron *(for clothes)* das Bügeleisen
(metal) das Eisen
to iron bügeln
ironing board das Bügelbrett
ironmonger's die Eisenwarenhandlung
is ist
island die Insel
it er/sie/es

Italian *adj* italienisch
m/f der Italiener/die Italienerin
Italy Italien
to itch jucken
item das Ding
itemized bill *(for telephone)* der Einzelverbindungsnachweis

J

jack *(for car)* der Wagenheber
jacket die Jacke
jacuzzi der Whirlpool
jam *(food)* die Marmelade
jammed *(camera, lock)* blockiert
January der Januar
jar *(honey, jam, etc)* das Glas
jaundice die Gelbsucht
jaw der Kiefer
jealous eifersüchtig
jeans die Jeans
jellyfish die Qualle
jet ski das Wassermotorrad
jetty die Mole
Jew der Jude/die Jüdin
jeweller's der Juwelier
jewellery der Schmuck
Jewish jüdisch
job *(employment)* die Stelle
to jog joggen
to join *(club)* beitreten
to join in mitmachen
joint *(of body)* das Gelenk
to joke scherzen
joke der Witz
journalist der Journalist/die Journalistin
journey die Reise
judge der Richter/die Richterin
jug der Krug
juice der Saft
carton of juice der Saftkarton
July der Juli
to jump springen
jumper der Pullover
jump leads *(for car)* das Starthilfekabel
junction *(road)* die Kreuzung
June der Juni
just: *just two* nur zwei
I've just arrived ich bin gerade angekommen

K

to keep *(retain)* behalten
  keep the change! stimmt so!
kettle der Wasserkocher
key der Schlüssel
  cardkey die Schlüsselkarte
keyboard *(computer)* die Tastatur
keyring der Schlüsselring
to kick *(ball)* schießen
  (person) treten
kidneys die Nieren
to kill töten
kilo das Kilo
kilogram das Kilogramm
kilometre der Kilometer
kind *(person)* nett
kind *(sort)* die Art
kiosk der Kiosk
kiss der Kuss
to kiss küssen
kitchen die Küche
kitchen paper das Küchenpapier
kite der Drachen
knee das Knie
kneehighs die Kniestrümpfe
knickers der Slip
knife das Messer
to knit stricken
to knock stoßen
to knock down *(in car)* überfahren
to knock over *(object)* umstoßen
knot der Knoten
to know *(facts)* wissen
  (to be acquainted with) kennen
  I don't know ich weiß nicht
to know how to können
  to know how to swim schwimmen
  können
kosher koscher

L

label das Schild
lace *(of shoe)* der Schnürsenkel
  (fabric) die Spitze
ladder die Leiter
ladies' *(toilet)* die Damentoilette
lady die Dame

lager das helle Bier
  bottled lager das Flaschenbier
  draught lager das Fassbier
lake der See
lamb das Lammfleisch
lamp *(for table)* die Lampe
lamppost der Laternenpfahl
lampshade der Lampenschirm
to land landen
landlady die Vermieterin
landlord der Vermieter
landslide der Erdrutsch
lane die Gasse
  (of motorway/road) die Spur
language die Sprache
language school die Sprachenschule
laptop der Laptop
large groß
last *(final)* letzte(r/s)
  the last bus der letzte Bus
  last night gestern Abend
  last week letzte Woche
  last year letztes Jahr
  last time letztes Mal
late spät
  the train is late der Zug hat Verspätung
  sorry we're late es tut uns leid, dass
  wir zu spät sind
later später
to laugh lachen
launderette der Waschsalon
laundry service der Wäschereiservice
lavatory die Toilette
law das Gesetz
lawn der Rasen
lawyer der Rechtsanwalt/
  die Rechtsanwältin
laxative das Abführmittel
layby die Haltebucht
lazy faul
lead *(metal)* das Blei
to lead führen
lead-free bleifrei
leaf das Blatt
leak *(of gas, liquid)* das Leck
to leak: *it's leaking* es hat ein Leck
to learn lernen
lease *(rental)* der Mietvertrag
leather das Leder
to leave *(a place)* weggehen/wegfahren
  when does the train leave? wann
  fährt der Zug ab?
  to leave behind zurücklassen
left: *on the left* links
  to the left nach links

27 **left-handed** *(person)* der Linkshänder/
die Linkshänder(in)

left-luggage locker das Schließfach

left-luggage office die Gepäckaufbewahrung

leg das Bein

lemon die Zitrone

lemon tea der Zitronentee

lemonade die Limonade

to lend leihen

length *(size)* die Länge
(duration) die Dauer

lens die Linse

lenses *(contact)* die Kontaktlinsen

lesbian lesbisch

less weniger
less than weniger als

lesson die Unterrichtsstunde

to let *(to allow)* erlauben
(room, house) vermieten

letter *(written)* der Brief
(of alphabet) der Buchstabe

letterbox der Briefkasten

lettuce der Kopfsalat

level crossing der Bahnübergang

library die Bibliothek

licence *(driving)* der Führerschein

lid der Deckel

lie *(untruth)* die Lüge

to lie down sich hinlegen

lifebelt der Rettungsring

lifeboat das Rettungsboot

lifeguard der Rettungsschwimmer/
die Rettungsschwimmerin

life insurance die Lebensversicherung

life jacket die Schwimmweste

life raft die Rettungsinsel

lift *(elevator)* der Aufzug
can you give me a lift? können Sie
mich mitnehmen?

lift pass *(on ski slopes)* der Liftpass

light *(not heavy)* leicht

light das Licht
have you a light? haben Sie Feuer?

light bulb die Glühbirne

lighter das Feuerzeug

lighthouse der Leuchtturm

lightning der Blitz

like *(preposition)* wie

to like mögen
I like coffee ich trinke gern Kaffee
I don't like... ich mag ... nicht
we'd like... wir möchten...

lilo® die Luftmatratze

lime *(fruit)* die Limone

eng-german   l

line *(row, of railway)* die Linie
(telephone) die Leitung

linen das Leinen

lingerie die Unterwäsche

lips die Lippen

lip-reading das Lippenlesen

lip salve der Lippenpflegestift

lipstick der Lippenstift

liqueur der Likör

list die Liste

to listen to zuhören

litre der Liter
a litre of milk ein Liter Milch

litter *(rubbish)* der Abfall

little *(small)* klein
a little... ein bisschen...

to live *(exist)* leben
(reside) wohnen
I live in London ich wohne in London

liver die Leber

living room das Wohnzimmer

loaf of bread das Brot

local *(wine, speciality)* hiesig

lock *(on door, box)* das Schloss
the lock is broken das Schloss ist
geöffnet worden

to lock zuschließen

locker *(luggage)* das Schließfach

locksmith der Schlosser

log *(for fire)* der Holzscheit

log book *(car)* die Zulassung

long lang
for a long time lange Zeit

long-sighted weitsichtig

to look after sich kümmern um

to look at anschauen

to look for suchen

loose *(screw, tooth)* locker
it's come loose es hat sich gelockert

lorry der Lastwagen

to lose verlieren

lost *(object)* verloren
I've lost my wallet ich habe meine
Brieftasche verloren
I'm lost (on foot) ich habe mich verlaufen
I'm lost (in car) ich habe mich verfahren

lost property office das Fundbüro

lot: *a lot* viel

lotion die Lotion

lottery das Lotto

loud laut

lounge *(hotel/airport)* die Lounge
(in house) das Wohnzimmer

love die Liebe
to love lieben
  I love you ich liebe dich
  I love swimming ich schwimme gern
lovely schön
low niedrig
low-alcohol alkoholarm
low-fat fettarm
low tide die Ebbe
luck das Glück
lucky glücklich
luggage das Gepäck
luggage allowance das Freigepäck
luggage rack die Gepäckablage
luggage tag der Kofferanhänger
luggage trolley der Gepäckwagen
lump *(swelling)* die Beule
lunch das Mittagessen
lunch break die Mittagspause
lung die Lunge
luxury der Luxus

M

machine die Maschine
mad verrückt
magazine die Zeitschrift
maggot die Made
magnet der Magnet
magnifying glass die Lupe
maid *(in hotel)* das Zimmermädchen
maiden name der Mädchenname
mail die Post
  by mail per Post
main *(principal)* Haupt-
main course *(of meal)* das Hauptgericht
main road die Hauptstraße
to make machen
  (meal) zubereiten
make-up das Make-up
male männlich
man der Mann
  men die Männer
to manage *(be able to)* schaffen
manager der Geschäftsführer/
die Geschäftsführerin
manual *(gear change)* das Schaltgetriebe
many viele
map die Karte
  (of region, country) die Landkarte
  (of town) der Stadtplan

March der März
margarine die Margarine
marina der Jachthafen
mark *(stain)* der Fleck
market der Markt
market place der Marktplatz
marmalade die Orangenmarmelade
married verheiratet
  I'm married ich bin verheiratet
  are you married? sind Sie verheiratet?
to marry heiraten
marsh der Sumpf
mascara die Wimperntusche
mass *(in church)* die Messe
mast der Mast
masterpiece das Meisterwerk
match *(sport)* der Wettkampf
matches die Streichhölzer
material das Material
matter: it doesn't matter das macht
nichts
  what's the matter? was ist los?
mattress die Matratze
May der Mai
mayonnaise die Mayonnaise
maximum das Maximum
me *(direct object)* mich
  (indirect object) mir
meal das Essen
to mean bedeuten
  what does this mean? was bedeutet
das?
measles die Masern
to measure messen
meat das Fleisch
  I don't eat meat ich esse kein Fleisch
mechanic der Mechaniker/
die Mechanikerin
medical insurance die Kranken-
versicherung
medical treatment die medizinische
Behandlung
medicine die Medizin
medieval mittelalterlich
medium rare *(meat)* halb durch
to meet *(by chance)* treffen
  (by arrangement) sich treffen mit
  pleased to meet you! sehr erfreut!
meeting das Treffen
to melt schmelzen
member *(of club, etc)* das Mitglied
membership card die Mitgliedskarte
memory das Gedächtnis
men die Männer
to mend reparieren

meningitis die Hirnhautentzündung
menu die Speisekarte
 set menu die Tageskarte
message die Nachricht
metal das Metall
meter der Zähler
metre der Meter
metro *(underground)* die U-Bahn
metro station die U-Bahn-Station
microwave oven die Mikrowelle
midday der Mittag
 at midday am Mittag
middle die Mitte
middle-aged in den mittleren Jahren
midge die Mücke
midnight die Mitternacht
 at midnight um Mitternacht
migraine die Migräne
 I have a migraine ich habe Migräne
mile die Meile
milk die Milch
 fresh milk frische Milch
 full cream milk Vollfettmilch
 hot milk heiße Milch
 long-life milk H-Milch
 powdered milk das Milchpulver
 semi-skimmed milk Halbfettmilch
 skimmed milk Magermilch
 soya milk die Sojamilch
 with/without milk mit/ohne Milch
millimetre der Millimeter
mince *(meat)* das Hackfleisch
mind: do you mind if...? haben Sie
 etwas dagegen, wenn...?
 I don't mind es ist mir egal
mineral water das Mineralwasser
minibar die Minibar
minimum das Minimum
minister *(church)* der Pfarrer/die Pfarrerin
 (political) der Minister/die Ministerin
minor road die Nebenstraße
mint *(herb)* die Minze
 (sweet) das Pfefferminzbonbon
minute die Minute
mirror der Spiegel
miscarriage die Fehlgeburt
to miss *(plane, train)* verpassen
Miss Fräulein
missing *(object)* verschwunden
 my son's missing mein Sohn ist weg
missing person der/die Vermisste
mistake der Fehler
misty dunstig
misunderstanding das Missverständnis
to mix mischen
mixer der Mixer

mobile phone das Handy
modem das Modem
modern modern
moisturizer die Feuchtigkeitscreme
mole *(on skin)* das Muttermal
moment: just a moment einen
 Moment, bitte
monastery das Kloster
Monday der Montag
money das Geld
 I have no money ich habe kein Geld
moneybelt die Gürteltasche
money order die Postanweisung
month der Monat
 this month diesen Monat
 last month letzten Monat
 next month nächsten Monat
monthly monatlich
monument das Denkmal
moon der Mond
mooring der Anlegeplatz
mop *(floor)* der Mopp
moped das Moped
more mehr
 more than mehr als
 more wine noch etwas Wein
morning der Morgen
 in the morning am Morgen
 this morning heute Morgen
 tomorrow morning morgen früh
morning-after pill die Pille danach
mosque die Moschee
mosquito die Stechmücke
mosquito net das Moskitonetz
mosquito repellent das Insektenschutzmittel
most: most of das meiste von
moth *(clothes)* die Motte
mother die Mutter
mother-in-law die Schwiegermutter
motor der Motor
motorbike das Motorrad
motorboat das Motorboot
motorway die Autobahn
mould der Schimmel
mountain der Berg
mountain bike das Mountainbike
mountain rescue die Bergwacht
mountaineering das Bergsteigen
mouse *(animal, computer)* die Maus
moustache der Schnurrbart
mouth der Mund

mouthwash das Mundwasser
to move bewegen
  it isn't moving es bewegt sich nicht
movie der Kinofilm
to mow mähen
Mr Herr
Mrs Frau
Ms Frau
much viel
  too much zu viel
muddy schlammig
mugging der Überfall
mumps der Mumps
Munich München
muscle der Muskel
museum das Museum
mushrooms die Pilze
music die Musik
musical das Musical
mussel die Muschel
must müssen
  I must ich muss
  we must wir müssen
  you musn't du darfst nicht
mustard der Senf
my *(with der words)* mein
  (with das words) mein
  (with die words) meine

N

nail *(fingernail)* der Fingernagel
  (metal) der Nagel
nailbrush die Nagelbürste
nail file die Nagelfeile
nail polish/varnish der Nagellack
nail polish remover der Nagellackentferner
nail scissors die Nagelschere
name der Name
  my name is... mein Name ist...
  what is your name? wie ist Ihr
  Name?
nanny das Kindermädchen
napkin die Serviette
nappy die Windel
narrow eng
national national
national park der Nationalpark
nationality die Nationalität
natural natürlich
nature die Natur

nature reserve das Naturschutzgebiet
nature trail der Naturlehrpfad
navy blue marineblau
near *(place, time)* nahe
  near the bank in der Nähe der Bank
  is it near? ist es in der Nähe?
necessary notwendig
neck der Hals
necklace die Halskette
nectarine die Nektarine
to need brauchen
  I need... ich brauche...
  we need... wir brauchen...
  I need to go ich muss gehen
needle die Nadel
  needle and thread Nadel und Faden
negative *(photo)* das Negativ
neighbour der Nachbar/die Nachbarin
nephew der Neffe
net das Netz
  the Net das Internet
never nie
  I never drink wine Wein trinke ich nie
new neu
news die Nachrichten
newsagent's der Zeitungsladen
newspaper die Zeitung
newsstand der Zeitungskiosk
New Year (1 Jan) Neujahr
  happy New Year! ein gutes neues
  Jahr!
New Year's Eve Silvester
New Zealand Neuseeland
next nächste(r/s)
  next to neben
  next week nächste Woche
  the next bus der nächste Bus
  the next train der nächste Zug
nice *(person)* nett
  (place, holiday) schön
niece die Nichte
night die Nacht
  at night am Abend
  last night gestern Abend
  per night pro Nacht
  tomorrow night (evening) morgen
  Abend
  tonight heute Abend
night club der Nachtklub
nightdress das Nachthemd
no nein
  no thanks nein danke
  no problem kein Problem
  (without) ohne
  no sugar ohne Zucker
  no ice ohne Eis
nobody niemand

131 noise der Lärm
noisy laut
  it's very noisy es ist sehr laut
non-alcoholic alkoholfrei
none keine(r/s)
non-smoker der Nichtraucher
non-smoking Nichtraucher-
north der Norden
Northern Ireland Nordirland
North Sea die Nordsee
nose die Nase
not nicht
  I do not know ich weiß nicht
note *(banknote)* der Geldschein
  (written) die Notiz
note pad der Notizblock
nothing nichts
  nothing else nichts weiter
notice *(sign)* das Schild
notice board das Anschlagbrett
novel der Roman
November der November
now jetzt
nowhere nirgends
nuclear nuklear
nudist beach der FKK-Strand
number die Zahl
number plate das Nummernschild
nurse die Krankenschwester/
  der Krankenpfleger
nursery die Kinderbetreuung
nursery school die Vorschule
nursery slope der Übungshang
nut *(to eat)* die Nuss
  (for bolt) die Schraubenmutter

O

oar das Ruder
oats der Hafer
to obtain erhalten
occupation *(work)* der Beruf
ocean der Ozean
October der Oktober
odd *(strange)* seltsam
of von
  a glass of water ein Glas Wasser
  made of... aus...
off *(light, radio, etc)* aus
  (rotten) schlecht
office das Büro
often oft
  how often? wie oft?
oil das Öl

oil filter der Ölfilter
oil gauge der Ölstandsanzeiger
ointment die Salbe
OK okay
old alt
  how old are you? wie alt sind Sie?
  I'm... years old ich bin... Jahre alt
old age pensioner der Rentner/
  die Rentnerin
on *(light, radio, etc)* an
on auf
  on the table auf dem Tisch
  on time pünktlich
once einmal
  at once sofort
one-way street die Einbahnstraße
onion die Zwiebel
only nur
open geöffnet
to open öffnen
opera die Oper
operation *(surgical)* die Operation
operator *(phone)* die Vermittlung
opposite gegenüber
  opposite the bank gegenüber
  der Bank
  quite the opposite ganz im Gegenteil
optician's der Optiker
or oder
orange *(colour)* orange
orange *(fruit)* die Orange
orange juice der Orangensaft
orchestra das Orchester
order *(in restaurant)* die Bestellung
to order *(in restaurant)* bestellen
organic organisch
to organize organisieren
ornament der Schmuckgegenstand
other: *the other one* der/die/das
  andere
  have you got any others? haben
  Sie noch andere?
our *(with der words)* unser
  (with das words) unser
  (with die words) unsere
out *(light, etc)* aus
  she's out sie ist nicht da
out of order kaputt
outdoor *(pool, etc)* im Freien
outside draußen
oven der Herd
ovenproof dish die feuerfeste Form

over (on top of, above) über
to overbook überbuchen
to overcharge zu viel berechnen
overdone (food) verkocht
overdose die Überdosis
to overheat überhitzen
to overload überladen
to oversleep verschlafen
to overtake (in car) überholen
to owe schulden
  I owe you... ich schulde Ihnen...
  you owe me... Sie schulden mir...
owner der Besitzer/die Besitzerin
oxygen der Sauerstoff

P

pace das Tempo
pacemaker der Herzschrittmacher
to pack (luggage) packen
package das Paket
package tour die Pauschalreise
packet das Paket
padded envelope der gefütterte
  Umschlag
paddling pool das Planschbecken
padlock das Vorhängeschloss
page die Seite
paid bezahlt
  I've paid ich habe bezahlt
pain der Schmerz
painful schmerzhaft
painkiller das Schmerzmittel
to paint malen
painting (picture) das Bild
pair das Paar
palace der Palast
pale blass
pan (saucepan) der Kochtopf
  (frying pan) die Bratpfanne
pancake der Pfannkuchen
panniers (for bike) die Satteltaschen
panties die Unterhose
pants (underwear) der Slip
panty liner die Slipeinlage
paper das Papier
paper hankies die Papiertaschentücher
paper napkins die Papierservietten
paragliding das Paragliding
paralysed gelähmt

parcel das Paket
pardon? wie bitte?
  I beg your pardon! Entschuldigung!
parents die Eltern
park der Park
to park parken
parking disk die Parkscheibe
parking fine der Strafzettel
parking meter die Parkuhr
parking ticket (fine) der Strafzettel
  (to display) der Parkschein
partner (business) der Geschäftspartner/
  die Geschäftspartnerin
  (boy/girlfriend) der Partner/
  die Partnerin
party (of tourists) die Reisegruppe
  (celebration) die Party
  (political) die Partei
pass der Pass
passenger der Passagier
passport der Reisepass
passport control die Passkontrolle
pasta die Nudeln
pastry der Teig
  (cake) das Gebäck
path der Weg
patient (in hospital) der Patient/die
  Patientin
pavement der Bürgersteig
to pay zahlen
  I'd like to pay ich möchte zahlen
  where do I pay? wo kann ich
  bezahlen?
payment die Bezahlung
payphone das Münztelefon
peace der Frieden
peach der Pfirsich
peak rate der Höchsttarif
peanut allergy die Erdnussallergie
pear die Birne
pearls die Perlen
peas die Erbsen
pedal das Pedal
pedalo der Wassertreter
pedestrian der Fußgänger/
  die Fußgängerin
pedestrian crossing der Fußgänger-
  übergang
to pee austreten
to peel (fruit) schälen
peg (clothes) die Wäscheklammer
  (tent) der Hering
pen der Füller
pencil der Bleistift

penfriend der Brieffreund/
die Brieffreundin
penicillin das Penizillin
penis der Penis
penknife das Taschenmesser
pension die Rente
pensioner der Rentner/die Rentnerin
people die Leute
pepper *(spice)* der Pfeffer
(vegetable) die Paprikaschote
per pro
per day pro Tag
per hour pro Stunde
per person pro Person
100 km per hour einhundert
Kilometer pro Stunde
perfect perfekt
performance die Vorstellung
perfume das Parfüm
perhaps vielleicht
period *(menstruation)* die Periode
perm die Dauerwelle
permit die Genehmigung
person die Person
personal organizer der Terminplaner
personal stereo der Walkman®
pet das Haustier
pet food das Tierfutter
pet shop die Zoohandlung
petrol das Benzin
4-star petrol Superbenzin
unleaded petrol bleifreies Benzin
petrol cap der Tankdeckel
petrol pump *(at petrol station)* die
Tanksäule
(in car) die Benzinpumpe
petrol station die Tankstelle
petrol tank der Tank
pharmacy die Apotheke
to phone telefonieren
phone das Telefon
by phone per Telefon
phonebook das Telefonbuch
phonebox die Telefonzelle
phone call der Anruf
phonecard die Telefonkarte
photocopy die Fotokopie
I need a photocopy ich brauche eine
Fotokopie
to photocopy fotokopieren
photograph das Foto
to take a photograph fotografieren
phrase book der Sprachführer
piano das Klavier

to pick *(choose)* auswählen
(pluck) pflücken
pickpocket der Taschendieb
picnic das Picknick
to have a picnic ein Picknick machen
picnic hamper der Picknickkorb
picnic rug die Picknickdecke
picnic table der Campingtisch
picture *(painting)* das Bild
(photo) das Foto
pie *(sweet)* der Obstkuchen
(savoury) die Pastete
piece das Stück
pier die Pier
pig das Schwein
pill die Pille
to be on the Pill die Pille nehmen
pillow das Kopfkissen
pillowcase der Kopfkissenbezug
pilot der Pilot/die Pilotin
pin die Stecknadel
pink rosa
pint: *a pint of beer* eine Halbe
pipe *(smoker's)* die Pfeife
(drain, etc) das Rohr
pity: *what a pity* wie schade
pizza die Pizza
place der Platz
place of birth der Geburtsort
plain *(unflavoured)* einfach
plait der Zopf
plane *(airplane)* das Flugzeug
plant die Pflanze
plaster *(sticking)* das Pflaster
(for broken limb) der Gips
plastic *(made of)* Plastik-
plastic bag der Plastikbeutel
plate der Teller
platform *(at station)* der Bahnsteig
which platform? welcher Bahnsteig?
play *(theatre)* das Stück
to play spielen
play area die Spielecke
playground der Spielplatz
play park der Spielplatz
playroom das Spielzimmer
please bitte
pleased erfreut
pleased to meet you sehr erfreut
pliers die Zange
plug *(electrical)* der Stecker
(in sink) der Stöpsel

to plug in einstecken
plum die Pflaume
plumber der Klempner
plumbing die Installationen
p.m. nachmittags
poached *(egg, fish)* pochiert
pocket die Tasche
points *(in car)* die Unterbrecherkontakte
poison das Gift
poisonous giftig
police *(force)* die Polizei
policeman/woman der Polizist/die Polizistin
police station das Polizeirevier
polish *(for shoes)* die Schuhcreme *(for furniture)* die Möbelpolitur
pollen der Pollen
polluted verschmutzt
pony das Pony
pony trekking das Ponyreiten
pool der Swimmingpool
pool attendant der Bademeister
poor arm
pop socks die Kniestrümpfe
popular beliebt
pork das Schweinefleisch
port *(seaport)* der Hafen
porter *(for door)* der Portier *(in station)* der Gepäckträger
portion die Portion
portrait das Portrait
possible möglich
post: *by post* per Post
to post aufgeben
postbox der Briefkasten
postcard die Ansichtskarte
postcode die Postleitzahl
postman/woman der Briefträger/die Briefträgerin
post office das Postamt
poster das Poster
to postpone verschieben
pot *(cooking)* der Topf
potato die Kartoffel
  baked potato die Folienkartoffel
  boiled potatoes die Salzkartoffeln
  fried potatoes die Bratkartoffeln
  mashed potatoes das Kartoffelpüree
  roast potatoes die Bratkartoffeln
  sautéed potatoes die Röstkartoffeln

potato peeler der Kartoffelschäler
potato salad der Kartoffelsalat
pothole das Schlagloch
pottery die Töpferwaren
pound das Pfund
to pour eingießen
powder: *in powder form* pulverförmig
powdered milk die Trockenmilch
power *(electricity)* der Strom
power cut der Stromausfall
pram der Kinderwagen
to pray beten
to prefer vorziehen
pregnant schwanger
  I'm pregnant ich bin schwanger
to prepare vorbereiten
to prescribe verschreiben
prescription das Rezept
present *(gift)* das Geschenk
preservative die Marmelade
president der Präsident
pressure: *tyre pressure* der Reifendruck
  blood pressure der Blutdruck
pretty hübsch
price der Preis
price list die Preisliste
priest der Priester
print *(photo)* der Abzug
printer der Drucker
prison das Gefängnis
private privat
prize der Preis
probably wahrscheinlich
problem das Problem
professor der Professor/die Professorin
programme das Programm
prohibited verboten
promise das Versprechen
to promise versprechen
to pronounce aussprechen
  how's it pronounced? wie spricht man das aus?
protein das Eiweiß
Protestant protestantisch
to provide zur Verfügung stellen
public öffentlich
public holiday der gesetzliche Feiertag
pudding die Nachspeise
to pull ziehen
  to pull a muscle sich einen Muskel verziehen
to pull over *(car)* anhalten
pullover der Pullover

35

pump (bike, etc) die Luftpumpe
  (in petrol station) die Tanksäule
puncture die Reifenpanne
puncture repair kit das Reifenflickzeug
puppet die Puppe
puppet show das Puppenspiel
purple violett
purpose der Zweck
  on purpose absichtlich
purse der Geldbeutel
to push stoßen
pushchair die Kinderkarre
to put (place) stellen
to put back verschieben
pyjamas der Pyjama

Q

quality die Qualität
quantity die Quantität
quarantine die Quarantäne
to quarrel streiten
quarter das Viertel
quay der Kai
queen die Königin
query die Frage
question die Frage
queue die Schlange
to queue anstehen
quick(ly) schnell
quiet ruhig
quilt die Bettdecke
quite (rather) ziemlich
  it's quite good es ist ganz gut
  it's quite expensive es ist ziemlich
  teuer
quiz show das Quiz

R

rabbit das Kaninchen
rabies die Tollwut
race das Rennen
race course die Rennbahn
racket (tennis, etc) der Schläger
radiator (car) der Kühler
  (heater) der Heizkörper
radio das Radio
railcard die Bahncard
railway die Eisenbahn
railway station der Bahnhof
rain der Regen
to rain regnen
  it's raining es regnet

raincoat der Regenmantel
raisins die Rosinen
rake die Harke
rape die Vergewaltigung
to rape vergewaltigen
rare (unique) selten
  (steak) blutig
rash (skin) der Ausschlag
rate (price) der Preis
rate of exchange der Wechselkurs
raw roh
razor der Rasierapparat
razor blades die Rasierklingen
to read lesen
ready fertig
  to get ready sich fertig machen
real echt
to realize erkennen
rearview mirror der Rückspiegel
receipt die Quittung
receiver (of phone) der Hörer
reception (desk) der Empfang
receptionist der Empfangschef/
  die Empfangsdame
to recharge (battery) wieder aufladen
recipe das Rezept
to recognize erkennen
to recommend empfehlen
to record aufnehmen
to recover (from illness) genesen
to recycle recyceln
red rot
to reduce reduzieren
reduction die Ermäßigung
refill (for pen) die Ersatzmine
  (for lighter) die Nachfüllpatrone
refund die Rückerstattung
to refund rückerstatten
to refuse ablehnen
region das Gebiet
to register (at hotel) sich anmelden
registered letter das Einschreiben
registration form das Anmeldeformular
to reimburse entschädigen
relation (family) der/die Verwandte
relationship das Verhältnis
to remain (to stay) bleiben
to remember sich erinnern
  I don't remember ich kann mich nicht
  erinnern
remote control die Fernbedienung

removal firm die Umzugsfirma
to remove entfernen
rent die Miete
to rent mieten
repair die Reparatur
to repair reparieren
to repeat wiederholen
to reply antworten
report der Bericht
to report berichten
request die Bitte
to request erbitten
to require benötigen
to rescue retten
reservation die Reservierung ; die Buchung
to reserve reservieren ; buchen
reserved reserviert
resident der Bewohner/die Bewohnerin
resort *(holiday)* das Urlaubsgebiet
rest *(repose)* die Ruhe
(remainder) der Rest
to rest ruhen
restaurant das Restaurant
restaurant car der Speisewagen
retired pensioniert
to return *(in car)* zurückfahren
(on foot) zurückgehen
(return something) zurückgeben
return ticket *(train)* die Rückfahrkarte
(plane) das Rückflugticket
to reverse *(car)* rückwärts fahren
to reverse the charges ein R-Gespräch führen
reverse charge call das R-Gespräch
reverse gear der Rückwärtsgang
rheumatism der Rheumatismus
rib die Rippe
ribbon das Band
rice der Reis
rich *(person)* reich
(food) reichhaltig
to ride *(horse)* reiten
right *(correct)* richtig
right: on the right rechts
to the right nach rechts
right of way die Vorfahrt
ring der Ring
to ring *(bell, phone)* klingeln
it's ringing es klingelt
to ring s.o. jemanden anrufen

ring road die Umgehungsstraße
ripe reif
river der Fluss
road die Straße
road map die Straßenkarte
road sign das Straßenschild
roadworks die Straßenarbeiten
roast Rost-
roll *(bread)* das Brötchen
roller blades die Rollerblades
romantic romantisch
roof das Dach
roof-rack der Dachgepäckträger
room *(in house, hotel)* das Zimmer
(space) der Platz
double room das Doppelzimmer
family room das Familienzimmer
single room das Einzelzimmer
room number die Zimmernummer
room service der Zimmerservice
root die Wurzel
rope das Seil
rose *(flower)* die Rose
rotten *(fruit, etc)* verfault
rough rau
round rund
roundabout *(traffic)* der Kreisverkehr
row *(in theatre, etc)* die Reihe
to row *(boat)* rudern
rowing *(sport)* das Rudern
rowing boat das Ruderboot
rubber *(eraser)* der Radiergummi
(material) das Gummi
rubber band das Gummiband
rubber gloves die Gummihandschuhe
rubbish der Abfall
rubella die Röteln
rucksack der Rucksack
rug der Teppich
ruin *(eg castle)* die Ruine
ruler *(for measuring)* das Lineal
to run rennen
rush hour die Rushhour
rusty rostig
rye bread das Roggenbrot

S

sad traurig
saddle der Sattel
safe *(for valuables)* der Safe
safe *(not dangerous)* ungefährlich
is it safe? ist das ungefährlich?

137

safety die Sicherheit
safety belt der Sicherheitsgurt
safety pin die Sicherheitsnadel
sail das Segel
to sail segeln
sailboard das Segelbrett
sailing *(sport)* das Segeln
sailing boat das Segelboot
salad der Salat
  green salad grüner Salat
  mixed salad gemischter Salat
  potato salad Kartoffelsalat
  tomato salad Tomatensalat
salad dressing die Salatsoße
salary das Gehalt
sale *(in general)* der Verkauf
  (seasonal bargains) der Schlussverkauf
salesperson der Verkäufer/die Verkäuferin
sales rep der Vertreter/die Vertreterin
salt das Salz
salt water das Salzwasser
salty salzig
same gleich
sample das Muster
sand der Sand
sandals die Sandalen
sandwich das Sandwich
  toasted sandwich das getoastete Sandwich
sanitary pads die Damenbinden
satellite dish die Satellitenschüssel
satellite TV das Satellitenfernsehen
Saturday der Samstag
sauce die Soße
  tomato sauce die Tomatensoße
saucepan der Kochtopf
saucer die Untertasse
sauna die Sauna
sausage die Wurst
to save *(person)* retten
  (money) sparen
savoury pikant
to say sagen
scales *(weighing)* die Waage
scarf *(headscarf)* das Kopftuch
  (round neck) das Halstuch
scenery die Landschaft
schedule der Plan
school die Schule
  primary school die Grundschule
  secondary school die Oberschule
scissors die Schere
score *(of match)* der Endstand
to score a goal ein Tor schießen

eng-german   s

Scot der Schotte/die Schottin
Scotland Schottland
Scottish schottisch
scouring pad der Topfschrubber
screen *(TV, etc)* der Bildschirm
screen wash das Scheibenputzmittel
screw die Schraube
screwdriver der Schraubenzieher
  (phillips) der Kreuzschlitzschraubenzieher
scuba diving das Sporttauchen
sculpture die Skulptur
sea das Meer
seafood die Meeresfrüchte
to search suchen
seasickness die Seekrankheit
seaside die Küste
  at the seaside an der Küste
seaweed die Alge
season *(of year)* die Jahreszeit
  (holiday) die Saison
  in season Saison haben
season ticket die Zeitkarte
seasonal saisonal
seasoning das Gewürz
seat *(chair)* der Sitz
  (in bus, train, theatre) der Platz
seat belt der Sicherheitsgurt
second *(time)* die Sekunde
second zweite(r/s)
second class *(travel)* zweite Klasse
second-hand gebraucht
secretary der Sekretär/die Sekretärin
security guard die Wache
sedative das Beruhigungsmittel
to see sehen
self-catering für Selbstversorger
self-employed freiberuflich
self-service die Selbstbedienung
to sell verkaufen
  do you sell...? verkaufen Sie...?
sell-by date das Haltbarkeitsdatum
Sellotape® der Tesafilm®
to send schicken
senior citizen der Rentner/die Rentnerin
separated *(couple)* getrennt
separately: *to pay separately* getrennt bezahlen
September der September
septic tank die Klärgrube
serious schlimm
to serve *(dish)* servieren

service *(church)* der Gottesdienst
(in shop, etc) die Bedienung
is service included? ist die Bedienung inbegriffen?
service charge die Bedienung
service station die Raststätte
set menu die Tageskarte
settee das Sofa
several verschiedene
to sew nähen
sex *(gender)* das Geschlecht
(intercourse) der Sex
shade der Schatten
in the shade im Schatten
to shake schütteln
shallow *(water)* seicht
shampoo das Shampoo
shampoo and set Waschen und Föhnen
to share teilen
sharp scharf
to shave rasieren
shaving cream die Rasiercreme
she sie
sheep das Schaf
sheet *(on bed)* das Betttuch
shelf das Regal
shell *(seashell)* die Muschel
(egg, nut) die Schale
sheltered geschützt
to shine scheinen
shingles die Gürtelrose
ship das Schiff
shirt das Hemd
shock der Schock
shock absorber der Stoßdämpfer
shoe der Schuh
shoelaces die Schnürsenkel
shoe polish die Schuhcreme
shoe shop der Schuhladen
shop der Laden
to shop einkaufen
shop assistant der Verkäufer/ die Verkäuferin
shop window das Schaufenster
shopping das Einkaufen
to go shopping einkaufen gehen
shopping centre das Einkaufszentrum
shore das Ufer
short kurz
shortage der Mangel

short circuit der Kurzschluss
short cut die Abkürzung
shorts die Shorts
short-sighted kurzsichtig
shoulder die Schulter
to shout rufen
show *(theatrical)* die Aufführung
to show zeigen
shower *(bath)* die Dusche
(of rain) der Schauer
shower cap die Duschhaube
shower gel das Duschgel
to shrink einlaufen
shut *(closed)* geschlossen
to shut schließen
shutter *(on window)* der Fensterladen
shuttle service der Shuttle-Service
sick *(ill)* krank
(nauseous) übel
I feel sick mir ist schlecht
side die Seite
side dish die Beilage
sidelight das Standlicht
sidewalk der Bürgersteig
sieve das Sieb
sight die Sehenswürdigkeit
sightseeing: *to go sightseeing* Sehenswürdigkeiten besichtigen
sightseeing tour die Besichtigungstour
sign *(notice)* das Schild
to sign unterschreiben
signature die Unterschrift
signpost der Wegweiser
silk die Seide
silver das Silber
similar ähnlich
since seit
to sing singen
single *(unmarried)* ledig
(not double) Einzel-
(ticket) einfach
single bed das Einzelbett
single room das Einzelzimmer
sink *(kitchen)* das Spülbecken
sister die Schwester
sister-in-law die Schwägerin
to sit sitzen
sit down please! bitte setzen Sie sich!
size *(of clothes, shoes)* die Größe
to skate *(on ice)* Schlittschuh laufen
skates *(ice)* die Schlittschuhe
(roller) die Rollschuhe
skateboard das Skateboard
skating rink die Eisbahn

139 ski der Ski

to ski Ski fahren
ski boots die Skistiefel
skiing das Skilaufen
ski instructor der Skilehrer/
die Skilehrerin
ski jump die Sprungschanze
ski lift der Skilift
ski pants die Skihose
ski pass der Skipass
ski run/piste die Abfahrt
ski stick/pole der Skistock
ski suit der Skianzug
skin die Haut
skirt der Rock
sky der Himmel
sledge der Schlitten
to sleep schlafen
to sleep in (oversleep) verschlafen
sleeper (on train) der Schlafwagen
sleeping bag der Schlafsack
sleeping car der Schlafwagen
sleeping pills die Schlaftabletten
slice die Scheibe
sliced bread geschnittenes Brot
slide (photograph) das Dia
to slip rutschen
slippers die Hausschuhe
slow(ly) langsam
to slow down langsamer werden
small klein
smaller than kleiner als
smell der Geruch
(unpleasant) der Gestank
a nice smell ein angenehmer Duft
to smell riechen
smile das Lächeln
to smile lächeln
smoke der Rauch
to smoke rauchen
I don't smoke ich bin Nichtraucher(in)
smoke alarm der Feuermelder
smoked (food) geräuchert
smokers (sign) Raucher
smooth weich
snack der Snack
to have a snack einen Imbiss essen
snack bar die Snackbar
snake die Schlange
snake bite der Schlangenbiss
to sneeze niesen
snorkel der Schnorchel
snow der Schnee

to snow: it's snowing es schneit
snow board das Snowboard
snowboarding: to go snowboarding
Snowboard fahren
snow chains die Schneeketten
snow plough der Schneepflug
snow tyres die Winterreifen
snowed up eingeschneit
soap die Seife
soap powder das Waschmittel
sober nüchtern
socket (for plug) die Steckdose
socks die Socken
soda water das Soda
sofa das Sofa
sofa bed das Sofabett
soft weich
soft drink das alkoholfreie Getränk
soldier der Soldat
sole (of shoe) die Sohle
soluble löslich
some einige
someone irgendjemand
something etwas
sometimes manchmal
somewhere irgendwo
son der Sohn
son-in-law der Schwiegersohn
song das Lied
soon bald
as soon as possible so bald wie möglich
sore throat die Halsschmerzen
sorry: I'm sorry! tut mir leid!
sort die Sorte
what sort? welche Sorte?
soup die Suppe
sour sauer
soured cream die saure Sahne
south der Süden
souvenir das Souvenir
spa das Bad
space der Platz
spade der Spaten
Spain Spanien
Spanish adj spanisch
spanner der Schraubenschlüssel
spare parts die Ersatzteile
spare room das Gästezimmer
spare tyre der Ersatzreifen
spare wheel das Ersatzrad

sparkling perlend
  sparkling water das Sprudelwasser
  sparkling wine der Schaumwein
spark plugs die Zündkerzen
to speak sprechen
  do you speak English? sprechen Sie Englisch?
special speziell
specialist der Spezialist/die Spezialistin
speciality die Spezialität
speed die Geschwindigkeit
speeding die Geschwindigkeitsübertretung
speeding ticket die Strafe für Geschwindigkeitsübertretung
speed limit die Geschwindigkeitsbegrenzung
  to exceed the speed limit die Geschwindigkeitsbegrenzung überschreiten
speedometer der Tachometer
to spell: *how's it spelt?* wie buchstabiert man das?
to spend ausgeben
spice das Gewürz
spicy würzig
to spill verschütten
spinach der Spinat
spin dryer die Wäscheschleuder
spine das Rückgrat
spirits *(alcohol)* die Spirituosen
splinter der Splitter
spoilt verdorben
spoke *(on wheel)* die Speiche
sponge der Schwamm
spoon der Löffel
sport der Sport
sports centre das Fitnesscenter
sports shop das Sportgeschäft
spot der Fleck
sprain die Verstauchung
spring *(season)* der Frühling
  (metal) die Feder
square *(in town)* der Platz
stadium das Stadion
staff das Personal
stain der Fleck
stairs die Treppe
stale *(bread)* trocken
stalls *(in theatre)* das Parkett
stamp die Briefmarke
to stand stehen
star der Stern
  (film) der Star

to start *(begin)* anfangen
starter *(in meal)* die Vorspeise
  (in car) der Anlasser
station der Bahnhof
stationer's die Schreibwarenhandlung
statue die Statue
stay der Aufenthalt
  enjoy your stay! angenehmen Aufenthalt!
to stay *(to remain)* bleiben
  I'm staying at the hotel Berlin ich wohne im Hotel Berlin
steak das Steak
to steal stehlen
steamed gedünstet
steel der Stahl
steep steil
steeple der Kirchturm
steering wheel das Lenkrad
step der Schritt
stepdaughter die Stieftochter
stepfather der Stiefvater
stepmother die Stiefmutter
stepson der Stiefsohn
stereo die Stereoanlage
sterling das Pfund Sterling
steward/stewardess der Steward/die Stewardess
to stick *(with glue)* kleben
sticking plaster das Heftpflaster
still *(yet)* noch
  (motionless) still
  still water stilles Wasser
sting der Stachel
to sting stechen
stitches: *the wound needs stitches* die Wunde muss genäht werden
stockings die Strümpfe
stolen gestohlen
stomach der Magen
stomach ache die Magenschmerzen
stone der Stein
stop *(sign)* das Stoppschild
to stop halten
store *(shop)* das Geschäft
storey das Geschoss
storm der Sturm
story die Geschichte
straight away sofort
straight on geradeaus
strange *(odd)* seltsam
straw *(for drinking)* der Strohhalm
strawberries die Erdbeeren
stream der Bach
street die Straße

street map der Stadtplan
strength die Stärke
stress der Stress
strike (of workers) der Streik
string die Schnur
striped gestreift
stroke (medical) der Schlaganfall
 to have a stroke einen Schlaganfall haben
strong stark
 strong coffee starker Kaffee
 strong tea starker Tee
stuck: *it's stuck* es klemmt
student der Student/die Studentin
student discount die Studenten-ermäßigung
stuffed gefüllt
stung gestochen
stupid dumm
subscription (fee) der Beitrag
subtitles die Untertitel
subway die Unterführung
suddenly plötzlich
suede das Wildleder
sugar der Zucker
sugar-free zuckerfrei
to suggest vorschlagen
suit (man's) der Anzug
 (woman's) das Kostüm
suitcase der Koffer
sum die Summe
summer der Sommer
summer holidays die Sommerferien
summit der Gipfel
sun die Sonne
to sunbathe sonnenbaden
sunblock die Sonnencreme
sunburn der Sonnenbrand
Sunday der Sonntag
sunglasses die Sonnenbrille
sunny sonnig
sunrise der Sonnenaufgang
sunroof (car) das Sonnendach
sunscreen das Sonnenschutzmittel
sunset der Sonnenuntergang
sunshade der Sonnenschirm
sunstroke der Sonnenstich
suntan die Sonnenbräune
suntan lotion das Sonnenöl
supermarket der Supermarkt
supper das Abendessen
supplement (to pay) der Zuschlag
to supply zur Verfügung stellen
sure: *I'm sure* ich bin mir sicher

eng-german s/t

to surf surfen
 to surf the Net im Internet surfen
surfboard das Surfbrett
surgery (treatment) die Operation
surname der Nachname
surprise die Überraschung
to survive überleben
suspension (in car) die Aufhängung
to swallow verschlucken
to sweat schwitzen
sweater der Pullover
sweatshirt das Sweatshirt
sweet (not savoury) süß
sweetener der Süßstoff
sweets die Süßigkeiten
to swell anschwellen
to swim schwimmen
swimming costume der Badeanzug
swimming pool das Schwimmbad
swimsuit der Badeanzug
swing (for children) die Schaukel
Swiss adj schweizerisch
 m/f der Schweizer/die Schweizerin
switch der Schalter
to switch off (light) ausschalten
 (machine) abschalten
 (gas, water) abstellen
to switch on (light, machine) einschalten
 (gas, water) anstellen
Switzerland die Schweiz
swollen geschwollen
synagogue die Synagoge
syringe die Spritze

T

table der Tisch
tablecloth die Tischdecke
tablet (pill) die Tablette
table tennis das Tischtennis
table wine der Tafelwein
to take nehmen; (medicine) einnehmen
 how long does it take? wie lange dauert es?
take-away food das Essen zum Mitnehmen
to take off abfliegen
talc der Körperpuder
to talk to sprechen mit
tall groß
tampons die Tampons

tangerine die Mandarine
tank *(petrol)* der Tank
(fish) das Aquarium
tap der Wasserhahn
tap water das Leitungswasser
tape die Kassette
tape measure das Maßband
tape recorder der Kassettenrekorder
target das Ziel
taste der Geschmack
to taste probieren
can I taste it? darf ich es probieren?
tax die Steuer
taxi das Taxi
taxi driver der Taxifahrer/
die Taxifahrerin
taxi rank der Taxistand
tea der Tee
herbal tea Kräutertee
lemon tea Zitronentee
tea with milk Tee mit Milch
tea bag der Teebeutel
teapot die Teekanne
teaspoon der Teelöffel
tea towel das Geschirrtuch
to teach unterrichten
teacher der Lehrer/die Lehrerin
team das Team
tear *(in material)* der Riss
teat *(on bottle)* der Sauger
teenager der Teenager
teeth die Zähne
telegram das Telegramm
telephone das Telefon
to telephone telefonieren
telephone box die Telefonzelle
telephone call der Anruf
telephone card die Telefonkarte
telephone directory das Telefonbuch
telephone number die Telefonnummer
television das Fernsehen
to tell erzählen
temperature die Temperatur
to have a temperature Fieber haben
temporary provisorisch
tenant der Mieter
tendon die Sehne
tennis das Tennis
tennis ball der Tennisball
tennis court der Tennisplatz
tennis racket der Tennisschläger

tent das Zelt
tent peg der Hering
terminal das Terminal
terrace die Terrasse
to test testen
testicles die Hoden
tetanus injection die Tetanusimpfung
than als
to thank danken
thank you danke
thanks very much vielen Dank
that das
that one das dort
the der, die, das
theatre das Theater
theft der Diebstahl
their *(with der words)* ihr
(with das words) ihr
(with die words) ihre
them ihnen
there *(over there)* dort
there is/there are es gibt
thermometer das Thermometer
these diese
these ones diese hier
they sie
thick *(not thin)* dick
thief der Dieb
thigh der Oberschenkel
thin dünn
thing das Ding
my things meine Sachen
to think denken
thirsty durstig
to be thirsty Durst haben
this dies
this one das hier
thorn der Dorn
those jene
those ones jene dort
thread der Faden
throat die Kehle
throat lozenges die Halspastillen
through durch
to throw away wegwerfen
thumb der Daumen
thunder der Donner
thunderstorm das Gewitter
Thursday der Donnerstag
ticket die Karte
(train, bus, etc) die Fahrkarte
(entrance fee) die Eintrittskarte
(parking fine) das Knöllchen
a single ticket eine einfache Fahrkarte
a return ticket eine Rückfahrkarte

143

a tourist ticket ein Touristenticket
a book of tickets ein Fahrscheinheft

ticket inspector der Schaffner/
die Schaffnerin

ticket office der Fahrkartenschalter

tide die Gezeiten
high tide die Flut
low tide die Ebbe

tidy ordentlich

to tidy up aufräumen

tie die Krawatte

tight eng

tights die Strumpfhose

tile die Fliese

till *(cash desk)* die Kasse

till *(until)* bis
till 2 o'clock bis zwei Uhr

time *(of day)* die Zeit
what time is it? wie spät ist es?
do you have time? haben Sie Zeit?

timer die Schaltuhr

timetable der Fahrplan

tin *(can)* die Dose

tinfoil die Alufolie

tin-opener der Dosenöffner

to tip Trinkgeld geben

tip *(to waiter, etc)* das Trinkgeld

tipped *(cigarettes)* Filter-

tired müde

tissues die Papiertaschentücher

to zu (zum/zur)
(with names of places) nach
to London nach London
to the airport zum Flughafen

toadstool der Giftpilz

toast der Toast

tobacco der Tabak

tobacconist's die Tabakwarenhandlung

today heute

toddler das Kleinkind

toe die Zehe

together zusammen

toilet die Toilette
disabled toilet die Behindertentoilette

toilet brush die Toilettenbürste

toilet paper das Toilettenpapier

toiletries die Toilettenartikel

token *(for bus)* der Fahrschein
(for phone, launderette, etc) die Marke

toll *(motorway)* die Maut

tomato die Tomate
tinned tomatoes die Dosentomaten

tomato juice der Tomatensaft

tomorrow morgen
tomorrow morning morgen früh

tomorrow afternoon morgen
Nachmittag
tomorrow evening morgen Abend

tongue die Zunge

tonic water das Tonic

tonight heute Abend

tonsillitis die Mandelentzündung

too *(also)* auch
too big zu groß
too small zu klein
too noisy zu laut

tools das Werkzeug

toolkit der Werkzeugkasten

tooth der Zahn

toothache die Zahnschmerzen
I have toothache ich habe
Zahnschmerzen

toothbrush die Zahnbürste

toothpaste die Zahnpasta

toothpick der Zahnstocher

top: *the top floor* das oberste
Stockwerk

top *(of mountain)* der Gipfel
(lid) der Deckel
(clothing) das Oberteil
on top of... oben auf...

topless oben ohne

torch *(flashlight)* die Taschenlampe

torn zerrissen

total *(amount)* die Endsumme

to touch anfassen

tough *(meat)* zäh

tour die Fahrt
guided tour die Besichtigungstour

tour guide der Reiseführer/
die Reiseführerin

tour operator der Reiseveranstalter

tourist der Tourist/die Touristin

tourist information die Touristen-
Information

tourist office das Fremdenverkehrsbüro

tourist route die Touristenroute

tourist ticket die Touristenkarte

to tow *(car)* abschleppen

towbar *(car)* die Abschleppstange

tow rope das Abschleppseil

towel das Handtuch

tower der Turm

town die Stadt

town centre das Stadtzentrum

town hall das Rathaus

town plan der Stadtplan

toxic giftig
toy das Spielzeug
toy shop der Spielzeugladen
tracksuit der Jogginganzug
traditional traditionell
traffic der Verkehr
traffic jam der Stau
traffic lights die Ampel
traffic warden die Politesse
trailer der Anhänger
train der Zug
  by train mit dem Zug
  the next train der nächste Zug
  the first train der erste Zug
  the last train der letzte Zug
trainers die Trainingsschuhe
tram die Straßenbahn
tranquilliser das Beruhigungsmittel
to translate übersetzen
translation die Übersetzung
to travel reisen
travel agent's das Reisebüro
travel documents die Reisepapiere
travel guide der Reiseführer
travel insurance die Reiseversicherung
travel sickness die Reisekrankheit
traveller's cheques die Reiseschecks
tray das Tablett
tree der Baum
trip der Ausflug
trolley *(luggage)* der Gepäckwagen
  (shopping) der Einkaufswagen
trouble der Ärger
  to be in trouble in Schwierigkeiten
  sein
trousers die Hose
truck der Laster
true wahr
trunk *(for luggage)* der Koffer
trunks *(swimming)* die Badehose
to try versuchen
to try on *(clothes, etc)* anprobieren
T-shirt das T-Shirt
Tuesday der Dienstag
tumble dryer der Wäschetrockner
tunnel der Tunnel
to turn *(right/left)* abbiegen
to turn around umdrehen
to turn off *(light)* ausmachen
  (TV, radio, etc) ausschalten
  (tap) zudrehen

to turn on *(light)* anmachen
  (TV, radio, etc) anschalten
  (tap) aufdrehen
turquoise *(colour)* türkis
tweezers die Pinzette
twice zweimal
twin-bedded room das Zweibett-
  zimmer
twins die Zwillinge
to type Maschine schreiben
typical typisch
tyre der Reifen
tyre gauge der Reifendruckmesser
tyre pressure der Reifendruck
Tyrol das Tirol

U

ugly hässlich
ulcer das Geschwür
umbrella der Regenschirm
  (sunshade) der Sonnenschirm
uncle der Onkel
uncomfortable unbequem
unconscious bewusstlos
under unter
undercooked nicht gar
underground *(metro)* die U-Bahn
underpants die Unterhose
underpass die Unterführung
understand verstehen
  I don't understand ich verstehe nicht
  do you understand? verstehen Sie?
underwear die Unterwäsche
unemployed arbeitslos
to unfasten aufmachen
United Kingdom das Vereinigte
  Königreich
United States die Vereinigten Staaten
university die Universität
unleaded petrol das bleifreie Benzin
unlikely unwahrscheinlich
to unlock aufschließen
to unpack auspacken
unpleasant unangenehm
to unplug herausziehen
to unscrew aufschrauben
until bis
unusual ungewöhnlich
up: *to get up* aufstehen
upside down verkehrt herum
upstairs oben
urgent dringend
urine der Urin

145 **us** uns
to use benutzen
useful nützlich
usual(ly) gewöhnlich
U-turn die Wende

V

vacancy *(in hotel)* Zimmer frei
vacant frei
vacation der Urlaub
vaccination die Impfung
vacuum cleaner der Staubsauger
vagina die Vagina
valid *(ticket, licence, etc)* gültig
valley das Tal
valuable wertvoll
valuables die Wertsachen
value der Wert
valve das Ventil
van der Lieferwagen
vase die Vase
VAT die Mehrwertsteuer (MWST)
vegan: *I'm vegan* ich bin Veganer
vegetables das Gemüse
vegetarian vegetarisch
I'm vegetarian ich bin Vegetarier
vehicle das Fahrzeug
vein die Ader
Velcro® das Klettband
vending machine der Automat
venereal disease die Geschlechts-krankheit
ventilator der Ventilator
very sehr
vest das Unterhemd
vet der Tierarzt
via über
to video *(from TV)* auf Video aufnehmen
(to film) filmen
video das Video
video camera die Videokamera
video cassette/tape die Videokassette
video game das Videospiel
video recorder der Videorekorder
Vienna Wien
view die Aussicht
villa die Villa
village das Dorf
vinegar der Essig
vineyard der Weinberg
virus der Virus
visa das Visum

visit der Besuch
to visit *(person)* besuchen
(place) besichtigen
visiting hours *(hospital)* die Besuchszeit
visitor der Besucher
vitamin das Vitamin
voice die Stimme
volcano der Vulkan
volleyball der Volleyball
voltage die Spannung
to vomit erbrechen
voucher der Gutschein

W

wage der Lohn
waist die Taille
waistcoat die Weste
to wait for warten auf
waiter/waitress der Kellner/die Kellnerin
waiting room der Warteraum
to wake up aufwachen
Wales Wales
walk der Spaziergang
to go for a walk einen Spaziergang machen
to walk spazieren gehen
(go on foot) zu Fuß gehen
walking boots die Wanderschuhe
walking stick der Wanderstock
Walkman® der Walkman®
wall die Mauer
wallet die Brieftasche
to want wollen
I want... ich möchte...
we want... wir möchten...
war der Krieg
ward *(hospital)* die Station
wardrobe der Kleiderschrank
warehouse die Lagerhalle
warm warm
it's warm (weather) es ist warm
to warm up *(milk, etc)* aufwärmen
warning triangle das Warndreieck
to wash waschen
(to wash oneself) sich waschen
wash and blow dry Waschen und Föhnen
washbasin das Waschbecken
washing machine die Waschmaschine
washing powder das Waschpulver
washing-up bowl die Abwaschschüssel

washing-up liquid das Spülmittel
wasp die Wespe
wasp sting der Wespenstich
waste bin der Abfalleimer
to watch zuschauen
watch die Armbanduhr
watch strap das Uhrarmband
water das Wasser
  hot water warmes Wasser
  cold water kaltes Wasser
  drinking water Trinkwasser
  mineral water Mineralwasser
  sparkling water Sprudelwasser
  still water stilles Wasser
water heater das Heißwassergerät
waterproof wasserdicht
water sports der Wassersport
to water ski Wasserski fahren
water wings die Schwimmflügel
waves *(on sea)* die Wellen
waxing die Wachsbehandlung
way der Weg
  which is the way to...? wie kommt
  man zu/nach...?
way in *(entrance)* der Eingang
way out *(exit)* der Ausgang
we wir
weak schwach
  (tea, coffee) dünn
to wear tragen
weather das Wetter
weather forecast die Wettervorhersage
website die Webseite
wedding die Hochzeit
wedding anniversary der Hochzeitstag
wedding present das Hochzeitsgeschenk
Wednesday der Mittwoch
week die Woche
  last week letzte Woche
  next week nächste Woche
  this week diese Woche
  per week pro Woche
  during the week im Verlauf der Woche
weekday der Werktag
weekend das Wochenende
  next weekend nächstes Wochenende
  this weekend dieses Wochenende
weekly wöchentlich
weekly ticket das Wochenticket
to weigh wiegen
weight das Gewicht
welcome willkommen

well gut
  he's not well ihm geht es nicht gut
well *(for water)* der Brunnen
well-done *(steak)* durch
wellington boots die Gummistiefel
Welsh *adj* walisisch
  m/f der Waliser/die Waliserin
west der Westen
wet nass
wetsuit der Taucheranzug
what was
wheat der Weizen
wheel das Rad
wheelchair der Rollstuhl
wheel clamp die Parkkralle
when wann
where wo
which: which man? welcher Mann?
  which woman? welche Frau?
  which book? welches Buch?
while während
  in a while bald
white weiß
who wer
whole vollständig
wholemeal bread das Vollkornbrot
whose wessen
why warum
wide breit
widow die Witwe
widower der Witwer
width die Breite
wife die Frau
wig die Perücke
to win gewinnen
wind der Wind
windbreak *(camping)* der Windschutz
windmill die Windmühle
window das Fenster
  (of shop) das Schaufenster
windscreen die Windschutzscheibe
windscreen wipers die Scheibenwischer
to windsurf surfen
windy: it's windy es ist windig
wine der Wein
  dry wine trockener Wein
  house wine Hauswein
  red wine Rotwein
  rosé wine Roséwein
  sparkling wine Schaumwein
  sweet wine süßer Wein
  white wine Weißwein
wine list die Weinkarte
wing der Flügel
wing mirror der Seitenspiegel

winter der Winter
wire der Draht
with mit
  with ice mit Eis
  with milk mit Milch
  with sugar mit Zucker
without ohne
  without ice ohne Eis
  without milk ohne Milch
  without sugar ohne Zucker
witness der Zeuge
woman die Frau
wonderful wunderbar
wood *(material)* das Holz
wooden hölzern
woods *(forest)* der Wald
wool die Wolle
word das Wort
work die Arbeit
work permit die Arbeitsgenehmigung
to work *(person)* arbeiten
  (machine) funktionieren
  it doesn't work es funktioniert nicht
world die Welt
worried besorgt
worse schlechter
worth: *it's worth £50* es ist fünfzig
  Pfund wert
to wrap up *(parcel)* einwickeln
wrapping paper das Geschenkpapier
wrinkles die Falten
wrist das Handgelenk
to write schreiben
  please write it down bitte schreiben
  Sie das auf
writing paper das Briefpapier
wrong falsch
  what's wrong? was stimmt nicht?
wrought-iron schmiedeeisern

X

X-ray die Röntgenaufnahme
to x-ray röntgen

Y

yacht die Jacht
year das Jahr
  this year dieses Jahr
  next year nächstes Jahr
  last year letztes Jahr
yearly jährlich
yellow gelb
Yellow Pages die Gelben Seiten
yes ja
yesterday gestern
yet: *not yet* noch nicht
yoghurt der Joghurt
  plain yoghurt Naturjoghurt
yolk das Eigelb
you *(polite sing. and pl.)* Sie
  (familiar sing.) du ; ihr *(pl.)*
young jung
your dein/Ihr
  (with der words) dein/Ihr
  (with das words) dein/Ihr
  (with die words) deine /Ihre
youth hostel die Jugendherberge

Z

zebra crossing der Zebrastreifen
zero null
zip der Reißverschluss
zone die Zone
zoo der Zoo
zoom lens der Zoom

Aal m eel
ab off ; from
  ab 8 Uhr from 8 o'clock
  ab Mai from May onward
abbestellen to cancel
abbiegen to turn *(right/left)*
Abbildung f illustration
abblenden to dip *(headlights)*
Abblendlicht nt dipped headlights
Abend m evening
Abendessen nt dinner ; supper
Abendgarderobe f formal dress
Abendkleid nt evening dress
abends in the evening(s)
aber but
abfahren to depart ; to leave
Abfahrt f departures *(train, bus)*
Abfahrtszeit f departure time
Abfall m rubbish
Abfertigungsschalter m check-in desk
abfliegen to take off *(plane)*
Abflug m departures *(plane)*
  Abflug Inland domestic departures
  Abflug Ausland international
  departures
Abflughalle f departure lounge
Abflugzeit f departure time
Abfluss m drain
Abführmittel nt laxative
abheben to withdraw *(money)*
abholen to fetch ; to claim *(baggage, etc)*
  abholen lassen to send for
Abkürzung f short cut
abladen to dump ; to offload
ablaufen to expire
ablehnen to refuse
Abonnement nt subscription
Abreise f departure
absagen to cancel
Absatz m heel
abschalten to switch off *(machine)*
abschicken to dispatch
Abschleppdienst m breakdown service
abschleppen to tow *(car)*
Abschleppseil nt towrope
Abschleppstange f towbar
Abschleppwagen m breakdown van
Absender m sender
abstellen to turn off ; to park car
Abszess m abscess
Abtei f abbey

Abteil nt compartment *(on train)*
Abteilung f department
Abtreibung f abortion
Abtreibungspille f abortion pill
Abwaschlappen m J cloth®
Abzug m print *(photo)*
Achse f axle
achten auf to pay attention to
Achtung f caution ; danger
Ader f vein
Adler m eagle
Adressbuch nt address book
Adresse f address
adressieren to address *(letter)*
Affe m monkey
ähnlich similar
Aktentasche f briefcase
Akzent m accent *(pronunciation)*
akzeptieren to accept
Alarmanlage f alarm
Alge f seaweed
Alkohol m alcohol
alkoholfrei non-alcoholic
alkoholisch alcoholic *(drink)*
alle all ; everybody ; everyone
  alle zwei Tage every other day
Allee f avenue
allein alone
Allergie f allergy
allergisch gegen allergic to
Allerheiligen nt All Saints' Day
alles everything ; all *(singular)*
allgemein general ; universal
Allradantrieb m four wheel drive
Alpen pl Alps
als than ; when *(with past tense)*
alt old
Altar m altar
Altbier nt top-fermented dark beer
Alter nt age *(of person)*
ältere(r/s) older ; elder
Altglascontainer m bottle bank
Alufolie f aluminium foil
am at ; in ; on
  am Bahnhof at the station
  am Abend in the evening
  am Freitag on Friday
Ameise f ant
Amerika nt America
Amerikaner(in) m/f American

amerikanisch *adj* American
Ampel *f* traffic light
Amtszeichen *nt* dialling tone
Amüsierviertel *nt* nightclub district
an at ; on *(light, radio, etc)* ; near
  Frankfurt an 1300 arriving Frankfurt
  at 1300
  an/aus on/off
Ananas *f* pineapple
anbauen to grow *(cultivate)*
anbieten to offer
andere(r/s) other
ändern to change *(to alter)*
Änderung *f* change
Anfall *m* fit *(seizure)*
Anfang *m* start *(beginning)*
anfangen to begin ; to start
Anfänger(in) *m/f* beginner
Anfängerhügel *m* nursery slope
Anfrage *f* enquiry
Angaben *pl* details ; directions *(to a place)*
angeben to give
Angebot *nt* offer
  im Angebot on offer
Angehörige(r) *m/f* relative
angeln to fish
Angeln *nt* fishing ; angling
  Angeln verboten no fishing
Angelrute *f* fishing rod
Angelschein *m* fishing permit
angenehm pleasant
Angestellte(r) *m/f* employee
Angina *f* angina
angreifen to attack
Angst haben vor to be afraid of
Anhänger *m* trailer ; fan *(supporter)*
Anker *m* anchor
ankommen to arrive
ankündigen to announce
Ankunft *f* arrivals
Anlage *f* park ; grounds ; facilities
  öffentliche Anlage public park
Anlasser *m* starter *(in car)*
Anlegeplatz *m* mooring
Anlegestelle *f* landing stage ; jetty
anmachen to turn on *(light, radio)*
Anmeldeformular *nt* registration form
Anmeldung *f* registration ; reception *(place)*
Annahme *f* acceptance ; reception

annehmen to assume ; to accept
anprobieren to try on *(clothes, etc)*
Anruf *m* phone call
Anrufbeantworter *m* answerphone
anrufen to phone
anschalten to turn on *(TV, etc)*
anschauen to look at
Anschlagbrett *nt* notice board
Anschluss *m* connection *(train, etc)*
Anschlussflug *m* connecting flight
anschnallen to fasten *(seatbelt)*
Anschrift *f* address
anschwellen to swell
Ansicht *f* view
Ansichtskarte *f* picture postcard
anstatt instead of
ansteckend infectious
anstehen to queue
anstellen to switch on *(gas, water)*
Anteil *m* share *(part)*
Antenne *f* aerial
Antibiotikum *nt* antibiotic
antik ancient
Antiquitäten *pl* antiques
Antiquitätenladen *m* antique shop
Antiseptikum *nt* antiseptic
Antwort *f* answer ; reply
antworten to answer ; to reply
Anweisungen *pl* instructions
Anzahl *f* number
Anzahlung *f* deposit
Anzeige *f* advertisement ; report *(to police)*
Anzug(-züge) *m* suit(s) *(man's)*
anzünden to light ; to set fire to
Apfel (Äpfel) *m* apple(s)
Apfelkuchen *m* apple cake
Apfelsaft *m* apple juice
Apfelsine(n) *f* orange(s)
Apfelwein *m* cider
Apotheke *f* pharmacy
Apparat *m* appliance ; camera ; extension
Aprikose(n) *f* apricot(s)
April *m* April
Aquarium *nt* fish tank
Arbeit *f* employment ; work
arbeiten to work *(person)*
arbeitslos unemployed
Architekt(in) *m/f* architect
Architektur *f* architecture
arm poor
Arm *m* arm

1

Armband nt bracelet
Armbanduhr f watch
Ärmelkanal m English Channel
Art f type ; sort ; manner
Arthritis f arthritis
Artikel m article ; item
Arznei f medicine
Arzt (Ärztin) m/f doctor
Aschenbecher m ashtray
Aspirin nt aspirin
Ast m branch (of tree)
Asthma nt asthma
Atlantik m Atlantic Ocean
atmen to breathe
attraktiv attractive
auch also ; too ; as well
auf onto ; on ; upon ; on top of
  auf Deutsch in German
  auf Wiedersehen goodbye
aufdrehen to turn on (tap)
Aufenthalt m stay ; visit
Aufenthaltsraum m lounge
Auffahrt f slip-road
Aufführung f performance ; show
aufgeben to quit ; to post ; to check
  in (baggage)
aufhalten to delay ; to hold up
  sich aufhalten to stay
auflegen to hang up (phone)
aufmachen to open (shop, bank etc) ;
  to unfasten
  sich aufmachen to set off
aufregend exciting
aufschließen to unlock
aufschrauben to unscrew
aufschreiben to write down
aufstehen to get up
Aufstieg m ascent
aufwachen to wake up
aufwärmen to heat up (food, milk)
Aufzug m lift/elevator
Auge(n) nt eye(s)
Augenblick m moment ; instant
Augentropfen pl eye drops
August m August
Auktion f auction
Au-pair-Mädchen nt au pair
aus off (light, radio, etc) ; made of... ;
  from ; out of
Ausdruck m expression ; print-out ;
  term (word)
Ausfahrt f exit (motorway)
Ausfall m failure (mechanical)
Ausflug(-flüge) m trip(s) ; excursion(s)

Ausfuhr f export(s)
ausführen to export ; to carry out (job)
ausfüllen to fill in (form)
  bitte nicht ausfüllen please leave
  blank (on form)
Ausgabe f issue (of magazine) ; issuing
  counter
Ausgaben pl expenses
Ausgang m exit ; gate (at airport)
ausgeben to spend (money)
ausgehen to go out (for amusement)
ausgeschaltet off (radio)
ausgestellt issued at (passport)
ausgezeichnet excellent
auskugeln to dislocate (joint)
Auskunft information
Ausland nt foreign countries ; abroad ;
  international
  aus dem Ausland from overseas
Ausländer(in) m/f foreigner
ausländisch foreign
Auslandsgespräch nt international call
auslassen to leave out ; to omit
auslaufen to sail (ship)
ausmachen to turn off (light) ; to put
  out (fire, cigarette)
Ausnahme(n) f exception(s)
auspacken to unpack
Auspuffrohr nt exhaust pipe
Ausrüstung f kit ; equipment
ausschalten to switch off (light, TV,
  radio)
Ausschank m bar ; drinks
Ausschlag m cold sore ; skin rash
ausschließlich excluding ; exclusive(ly)
Außenseite f outside
Außenspiegel m outside mirror
außer betrieb out of order
äußerlich exterior
Aussicht f view ; prospect
aussprechen to pronounce
Ausstattung f equipment (of car)
aussteigen to get out of (vehicle)
Ausstellung f show ; exhibition
Ausstellungsdatum nt date of issue
Austausch m exchange
Australien nt Australia
Australier(in) m/f Australian
australisch adj Australian
Ausverkauf m sale
ausverkauft sold out

Auswahl f choice
auswählen to choose
auswärts essen to eat out
ausweichen to avoid (obstacle)
Ausweis m identity card ; pass (permit)
auszahlen to pay
Auto(s) nt car(s)
Autobahn f motorway
Autobahngebühr f toll
Autofähre f car-ferry
Autokarte f road map
Automat m vending machine
　Automat wechselt change given
Automatikauto nt automatic car
automatisch automatic
Automobilklub m automobile association
Autor(in) m/f author
Autoreisezug m motorail service
Autoschlüssel pl car keys
Autovermietung f car hire

B

Baby nt baby
Babyflasche f baby's bottle
Babymilch f baby milk
Babynahrung f baby food
Babyraum m mother and baby room
Babysitter(in) m/f babysitter
Babytücher pl baby wipes
Bach m stream
Bäckerei f baker's
Backofen m oven
Bad nt bath ; spa
Badeanzug m swimsuit
Badehose f swimming trunks
Badekappe f bathing cap
Badelatschen pl flip flops
baden to bathe ; to swim
　Baden verboten no swimming
Badezimmer nt bathroom
Baguette nt French bread
Bahn f railway ; rink
　per Bahn by rail
Bahnhof m station ; depot
Bahnlinie f line (railway)
Bahnsteig m platform
Bahnübergang m level crossing
bald soon
Balkon m balcony

Ball m ball
Ballett nt ballet
Ballon m balloon
Banane(n) f banana(s)
Band (Bänder) nt ribbon(s) ; tape(s)
Band f band (musical)
Bank f bank (financial) ; bench
Bankkonto nt bank account
Bar f nightclub ; bar
Bär m bear (animal)
Bargeld nt cash
Bart m beard
Basel Basle
Batterie f battery
Bauarbeiten pl roadworks ; construction work
bauen to build
Bauer (Bäuerin) m/f farmer
Bauernhaus nt farmhouse
Bauernhof m farm(yard)
Baum m tree
Baumarkt m DIY shop
Baumwolle f cotton (fabric)
Baustelle f roadworks ; construction site
Bayern nt Bavaria
beachten to observe ; to obey
beantworten to answer
Bedarfshaltestelle f request stop
bedeckt cloudy (weather)
Bedeutung f meaning
bedienen to serve ; to operate
　sich bedienen to help oneself
Bedienung f service (charge)
Bedingung f condition (proviso)
Beefsteak nt steak
　deutsches Beefsteak hamburger; beefburger
beenden to end ; to finish
Beerdigung f funeral
Beere f berry
beginnen to begin
begrüßen to greet ; to welcome
behalten to keep (retain)
Behandlung f treatment
beheizt heated
behindert disabled (person)
Behindertentoilette f toilet for disabled
Behinderung f obstruction ; handicap
bei near ; by (beside) ; at ; on ; during
beide both
Beilage f side-dish ; vegetables ; side-salad
Bein nt leg

3 **Beisel** nt pub (Austria)
Beispiel(e) nt example(s)
  zum Beispiel for example
beißen to bite
Beitrag m contribution ; subscription (to club)
beitreten to join (club)
Bekleidungsgeschäft nt clothes shop
bekommen to get (receive, obtain)
beladen to load (truck, ship)
Belastung f load
belegt no vacancies
Beleuchtung f lighting
Belgien nt Belgium
Belichtung f exposure (film)
beliebt popular
Belohnung f reward
benachrichtigen to inform
Benachrichtigung f advice note
benötigen to require
benutzen to use
Benzin nt petrol
Benzinpumpe f fuel pump (in car)
bequem comfortable
Beratungsstelle f advice centre
berechtigt zu entitled to
Berechtigte(r) m/f authorized person
bereit ready
Bereitschaftsdienst m emergency service
Berg(e) m mountain(s)
bergab downhill
bergauf uphill
Bergführer(in) m/f mountain guide
Bergschuhe pl climbing boots
Bergsteigen nt mountaineering
Bergtour f hillwalk ; climb
Bergwacht f mountain rescue
Bergwanderung f hill-walking
Bericht(e) m report(s) ; bulletin(s)
berichten to report
Berliner m doughnut
Beruf m profession ; occupation
beruflich professional
Beruhigungsmittel nt tranquilliser
berühmt famous
berühren to handle ; to touch
beschädigen to damage
beschäftigt busy
Beschäftigung f employment ; occupation
Bescheinigung f certificate
beschreiben to describe
Beschreibung f description

Besen m brush (for sweeping floor)
besetzt engaged ; occupied
besichtigen to visit (place)
Besichtigungen pl sightseeing
Besichtigungstour f guided tour
Besitzer(in) m/f owner
besondere(r/s) particular ; special
besorgt worried
besser better
Besserung(en) f improvement(s)
  gute Besserung get well soon
bestätigen to confirm
Bestätigung f confirmation (flight, etc)
beste(r/s) best
Besteck nt cutlery
bestellen to book ; to order
Bestellung f order (in restaurant)
Bestimmungen pl regulations
Bestimmungsort m destination
besuchen to visit (person)
Besucher(in) m/f visitor
Besuchszeit f visiting hours
beten to pray
Betrag m amount
  Betrag erhalten payment received
betreffs concerning
betreten to enter
  Betreten verboten keep off
Betrieb m business
betrunken drunk
Bett(en) nt bed(s)
Bettbezug m duvet cover
Bettdecke f duvet ; quilt
Betttuch nt sheet (on bed)
Bettzeug nt bedclothes
Beule f lump (swelling)
bewacht guarded
bewegen to move
Bewohner(in) m/f resident
bewölkt cloudy
bewusstlos unconscious
bezahlen to pay ; to settle (bill)
bezahlt paid
Bezahlung f payment
Bezirk m district
BH m bra
Bibliothek f library
Biene f bee
Bienenstich m bee sting ; type of cream cake

Bier nt beer
  Bier vom Fass draught beer
Biergarten m beer garden
Bierkeller m beer cellar
Bierstube f pub that specializes in beer
bieten to offer
Bikini m bikini
Bild(er) nt picture(s)
Bilderrahmen m picture frame
Bildschirm m screen *(TV, computer)*
billig cheap ; inexpensive
billiger cheaper
Billigtarif m cheap rate *(phone)*
Birne(n) f pear(s) ; lightbulb(s)
bis until ; till
  bis jetzt up till now
  bis zu 6 up to 6
  bis bald see you soon
bisschen: *ein bisschen* a little ; a bit of
bitte please
bitte? pardon?
bitten um to ask for
bitter bitter *(taste)*
blass pale
Blase f blister
Blasenentzündung f cystitis
Blatt (Blätter) nt sheet(s) *(of paper)* ;
  leaf (leaves)
blau blue
Blaue Zone f limited parking zone
  (parking disk required)
Blei nt lead *(metal)*
bleiben to stay *(to remain)*
Bleichmittel nt bleach
Bleiersatz-Additiv nt lead additive
bleifreies Benzin nt unleaded petrol
Bleistift m pencil
blind blind *(person)*
Blinddarmentzündung f appendicitis
Blinker m indicator *(in car)*
Blitz m lightning
Blitzlicht nt flash *(for camera)*
blockiert jammed *(camera, lock)*
Blockschrift f block letters
blond fair *(hair)* ; blond
Blumen pl flowers
Blumenladen m florist's shop
Bluse f blouse
Blut nt blood
Blutdruck m blood pressure
bluten to bleed

Bluterguss m bruise
Blutgruppe f blood group
blutig rare *(steak)*
Bluttest m blood test
Blutvergiftung f blood poisoning
Bockbier nt bock *(strong beer)*
Boden m floor *(of room)* ; ground
Bodensee m Lake Constance
Bohnen pl beans
  grüne Bohnen french beans
Bohrer m drill *(tool)*
Boiler m immersion heater
Bombe f bomb
Bonbon nt sweet
Boot nt boat *(small)*
Bootsfahrt f cruise
Bootsrundfahrt f round boat trip
Bootsverleih m boat hire
Bordkarte f boarding pass
borgen to borrow
Böschung f embankment
botanischer Garten m botanical gardens
Botschaft f embassy
Bowle f punch *(drink)*
Brandwunde f burn *(on skin)*
Brat- fried ; roast
braten to fry ; to roast
Bratkartoffeln pl fried potatoes
Bratpfanne f frying pan
Bratwurst f sausage
Brauch m custom *(tradition)*
brauchen to need
Brauerei f brewery
braun brown
Bräune f suntan
Braut f bride
Bräutigam m bridegroom
Brechreiz m nausea
breit wide
Bremse(n) f brake(s)
bremsen to brake
Bremsflüssigkeit f brake fluid
Bremslicht nt brake light
brennen to burn
Brief m letter *(message)*
Briefkasten m letterbox ; postbox
Briefmarke(n) f stamp(s)
Briefpapier nt writing paper
Brieftasche f wallet
Briefträger(in) m/f postman/woman
Brille f glasses *(spectacles)*
Brillenetui nt glasses case
bringen to bring

britisch British
Brombeeren pl blackberries
Bronchitis f bronchitis
Bronze f bronze
Brosche f brooch
Broschüre f brochure
Brot nt bread ; loaf
Brötchen nt bread roll
Bruch m fracture
Brücke f bridge
Bruder(Brüder) m brother(s)
Brühe f stock (for soup, etc)
Brühwürfel pl stock cubes
Brunnen m well (for water) ; fountain
Brust f breast ; chest
Buch nt book
buchen to book
Buchhandlung f bookshop
Büchsen- canned
Büchsenöffner m can-opener
Buchstabe m letter (of alphabet)
Bucht f bay (along coast)
Buchung f booking
Bügel m coat hanger
  Bügel drücken! press down!
Bügelbrett nt ironing board
Bügeleisen nt iron (for clothes)
bügeln to iron
Bundes- federal
Bundesrepublik Deutschland f Federal Republic of Germany
Bungee-Springen nt bungee jumping
bunt coloured
Burg f castle ; fortress (medieval)
Bürger(in) m/f citizen
bürgerlich middle-class
Bürgermeister(in) m/f mayor(-ess)
Bürgersteig m pavement ; sidewalk
Büro nt agency ; office
Bürogebäude nt office block
Bürste f brush
Bus(se) m bus(es) ; coach(es)
Busbahnhof m bus/coach station
Busfahrschein m bus ticket
Busfahrt f bus tour
Bushaltestelle f bus stop
Buslinie f bus route
Busreise f coach trip
Busverbindung f bus service
Büstenhalter m bra
Butangas nt Calor gas®
Butter f butter

C

campen to camp
Campingführer m camping guide(book)
Campingkocher m camping stove
Campingplatz m campsite
Campingtisch m picnic table
CD-Spieler m CD player
Champignon(s) m mushroom(s)
Charterflug m charter flight
Check-in m check-in
Chef(in) m/f boss
chemische Toilette f chemical loo
Chinarestaurant nt Chinese restaurant
Chips pl crisps ; chips (gambling)
Chor m choir
Cola f Coke®
Computer m computer
Computerprogramm nt computer program
Computerspiel nt computer game
Conditioner m conditioner (hair)
Cousin(e) m/f cousin
Creme f cream (lotion)
Creme(speise) f mousse

D

da there
  nicht da out (not at home)
Dach nt roof
Dachboden m attic
Dachgepäckträger m roof-rack
daheim at home
Damen ladies
Damenbinde(n) f sanitary towel(s)
Dampfer m steamer (boat)
danach after (afterwards)
Dänemark nt Denmark
danke thank you
danken to thank
Darmgrippe f gastric flu
das the ; that ; this ; which
Datei f file (computer)
Datum nt date (day)
Dauer f length ; duration
Dauerwelle f perm
Daumen m thumb
Decke f blanket ; ceiling

Deckel m top ; lid
dein your (singular familiar)
denken to think
Denkmal(-mäler) nt monument(s)
Deo nt deodorant
der the ; who(m) ; that ; this ; which
Desinfektionsmittel nt disinfectant
desinfizieren to disinfect
destilliertes Wasser nt distilled water
Details pl details
deutsch adj German
Deutsch nt German (language)
Deutsche(r) m/f German
Deutschland nt Germany
Devisen pl foreign currency
Dezember m December
Dia(s) nt slide(s)
Diabetes m diabetes
Diabetiker(in) m/f diabetic person
Diamant m diamond
Diät f diet (special)
dick fat
die the ; who(m) ; that ; this ; which
Dieb(in) m/f thief
Diebstahl m theft
Dienst m service
  im Dienst on duty
Dienstag m Tuesday
dienstbereit open (pharmacy) ; on duty (doctor)
Dienstreise f business trip
Dienstzeit f office hours
dies this
diese these
diese(r/s) this (one)
Diesel m diesel
Dieselöl nt diesel oil
Ding(e) nt thing(s)
Diplomat(in) m/f diplomat
direkt direct (route, train)
Direktflug m direct flight
Direktor(in) m/f managing director
Diskette f computer disk (floppy)
Disko f disco
Dokumente pl documents
Dollar m dollar
Dolmetscher(in) m/f interpreter
Dom m cathedral
Donner m thunder
Donnerstag m Thursday

Doppel- double
Doppelbett nt double bed
doppelt double
Doppelzimmer nt double room
Dorf(Dörfer) nt village(s)
Dorn m thorn
dort there (over there) ; that one
Dose f box ; tin ; can
Dosenöffner m tin-opener
Dozent(in) m/f teacher (university)
Drachenfliegen nt hang gliding
Draht m wire
Drahtseilbahn f cable railway
draußen outdoors ; outside
drehen to turn ; to twist
Dreibettabteil nt three-berth compartment
Dreieck nt triangle
Dreikönigstag m Epiphany
dringend urgent
drinnen indoors
Droge f drug
Drogerie f chemist's (not for prescriptions)
drücken push
Druckschrift f block letters
du you (familiar form)
dumm stupid
dunkel dark
dunkelblau dark blue
dünn thin ; weak (tea)
dunstig misty
durch through ; well-done (steak)
Durchfahrt verboten no through traffic
Durchfall m diarrhoea
Durchgang m way ; passage
Durchgangsverkehr m through traffic
durchgehend direct (train, bus) ; 24 hour
Durchsage f announcement
durchwählen to dial direct
Durchzug m draught (of air)
dürfen to be allowed
Dürre f drought
Durst haben to be thirsty
durstig thirsty
Dusche f shower
Duschhaube f shower cap
Duschvorhang m shower curtain
Dutzend nt dozen

E

Ebbe f low tide
echt real ; genuine

Ecke f corner
Edelstein m jewel ; gem
ehemalig ex-
ehrlich honest
Ei(er) nt egg(s)
Eiche f oak
eifersüchtig jealous
Eigelb nt egg yolk
Eigentum nt property
Eigentümer(in) m/f owner
Eil- urgent
Eilbrief m express letter
Eilzustellung f special delivery
Eimer m bucket
ein (with 'das'/'der' words) a ; one
ein(geschaltet) on (machine)
Einbahnstraße f one-way street
Einbrecher(in) m/f burglar
einchecken to check in
eine (with 'die' words) a ; one
einfach simple ; single ticket ; plain (unflavoured)
Einfuhr f import
einführen to insert ; to import
Eingang m entrance
Eingangstür f front door
eingeschlossen included (in price)
eingeschneit snowed up
Eingeweidebruch m hernia
eingießen to pour
einige(r/s) some ; a few
einkaufen to shop
Einkaufswagen m shopping trolley
Einkaufszentrum nt shopping centre
einladen to invite
Einladung f invitation
Einlass ab 18 no entry for under 18s
einlaufen to shrink
einlösen to cash (cheque)
einmal once
einnehmen to take (medicine)
einordnen to get in lane
Einrichtungen pl facilities
eins one
einschalten to switch on (light, TV)
einschieben to insert
einschließlich including
Einschreiben nt registered letter
  per Einschreiben by recorded delivery
einsteigen to get in(to) (bus, etc)
einstellen to adjust ; to appoint ; to stop
Eintopfgericht nt stew
eintreten to enter

Eintritt m entry ; admission (fee)
Eintritt frei free entry
Eintrittskarte(n) f ticket(s)
Eintrittspreis m admission charge/fee
einwerfen to post ; to insert
einwickeln to wrap up (parcel)
Einwurf m slot ; slit
  Einwurf 2 Mark insert 2 marks
Einzahlung f deposit
Einzel- (not double)
Einzelbett nt single bed
Einzelfahrschein m single ticket
einzeln single ; individual
Einzelzimmer nt single room
Eis nt ice cream ; ice
Eisbahn f skating rink
Eisbecher m knickerbocker glory
Eisdiele f ice-cream parlour
Eisen nt iron (metal)
Eisenbahn f railway
Eisenwarenhandlung f hardware shop
Eiskaffee m iced coffee
Eistee m iced tea
Eiswürfel pl ice cubes
Eiweiß nt egg white
Elastikbinde f elastic bandage
elastisch elastic
Elektriker(in) m/f electrician
elektrisch electric(al)
elektrischer Schlag m electric shock
Elektrizität f electricity
Elektrorasierer m electric razor
Ellbogen m elbow
Eltern pl parents
E-Mail f e-mail
E-Mail-Adresse f e-mail address
Empfang m reception
empfangen to receive (guest) ; to greet
Empfangschef m receptionist
Empfangsdame f receptionist
Empfangsschein m receipt
empfehlen to recommend
Ende nt end ; bottom (of page, etc)
Endstand m final score (of match)
Endstation f terminal
Endsumme f total (amount)
eng narrow ; tight (clothes)
England nt England
Engländer(in) m/f Englishman/woman
Englisch nt English (language)

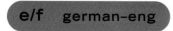

e/f german–eng

Enkel m grandson
Enkelin f granddaughter
entdecken to discover
Ente f duck
enteisen to de-ice
entfernt distant
  2 Kilometer entfernt 2 km away
Entfernung f distance
entfrosten to defrost
Enthaarungscreme f depilatory cream
enthalten to hold *(to contain)*
entkoffeinierter Kaffee m decaffeinated coffee
entkommen to escape
entrahmte Milch f skimmed milk
entschädigen to reimburse
Entschuldigung f pardon ; excuse me
entweder ... oder either ... or
entwickeln to develop *(photos)*
Entzündung f inflammation
Epileptiker(in) m/f epileptic
epileptischer Anfall m epileptic fit
er he ; it
erbrechen to vomit
Erbsen pl peas
Erdbeben nt earthquake
Erdbeeren pl strawberries
Erde f earth
Erdgeschoss nt ground floor
Erdnuss(-nüsse) f peanut(s)
Erdrutsch m landslide
erfreut pleased
Erfrischungen pl refreshments
erhalten to obtain ; to receive
erhältlich available
Erkältung f cold *(illness)*
erkennen to realize ; to recognize
erklären to explain
Erklärung f explanation
erlauben to permit *(something)* ; to allow
Ermäßigung f reduction
Ernte f harvest
Ersatz m substitute ; replacement
Ersatzrad nt spare wheel
Ersatzteile pl car parts
erste(r/s) first
  erste Hilfe first aid
  erste Klasse first class
ertrinken to drown

Erwachsene(r) m/f adult
erzählen to tell
es it
essbar edible
essen to eat
Essen nt food ; meal
Essen zum Mitnehmen take-away food
Essig m vinegar
Esslöffel m tablespoon
Esszimmer nt dining room
Etage f floor , storey
Etagenbetten pl bunk beds
etwas something
Eule f owl
Euro m Euro *(currency)*
Europa nt Europe
europäisch European
Europäische Union (EU) f European Union (EU)
Euroscheck m Eurocheque
Exemplar nt copy *(of book, etc)*
Experte (Expertin) m/f expert
exportieren to export

F

Fabrik f works ; factory
Facharzt (Fachärztin) m/f specialist *(medical)*
Fächer m fan *(hand-held)*
Faden m thread
Fahne f flag
Fahrbahn f carriageway
Fähre f ferry
fahren to drive ; to go
Fahrer(in) m/f driver *(of car)*
Fahrgast m passenger
Fahrkarte f ticket *(train, bus, etc)*
Fahrkartenschalter m ticket office
Fahrplan m timetable *(trains, etc)*
Fahrplanhinweise pl travel information
Fahrpreis(e) m fare(s)
Fahrrad(-räder) nt bicycle(s)
Fahrradflickzeug nt bicycle repair kit
Fahrradschloss nt bicycle lock
Fahrradvermietung f bike hire
Fahrschein(e) m ticket(s)
Fahrscheinentwerter m ticket stamping machine
Fahrscheinheft nt book of tickets
Fahrspur(en) f lane(s)
Fahrstuhl m lift ; elevator
Fahrt f journey ; drive ; ride *(in vehicle)*
  gute Fahrt! safe journey!

Fahrzeug nt vehicle
Fall m instance
 im Falle von in case of
fallen to fall
fällig due (owing)
falsch false (name, etc) ; wrong
Falten pl wrinkles
Familie f family
Familienname m surname
Familienstand m marital status
Familienzimmer nt family room
Fan m fan (football)
Farbe f colour ; paint ; suit (cards)
färben dye
farbenblind colour-blind
Farbfilm m colour film
farbig coloured
Farbstoff m dye
Fasching m carnival
Fass nt barrel
 vom Fass on tap ; on draught
Fassbier nt draught beer
Fastnachtsdienstag m Shrove Tuesday
faul lazy
Fax nt fax
faxen to fax
Faxnummer f fax number
Februar m February
Feder f spring (coil) ; feather
Federball m badminton
Federung f suspension (in car)
fehlen to be missing
Fehler m fault ; mistake
Fehlgeburt f miscarriage
feiern to celebrate
Feiertag m holiday
Feile f file (nail)
Feinkostgeschäft nt delicatessen
Feld nt field
Felsen m cliff (in mountains)
Fenster nt window
Fensterladen m shutter (on window)
Fensterplatz m window seat
Ferien pl holiday(s)
Ferienhaus nt chalet (holiday)
Ferienwohnung f holiday flat
Fern- long-distance
Fernbedienung f remote control
Ferngespräch nt long-distance call
Fernglas nt binoculars
Fernlicht nt full beam (headlights)
Fernsehen nt television
Fernseher m TV set

Fernsprecher m public phone
fertig ready ; finished
Fest nt celebration ; party ; festival
Festplatte f hard disk
Fett nt fat ; grease
fettarm low-fat
fettarme Milch f low-fat milk
fettig greasy
feucht damp
Feuchtigkeitscreme f moisturizer
Feuer nt fire
feuerfeste Form f ovenproof dish
feuergefährlich inflammable
Feuerlöscher m fire extinguisher
Feuermelder m fire/smoke alarm
Feuertreppe f fire escape
Feuerwehr f fire brigade
Feuerwehrauto nt fire engine
Feuerwerk nt fireworks
Feuerzeug nt cigarette lighter
Fieber nt fever
 Fieber haben to have temperature
Filet nt sirloin ; fillet (of meat, fish)
Filiale f branch (of store, bank, etc)
Film m film (at cinema, for camera)
filmen to film
Filter m filter
Filzstift m felt-tip pen
finden to find
Finger m finger
Fingernagel m fingernail
Firma f company (firm)
Fisch m fish
Fischladen m fishmonger's
FKK-Strand m nudist beach
flach flat (level)
Flamme f flame
Flasche f bottle
Flaschenbier nt bottled beer
Flaschenöffner m bottle opener
Fleck m mark (stain)
Fleckenmittel nt stain-remover
Fleisch nt meat ; flesh
Fleischerei f butcher's
Flickzeug nt puncture repair kit
Fliege f bow tie ; fly
fliegen to fly
Flitterwochen pl honeymoon
Flöhe pl fleas
Flohmarkt m flea market

Flug(Flüge) m flight(s)
Fluggast m passenger
Fluggesellschaft f airline
Flughafen m airport
Flughafenbus m airport bus
Flugplan m flight schedule
Flugauskunft f flight information
Flugschein(e) m plane ticket(s)
Flugsteig m gate
Flugstrecke f route ; flying distance
Flugticket(s) nt plane ticket(s)
Flugzeug nt plane, aircraft
Flur m corridor
Fluss(Flüsse) m river(s)
Flussfahrt f river trip
Flüssigkeit f liquid
Flut f flood ; high tide
Föhn m hairdryer
föhnen to blow-dry
folgen to follow
Forelle f trout
Form f shape ; form
Formular nt form (document)
Fortsetzung f sequel (book, film)
Foto nt photo
Fotoapparat m camera
Fotogeschäft nt photo shop
Fotografie f photography
fotografieren to take a photo
Fotokopie f photocopy
fotokopieren to photocopy
Fracht f cargo ; freight
Frage f question
fragen to ask
frankieren to stamp (letter)
Frankreich nt France
Franzose (Französin) m/f Frenchman/
  woman
französisch adj French
Frau f wife ; Mrs ; Ms ; woman
Fräulein nt Miss
frei free / vacant
  im Freien outdoor ; open-air
Freibad nt open-air pool
freiberuflich freelance ; self-employed
Freigepäck nt baggage allowance
freimachen to stamp
Freitag m Friday
Freizeichen nt ringing tone
Freizeit f spare time ; leisure

Freizeitzentrum nt leisure centre
fremd foreign ; strange (unknown)
Fremde(r) m/f stranger
Fremdenführer(in) m/f tourist guide
Fremdenverkehrsbüro nt tourist office
Freude f joy
Freund m friend ; boyfriend
Freundin f friend ; girlfriend
freundlich friendly
Frieden m peace
Friedhof m cemetery
frisch fresh ; wet (paint)
Frischhaltefolie f cling film
Frischkäse m cream cheese
Friseur (Friseuse) m/f hairdresser
Frosch m frog
Frost m frost
Frostschutzmittel nt antifreeze
Früchte pl fruit
Früchtetee m fruit tea
Fruchtsaft m fruit juice
früh early
früher earlier
Frühling m spring (season)
Frühstück nt breakfast
Fuchs m fox
fühlen to feel
führen to lead
Führer(in) m/f guide
Führerschein m driving licence
Führung(en) f guided tour(s)
füllen to fill
Füller m pen
Fundbüro nt lost property office
Fundsachen pl lost property
funktionieren to work (machine)
für for
  Benzin für DM 50 DM 50 worth of
  petrol
  für immer forever
Fuß(Füße) m foot(feet)
  zu Fuß gehen to walk
Fußball m football ; soccer
Fußballer(in) m/f football player
Fußballplatz m football pitch
Fußballspiel nt football match
Fußgänger(in) m/f pedestrian
Fußgängerüberweg m pedestrian
  crossing
Fußgängerzone f pedestrian precinct
Fußweg m footpath
füttern to feed

Gabel f fork (for eating)
Gabelung f fork (in road)
Galerie f gallery
Gang m course (of meal) ; aisle (theatre, plane)
Gangschaltung f gears
Gans f goose
ganz whole ; quite
ganztägig full-time
Garage f garage (private)
Garantie f guarantee ; warrant(y)
Garderobe f cloakroom
Garten m garden
Gartenlokal nt garden café
Gärtner(in) m/f gardener
Gas nt gas
Gasflasche f gas cylinder
Gasherd m gas cooker
Gaspedal nt accelerator
Gasse f alley ; lane (in town)
Gast m guest
  nur für Gäste patrons only
Gästezimmer nt guest-room
Gasthaus nt inn
Gasthof m inn ; guesthouse
Gastritis f gastritis
Gaststätte f restaurant
Gaststube f lounge
Gate nt gate (airport)
Gebäck nt pastry (cake)
gebacken baked
Gebäude nt building
gebeizt cured ; marinated
geben to give
Gebiet nt region ; area
Gebiss nt dentures
geboren born
  geborene Schnorr née Schnorr
gebraten fried
gebrauchen to use
Gebraucht- used (car, etc)
gebrochen broken
Gebühr f fee
gebührenpflichtig subject to fee
Geburt f birth
Geburtsdatum nt date of birth
Geburtsort m place of birth
Geburtstag m birthday
Geburtstagsgeschenk nt birthday present
Geburtstagskarte f birthday card
Geburtsurkunde f birth certificate

Gedeckkosten pl cover charge (in restaurant)
gedünstet steamed
Gefahr f danger
gefährlich dangerous
Gefälle nt gradient
Gefängnis nt prison
Geflügel nt poultry ; fowl
gefroren frozen (food)
gefüllt stuffed
gegen versus ; against ; toward(s)
Gegend f district ; region
gegenüber opposite ; facing
Gegenverkehr m two-way traffic
gegrillt grilled
gehen to go ; to walk
  wie geht es Ihnen? how are you?
Gehirnerschütterung f concussion
gehören to belong to
gekocht boiled ; cooked
gelb yellow ; amber (traffic lights)
Gelbe Seiten pl Yellow Pages
Gelbsucht f jaundice
Geld nt money
  Geld einwerfen insert money
Geldautomat m cash dispenser
Geldbeutel m purse
Geldrückgabe f coin return
Geldschein m banknote
Geldstrafe f fine (to be paid)
Geldstück nt coin
gelegentlich occasionally
Gelenk nt joint (of body)
Geltungsdauer f period of validity
gemischt mixed ; assorted
Gemüse nt vegetables
Gemüseladen m greengrocer's
genau accurate ; precise ; exact
Genehmigung f approval ; permit
genug enough
Genuss m enjoyment
geöffnet open
Gepäck nt luggage
Gepäckablage f luggage rack
Gepäckaufbewahrung f left-luggage office
Gepäckausgabe f baggage reclaim
Gepäckermittlung f luggage desk (for queries)
Gepäcknetz nt luggage rack (in train)

Gepäckschließfach nt left-luggage locker

Gepäckträger m luggage rack (on car) ; porter

Gepäckversicherung f luggage insurance

Gepäckwagen m luggage trolley

gerade even (number)

geradeaus straight ahead

Gerät nt appliance ; gadget

geräuchert smoked (food)

Gericht nt court (law) ; dish (food)

gerieben grated (cheese)

geröstet sauté ; fried ; toasted

Geruch m smell

Gesamtsumme f total amount

Geschäft(e) nt business ; shop(s)

Geschäftsadresse f business address

Geschäftsführer(in) m/f manager

Geschäftspartner(in) m/f partner (business)

Geschäftsstunden pl business hours

geschehen to happen

Geschenk(e) nt gift(s)

Geschenkeladen m gift shop

Geschenkpapier nt wrapping paper

Geschichte f history

geschieden divorced

Geschirrspülmaschine f dishwasher

Geschirrspülmittel nt washing-up liquid

Geschirrtuch nt tea/dish towel

Geschlecht nt gender ; sex

Geschlechtskrankheit f venereal disease

geschlossen closed/shut

Geschmack m taste ; flavour

geschmort braised

geschnittenes Brot nt sliced bread

Geschoss nt storey

geschützt sheltered

Geschwindigkeit f speed

geschwollen swollen

Geschwür nt ulcer

Gesellschaft f company

Gesetz nt law

gesetzlicher Feiertag m public holiday

Gesicht nt face

Gesichtswasser f cleanser (for face)

Gesichtspflege f facial (beauty treatment)

gesperrt closed

Gespräch nt talk ; phone call

Gestank m smell (unpleasant)

gestattet permitted

gestern yesterday

gestochen stung ; bitten (by insect)

gestreift striped

gesund healthy

Gesundheit f health ; bless you!

Getränk(e) nt drink(s)

Getränkekarte f list of beverages

getrennt separated (couple)
  getrennt bezahlen to pay separately

Getriebe nt gearbox ; gears

Gewehr nt gun

Gewicht nt weight

gewinnen to win

Gewitter nt thunderstorm

gewöhnlich usual(ly)

Gewürz nt spice ; seasoning

Gezeiten pl tide

gibt es...? is/are there...?

Gift nt poison

giftig poisonous

Gipfel m summit ; mountain top

Gips m plaster (for broken limb)

Gitarre f guitar

Glas nt glass ; lens (of glasses) ; jar

Glatteis nt black ice

Glatteisgefahr f danger-black ice

glatzköpfig bald (person)

glauben to believe ; to think (be of opinion)

gleich same

Gleise pl platforms ; tracks

Gletscher m glacier

Glocke f bell

Glück nt happiness ; luck

glücklich happy ; lucky

Glühbirne f light bulb

Gold nt gold

Golf nt golf

Golfplatz m golf course

Golfschläger m golf club

gotisch Gothic

Gott m God

Gottesdienst m church service

Grad m degree (of heat, cold)

Gramm nt gram(me)

Grapefruit f grapefruit

Gras nt grass

Gräte f fish bone

grau grey

Grenze f frontier ; border (of country)

Grenzpolizei f border police

Griff m handle ; knob

Grill *m* barbecue ; grill
grillen to grill
Grillstube *f* steak house ; grillroom
Grillteller *m* mixed grill
Grippe *f* flu
groß tall ; great ; big ; high *(number, speed)*
Großbritannien *nt* Great Britain
Großbuchstabe *m* capital letter
Größe *f* size *(of clothes, shoes)* ; height
Großeltern *pl* grandparents
Großmutter *f* grandmother
Großvater *m* grandfather
großzügig generous
grün green ; fresh *(fish)*
Grünanlage *f* park
Grundstücksmakler *m* estate agent's
grüne Versicherungskarte *f* green card *(car insurance)*
grüner Salat *m* green salad
Gruppe *f* group
Gruß *m* greeting
Grußkarte *f* greetings card
Gulasch *nt* goulash
gültig valid
Gummi *m* rubber ; elastic
Gummiband *nt* rubber band
Gummihandschuhe *pl* rubber gloves
Gummistiefel *pl* wellington boots
günstig convenient
Gurke(n) *f* cucumber(s) ; gherkin(s)
Gürtel *m* belt
Gürtelrose *f* shingles
Gürteltasche *f* bumbag ; moneybelt
gut good ; well ; all right *(yes)*
    alles Gute all the best ; with best wishes
guten Abend good evening
guten Appetit enjoy your meal
guten Morgen good morning
gute Nacht good night
guten Tag hello ; good day/afternoon
Güter *pl* goods
Gutschein *m* voucher ; coupon

H

H-Milch *f* long-life milk
Haar *nt* hair
Haarbürste *f* hairbrush
Haare *pl* hair
Haargel *nt* hair gel
Haarklemme *f* hairgrip
Haarschnitt *m* haircut

Haarspray *nt* hair spray
haben to have
Hackfleisch *nt* mince meat
Hacksteak *nt* hamburger
Hafen *m* harbour ; port
Hafer *m* oats
Haftung *f* liability
Hagel *m* hail
Hahn *m* tap *(for water)* ; cockerel
Hähnchen *nt* chicken
halb half
    zum halben Preis half-price
halb durch medium rare *(meat)*
halber Fahrpreis *m* half fare
Halbfettmilch *f* semi-skimmed milk
Halbinsel *f* peninsula
Halbpension *f* half board
Hälfte *f* half
hallo hello
Hals *m* neck ; throat
Halskette *f* necklace
Halspastillen *pl* throat lozenges
Halsschmerzen *pl* sore throat
Halstuch *nt* scarf *(round neck)*
Halt *m* stop
Haltbarkeitsdatum *nt* sell-by date
Haltebucht *f* layby
halten to hold ; to stop
Halten verboten no stopping
Haltestelle *f* bus stop
Hammer *m* hammer
Hämorrhoiden *pl* haemorrhoids
Hand *f* hand
Handel *m* trade ; commerce
Handgelenk *nt* wrist
handgemacht handmade
Handgepäck *nt* hand-luggage
Handschuhe *pl* gloves
Handtasche *f* handbag
Handtuch *nt* towel
Handwerker(in) *m/f* craftsperson
Harke *f* rake
hart hard *(not soft)*
hart gekochtes Ei *nt* hard-boiled egg
Hase *m* hare
Haselnuss(-nüsse) *f* hazelnut(s)
hässlich ugly
häufig frequent ; common
Haupt- major ; main
Hauptbahnhof *m* main station

Hauptgericht nt main course
Hauptstadt f capital (city)
Hauptstraße f major road
Hauptverkehrszeit f peak hours
Haus nt house ; home
  zu Hause at home
Hausarbeit f housework
Hausfrau (Hausmann) f/m housewife/househusband
Haushaltswaren pl household goods
Hausschuhe pl slippers
Haustier nt pet
Hauswein m house wine
Haut f hide (leather) ; skin
Hecht m pike
Hefe f yeast
Heft nt exercise book
Hefter m stapler
Heftklammern pl staples
Heftpflaster nt sticking plaster
Heidelbeeren pl blueberries
heilig holy
Heiligabend m Christmas Eve
Heim nt home (institution) ; hostel
Heimweh haben to be homesick
heiraten to marry (get married)
heiß hot
  heiße Schokolade f hot chocolate
heißen to be called
  wie heißen Sie? what's your name?
Heißwassergerät nt water heater
Heizgerät nt heater
Heizkörper m radiator
Heizung f heating
helfen to help
Helikopter m helicopter
hell light (pale) ; bright
hellblau light blue
helles Bier nt lager
helles Fleisch nt white meat
Helm m helmet
Hemd(en) nt shirt(s)
Hepatitis f hepatitis
Herbst m autumn
Herd m cooker ; oven
herein in ; come in
hereinkommen to come in
Hering m herring ; tent peg
Herr m gentleman ; Mr
Herren gents (toilet)

heruntergehen to go down
Herz nt heart
Herzanfall m heart attack
herzliche Glückwünsche! congratulations!
Herzschrittmacher m pacemaker
Heuschnupfen m hay fever
heute today
heute Abend tonight
hier here
hiesig local (wine, speciality)
Hilfe f help
Himbeeren pl raspberries
Himmel m heaven ; sky
hin there
Hin- und Rückfahrt f round trip
hineingehen to go in
hinten behind
hinten einsteigen enter at rear
hinter behind
Hinweis m notice ; information
Hirnhautentzündung f meningitis
historisch historic
hoch high
Hochsaison f high season
Höchstgeschwindigkeit f maximum speed
Höchsttarif m peak rate
Hochzeit f wedding
Hochzeitsgeschenk nt wedding present
Hochzeitskleid nt wedding dress
Hochzeitstag m wedding anniversary
Hochzeitstorte f wedding cake
Hoden pl testicles
Hof m court
hoffen to hope
höflich polite
Höhe f altitude ; height
hoher Blutdruck m high blood pressure
höher higher
  höher stellen to turn up (heat, volume)
Höhle f cave
holen to fetch
holländisch Dutch
Holz nt wood (material)
Holzkohle f charcoal
Homöopathie f homeopathy
homosexuell homosexual
Honig m honey
hören to hear
Hörer m receiver (phone)
Hörgerät nt hearing aid
Hörnchen nt croissant
Hose f trousers

165 **Hotel** nt hotel
Hotel garni nt bed and breakfast hotel
hübsch pretty
Hubschrauber m helicopter
Hüfte f hip
Hügel m hill
Huhn nt hen
Hühnchen nt chicken
Hummer m lobster
Hund m dog
Hundeleine f dog lead
hundert hundred
Hunger haben to be hungry
Hupe f horn (of car)
husten to cough
Husten m cough
Hustenbonbons pl cough sweets
Hustensaft m cough mixture
Hut m hat
Hütte f mountain hut

I

ich I
Idiotenhügel m nursery slope
ihm him
ihnen them
ihr(e) her ; their
Imbiss m snack
Imbissstube f snack bar
immer always
Immunisierung f immunisation
Impfung f vaccination
in in (place, position) ; inside ; into
  in Ordnung all right (agreed)
Infektion f infection
Informationsbüro nt information office
Ingenieur(in) m/f engineer
Inhalationsapparat m inhaler (medication)
Inhalt m contents
inklusive inclusive
Inland nt domestic (flight, etc)
Inlandsgespräch(e) nt national call(s)
innen inside
Innenstadt f city centre
innerlich for internal use (medicine)
Insekt nt insect
Insektenschutzmittel nt insect repellent
Insel f island
Insulin nt insulin
intelligent intelligent
interessant interesting
Internet nt internet

Internet-Café nt internet café
Internet-Seite f website
Ire (Irin) m/f Irishman/woman
irgend jemand someone
irgendwo somewhere
irisch adj Irish
Irland nt Ireland
Irrtum m mistake
Italien nt Italy
Italiener(in) m/f Italian
italienisch adj Italian

J

ja yes
Jacht f yacht
Jachthafen m marina
Jacke f jacket ; cardigan
Jagderlaubnis f hunting permit
jagen to hunt
Jahr nt year
Jahrestag m anniversary
Jahreszeit f season
Jahrgang m vintage
Jahrhundert nt century
jährlich annual ; yearly
Jahrmarkt m fair
Januar m January
je everyone
Jeans pl jeans
jede(r/s) each
jemand somebody ; someone
jene those
jetzt now
Jod nt iodine
joggen to jog
Jogginganzug m tracksuit
Joghurt m yoghurt
Johannisbeere(n) f currant(s)
Journalist(in) m/f journalist
jucken to itch
Jude/Jüdin m/f Jew
Jugendherberge f youth hostel
Jugendliche(r) m/f teenager
Juli m July
jung young
Junge m boy
Junggeselle m bachelor
Juni m June
Juwelier m jeweller's

K

Kabel nt cable ; lead (electrical)
Kabelfernsehen nt cable TV
Kabine f cabin ; berth (train, ship)
Kaffee m coffee
Kaffeehaus nt café
Kaffeemaschine f percolator
Kai m quayside
Kakao m cocoa
Kakerlake f cockroach
Kalb nt calf (young cow)
Kalbfleisch nt veal
kalt cold
Kamera f camera
Kameratasche f camera case
Kamillentee m camomile tea
Kamin m fireplace
Kamm m comb ; ridge
kämpfen to fight
Kanada nt Canada
Kanadier(in) m/f Canadian
kanadisch adj Canadian
Kanal m canal ; (English) Channel
kandiert glacé
Kaninchen nt rabbit
Kanister m (petrol) can
Kanu nt canoe
Kapelle f chapel ; orchestra
kaputt broken ; out of order
kaputtmachen to break (object)
Kapuze f hood (of jacket)
Karaffe f decanter ; carafe
Karfreitag m Good Friday
Karotten pl carrots
Karte f card ; ticket ; map ; menu
Kartentelefon nt cardphone
Kartoffel(n) f potato(es)
Kartoffelpüree nt mashed potato
Kartoffelsalat m potato salad
Karton m box (cardboard) ; carton
Käse m cheese
Kasino nt casino
Kasse f cash desk
Kasserolle f casserole
Kassette f cassette ; cartridge ; tape
Kassettenrecorder m cassette player ; tape recorder
Kassierer(in) m/f cashier

Kastanie f chestnut
Katalog m catalogue
Kater m hangover
katholisch Catholic
Katze f cat
kaufen to buy
Kaufhaus nt department store
Kaugummi m chewing gum
Kaution f deposit
Kehle f throat
Keilriemen m fan belt
kein... no...
keine(r/s) no ; none
Keks(e) m biscuit(s) (sweet)
Keller m cellar
Kellner(in) m/f waiter/waitress
kennen to be acquainted with
Keramik f pottery
Kern m pip
Kerze f candle
Kette f chain
Kfz-Versicherung f car insurance
Kiefer f pine
Kiefer m jaw
Kilo(gramm) nt kilo(gram)
Kilometer m kilometre
Kind(er) nt child(ren)
Kinderbett nt cot
Kindermädchen nt nanny
Kindersitz m child seat (car)
Kinderstuhl m high chair
Kinderteller m child's helping
Kinderwagen m pram
Kinn nt chin
Kino nt cinema
Kiosk m kiosk
Kirche f church
Kirmes f funfair
Kirsche(n) f cherry(cherries)
Kissen nt cushion ; pillow
Kiste f box (wooden)
Klage f complaint
klar clear
Klarer m schnapps
Klärgrube f septic tank
Klasse f class ; grade
Klavier nt piano
Klebeband f adhesive tape
kleben to stick (with glue)
Klebstoff m glue
Kleid nt dress
Kleider pl clothes
Kleiderbügel m coat hanger

Kleiderschrank m wardrobe
klein little (small) ; short
Kleingeld nt change (money)
Klempner(in) m/f plumber
Klettband nt Velcro®
klettern to climb (mountains)
Klimaanlage f air-conditioning
klimatisiert air-conditioned
Klingel f doorbell
klingeln to ring (bell, phone)
Klinik f clinic
Klippe f cliff (along coast)
klopfen to knock (on door)
Kloß m dumpling
Kloster nt monastery ; convent
Kneipe f pub
Knie nt knee
Kniestrümpfe pl pop socks
Knoblauch m garlic
Knöchel m ankle
Knochen m bone
Knödel m dumpling
Knopf m button ; knob (radio, etc)
Knoten m knot
Koch m chef
kochen to boil ; to cook
Kocher m cooker ; stove
Köchin f cook
Kochschinken m cooked ham
Kochtopf m saucepan
Kode m code
Köder m bait (for fishing)
koffeinfreier Kaffee m decaffeinated coffee
Koffer m suitcase ; trunk
Kofferanhänger m luggage tag
Kofferraum m carboot
Kognak m brandy
Kohl m cabbage
Kohle f coal
Kohlrübe f swede
Koje f berth (in ship) ; bunk
Kollege (Kollegin) m/f colleague
Köln Cologne
Kölnischwasser nt eau de cologne
komisch funny (amusing)
kommen to come
Kommode f chest of drawers
Komödie f comedy
Kompass m compass
Komponist(in) m/f composer
Kondensmilch f condensed milk
Konditorei f cake shop ; café

Kondom nt condom
Konfektions- ready-made (clothes)
Konferenz f conference
Konfitüre f jam
König m king
Königin f queen
königlich royal
können to be able to ; to know how to
Konsulat nt consulate
Kontaktlinsen pl contact lenses
Kontaktlinsenreiniger m contact lens cleaner
Konto nt bank account
Kontrolle f check ; control
kontrollieren to check (passports, tickets)
Konzert nt concert
Konzertsaal m concert hall
Kopf m head
Kopfhörer pl headphones
Kopfkissen nt pillow
Kopfsalat m lettuce
Kopfschmerzen pl headache
Kopftuch nt scarf (headscarf)
Kopie f copy (duplicate)
kopieren to copy
Korb m basket
Korinthe f currant
Korken m cork (of bottle)
Korkenzieher m corkscrew
Körper m body
Körperpuder m talc
Kortison nt cortisone
Kosmetiksalon m beauty salon
Kosmetiktücher pl paper tissues
kosten to cost
Kosten pl cost (price)
kostenlos free (costing nothing)
köstlich delicious
Kostüm nt suit (woman's)
Krabbe f crab
Kräcker m cracker
Kraftstoff m fuel
Kragen m collar
Krämpfe pl cramps
krank ill ; sick
Krankenhaus nt hospital
Krankenkasse f medical insurance
Krankenwagen m ambulance
Krankheit f disease
Kräuter pl herbs

Kräutertee m herbal tea
Krawatte f tie
Krebs m crab (animal) ; cancer (illness)
Kreditkarte f credit card
Kreisverkehr m roundabout
Kreuz nt cross (also crucifix)
Kreuzfahrt f cruise
Kreuzschlitzschraubenzieher m Phillips screwdriver®
Kreuzung f junction ; crossroads
Kreuzworträtsel nt crossword
Krieg m war
Kristall nt crystal
Krone f crown
Krücken pl crutches
Krug m jug
Küche f kitchen ; cuisine
Kuchen m flan ; cake
Küchenbrett nt chopping board
Küchenpapier nt kitchen paper
Kugel f ball ; scoop (of ice cream)
Kugelschreiber m pen ; biro
Kuh f cow
kühl cool
Kühlbox f cool-box (for picnic)
kühlen to chill (wine, food)
Kühler m radiator (of car)
Kühlschrank m fridge
Kümmel m caraway seed ; cumin ; schnapps
Kunde (Kundin) m/f client ; customer
Kunst f art
Kunstfaser f man-made fibre
Kunstgewerbearbeiten pl crafts
Kunsthalle f art gallery
Künstler(in) m/f artist
künstlich artificial ; man-made
künstliche Hüfte f hip replacement
Kupfer nt copper
Kupplung f clutch (of car)
Kurierdienst m courier service
Kurort m spa
Kurs m course ; exchange rate
Kurve f curve ; corner ; bend
kurz short ; brief
Kurz(zeit)parkplatz m short-stay car park
kurzsichtig short-sighted
Kurzwarengeschäft nt haberdasher's
Kuss m kiss

küssen to kiss
Küste f coast ; seaside
Küstenwache f coastguard

L

lächeln to smile
Lächeln nt smile
lachen to laugh
Lachs m salmon
Lack m varnish
Laden m shop ; store
Lagerhalle f warehouse
Lakritze f liquorice
Lamm nt lamb
Lampe f lamp
Land nt country (Italy, France, etc) ; land
landen to land
Landkarte f map (of country)
Landschaft f countryside
Landung f landing (of plane)
Landwein m table wine
lang long
Länge f length
Langlauf m cross-country skiing
langsam slow(ly)
langsamer werden to slow down
langweilig boring
Langzeitparkplatz m long-stay car park
Lappen m cloth (rag)
Laptop m laptop
Lärm m noise
lassen to let (allow)
Last f load
Laster m truck
Lastwagen m truck ; lorry
Lätzchen nt bib (baby's)
Lauch m leek
laufen to run
Laugenbrezel f soft pretzel
laut noisy ; loud(ly) ; aloud
läuten to ring (doorbell)
Lautsprecher m loudspeaker
Lautstärke f volume (of sound)
Lawine f avalanche
Lawinengefahr f danger of avalanches
leben to live (exist)
Lebensgefahr f danger to life
Lebensmittel pl groceries
Lebensmittelvergiftung f food poisoning
Lebensversicherung f life insurance
Leber f liver

169

Lebkuchen *m* gingerbread
Leck *nt* leak *(of gas, liquid)*
Lederwaren *pl* leather goods
ledig single *(not married)*
leer empty ; flat *(battery)* ; blank
Leerlauf *m* neutral *(gear)*
legen to lay
Lehrer(in) *m/f* teacher *(school)* ; instructor
leicht light *(not heavy)* ; easy
Leid *nt* grief
 es tut mir Leid (I'm) sorry
leider unfortunately
leihen to rent *(car)* ; to lend
Leihgebühr *f* rental
Leinen *nt* linen *(cloth)*
leise quietly ; soft ; faint
 leiser stellen to turn down *(volume)*
Leiter *f* ladder
Leitung *f* telephone line
Lenker *m* handlebars
Lenkrad *nt* steering wheel
lernen to learn
lesbisch lesbian
lesen to read
letzte(r/s) last ; final
Leuchtturm *m* lighthouse
Leute *pl* people
Licht *nt* light
 das Licht anschalten to switch on lights
Lichtmaschine *f* alternator
Lichtschalter *m* light switch
Lidschatten *m* eye shadow
liebe(r) dear *(in letter)*
Liebe *f* love
lieben to love
liebenswürdig kind
lieber rather
Lieblings- favourite
Lied *nt* song
Lieferwagen *m* van
Liegestuhl *m* deckchair
Liegewagen *m* couchette
Lift *m* elevator ; lift
Liftpass *m* lift pass *(on ski slopes)*
Likör *m* liqueur
Limonade *f* lemonade
Limone *f* lime *(fruit)*
Lineal *nt* ruler
Linie *f* line *(row, of railway)*
Linienflug *m* scheduled flight
linke(r/s) left(-hand)
links to the left ; on the left
Linkshänder(in) *m/f* left-handed person

Linse *f* lens
Linsen *pl* lentils
Lippen *pl* lips
Lippenpflegestift *m* lip salve
Lippenstift *m* lipstick
Liste *f* list
Liter *m* litre
Loch *nt* hole
lochen to punch *(ticket, etc)*
locker loose *(screw, tooth)*
Löffel *m* spoon
Loge *f* box *(in theatre)*
Lohn *m* wage
Loipe *f* cross-country ski run
Lokal *nt* pub
Lorbeerblatt *nt* bayleaf
los loose
 was ist los? what's wrong?
Los *nt* lot *(at auction)* ; ticket *(lottery)*
lösen to buy *(ticket)*
löslich soluble
Lounge *f* lounge
Löwe *m* lion
Luft *f* air
Luftfilter *m* air filter
Luftfracht *f* air freight
Luftkissenboot *nt* hovercraft
Luftmatratze *f* air bed/mattress
Luftpost *f* air mail
Luftpumpe *f* pump *(bike/airmattress)*
Lüge *f* lie *(untruth)*
Lunge *f* lung
Lupe *f* magnifying glass
Lutscher *m* lollipop
Luxus *m* luxury

M

machen to make ; to do
Mädchen *nt* girl
Mädchenname *m* maiden name
Made *f* maggot
Magen *m* stomach
Magenschmerzen *pl* stomachache
Magentabletten *pl* indigestion tablets
Magenverstimmung *f* indigestion
Magermilch *f* skimmed milk
Magnet *m* magnet
Mai *m* May
Mais *m* sweetcorn

Make-up nt make-up
malen to paint
Malzbier nt malt beer
man one
managen to manage (be in charge)
manchmal sometimes
Mandarine f tangerine
Mandel f almond ; tonsil
Mandelentzündung f tonsillitis
Mangel m flaw
Mann m man ; husband
Männer pl men
männlich masculine ; male
Manschettenknöpfe pl cufflinks
Mantel m coat
Margarine f margarine
marineblau navy blue
mariniert marinated
Marke f brand (of product) ; token (for phone)
Markt m market
Marktplatz m market place
Marmelade f jam
Marmor m marble
März m March
Maschine f machine
Maschine schreiben to type
Masern pl measles
Maßband nt tape measure
Maße pl measurements
Mast m mast
Material nt material
Matratze f mattress
Mauer f wall
Maus f mouse (animal/computer)
Maut f toll (motorway)
Mayonnaise f mayonnaise
Mechaniker(in) m/f mechanic
Medikament nt drug ; medicine
Medizin f medicine
Meer nt sea
Meeresfrüchte pl seafood
Mehl nt flour
mehr more
Mehrwertsteuer (MWST) f value-added tax (VAT)
meiden to avoid (person)
Meile f mile
mein my
meiste(n) most

Meisterwerk nt masterpiece
melden to report (tell about)
Melone f melon ; bowler hat
Menge f crowd
Messe f fair (commercial) ; mass (church)
Messegelände nt exhibition centre
messen to measure
Messer nt knife
Messing nt brass
Metall nt metal
Meter m metre
Metro f metro (underground)
Metzgerei f butcher's
mich me (direct object)
Mietauto nt hire car
Miete f rent
mieten to hire ; to rent (house, etc)
Mietgebühr f rental (amount)
Mietvertrag m lease (rental)
Migräne f migraine
Mikrowelle f microwave oven
Milch f milk
Milchprodukte pl dairy produce
Milchpulver nt powdered milk
Millimeter m millimetre
Million f million
minderwertig low-quality
Mindest- minimum
Mineralwasser nt mineral water
Minimum nt minimum
Minister(in) m/f minister (politics)
Minute(n) f minute(s)
Minze f mint (herb)
mir me (indirect object)
mischen to mix
Missverständnis nt misunderstanding
mit with
Mitfahrgelegenheit f lift (in car)
Mitglied nt member (of club, etc)
mitnehmen to give a lift to
  zum Mitnehmen take-away (food)
Mittag m midday
Mittagessen nt lunch
Mitte f middle
Mitteilung f message
Mittel nt means
  ein Mittel gegen a remedy for
mittelalterlich medieval
Mittelmeer- Mediterranean
Mitternacht f midnight
Mittwoch m Wednesday
Mixer m blender ; mixer
Möbel pl furniture

Möbelpolitur f furniture polish
Mobiltelefon nt mobile phone
möbliert furnished
Modem nt modem
modern fashionable ; modern
mögen to enjoy (to like)
möglich possible
Mohn m poppy
Möhre(n) f carrot(s)
Mole f jetty
Monat m month
monatlich monthly
Mond m moon
Montag m Monday
Moped nt moped
Morgen m morning ; tomorrow
morgen tomorrow
Morgendämmerung f dawn
Morgenmantel m dressing gown
Moschee f mosque
Moskitonetz nt mosquito net
Motor m motor ; engine
Motorboot nt motor boat
Motorhaube f bonnet (car)
Motorrad nt motorbike
Motte f moth (clothes)
Mountainbike nt mountain bike
Mücke f midge
müde tired
Müll m rubbish
Müllbeutel m bin liner
Mülleimer m bin (dustbin)
Mumps m mumps
München Munich
Mund m mouth
Mundwasser nt mouthwash
Münster nt cathedral
Münze(n) f coin(s)
Münzfernsprecher m payphone
Münztelefon nt payphone
Muscheln pl mussels
Museum nt museum
Musik f music
Muskat m nutmeg
Muskel m muscle
müssen to have to ; to must
mutig brave
Mutter f mother
Mütze f cap (hat)
MWST f VAT

N

nach after ; according to ; to ; to (with names of places)
Nachbar(in) m/f neighbour
Nachmittag m afternoon
nachmittags pm ; in the afternoon
Nachname m surname
Nachricht f note (letter) ; message
Nachrichten pl news
Nachspeise f dessert ; pudding
nächste(r/s) next
Nacht f night
 über Nacht overnight
Nachtdienst m night duty (chemist)
Nachthemd nt nightdress
Nachtisch m dessert
Nachtklub m night club
nachzahlen to pay extra
nackt nude ; naked ; bare
Nadel f needle
Nagel m nail (metal)
Nagelbürste f nailbrush
Nagelfeile f nail file
Nagellack m nail polish/varnish
Nagellackentferner m nail polish remover
Nagelschere f nail scissors
Nähe f proximity
 in der Nähe nearby
nähen to sew
Name m name ; surname
Narkose f anaesthetic
Nase f nose
nass wet
national national
Nationalität f nationality
Natur- natural
Naturlehrpfad m nature trail
Naturschutzgebiet nt nature reserve
Nebel m mist ; fog
neben by (next to) ; beside
Nebenstraße f minor road
neblig foggy
Neffe m nephew
Negativ nt negative (photo)
nehmen to catch (bus, train) ; to take (remove)
nein no
Nektarine f nectarine

Nelke f carnation
nennen to quote (price)
Nervenzusammenbruch m nervous breakdown
Nest nt nest
nett nice (person) ; kind
Netto- net (income, price)
Netz nt net ; network
neu new
neueste(r/s) newest ; latest
Neujahr(stag) m New Year's Day
Neuseeland nt New Zealand
nicht not ; non-
Nichte f niece
Nichtraucher m non-smoker
nichts nothing
nie never
Niederlande pl Netherlands
Niedersachsen nt Lower Saxony
niedrig low
Niedrigwasser nt low tide
niemand no one ; nobody
Niere(n) f kidney(s)
niesen to sneeze
nirgends nowhere
noch still (up to this time) ; yet
noch ein(e) extra (more) ; another
Norden m north
Nordirland nt Northern Ireland
nördlich north ; northern
Nordsee f North Sea
Normal(benzin) nt regular (petrol)
Normal- standard (size)
Notarzt m emergency doctor
Notaufnahme f accident & emergency department
Notausgang m emergency exit
Notdienstapotheke f on-duty chemist
Notfall m emergency
notieren to make a note of
nötig necessary
Notizblock m note pad
Notruf m emergency number
Notrufsäule f emergency phone (on motorway)
Notsignal nt distress signal
notwendig essential ; necessary
November m November
nüchtern sober
Nudeln pl pasta ; noodles

Null f nil ; zero ; nought
numerieren to number
Nummer f number ; act
Nummernschild nt numberplate
nur only
Nürnberg Nuremberg
Nuss (Nüsse) f nut(s)
nützlich useful

O

oben upstairs ; above ; this side up
oben auf on top of...
Oberschenkel m thigh
obligatorisch compulsory
Obst nt fruit
Obstkuchen m fruit tart
oder or
offen open
    offene Weine pl wine served by the glass
öffentlich public
öffnen to open ; to undo
Öffnungszeiten pl business hours
oft often
ohne without
ohnmächtig fainted
ohnmächtig werden to faint
Ohr(en) nt ear(s)
Ohrenschmerzen pl earache
Ohrringe pl earrings
okay OK
ökonomisch economic
Oktober m October
Öl nt oil
Ölfilter m oil filter
Olive f olive
Olivenöl nt olive oil
Ölstandsanzeiger m oil gauge
Ölwechsel m oil change
Omelett nt omelette
Onkel m uncle
Oper f opera
Operation f operation (surgical)
Optiker m optician's
orange orange (colour)
Orange f orange (fruit)
Orangensaft m orange juice
Orchester nt orchestra
Ordner m file (for papers)
Oregano m oregano
organisch organic
organisieren to organize

73 **Organspenderausweis** m donor card
Ort m place
  an Ort und Stelle on the spot
örtlich local
örtliche Betäubung f local anaesthetic
Ortschaft f village ; town
Ortsgespräch nt local call
Ortszeit f local time
Osten m east
Osterei nt Easter egg
Ostermontag m Easter Monday
Ostern nt Easter
Österreich nt Austria
Österreicher(in) m/f Austrian
österreichisch adj Austrian
Ostersonntag m Easter Sunday
östlich eastern
Ozean m ocean

P

Paar nt pair ; couple (persons)
  ein paar a couple of (a few)
packen to pack (luggage)
Paket nt parcel ; packet
Palast m palace
Pampelmuse(n) f grapefruit(s)
Panne f breakdown (of car)
Papier(e) nt paper(s)
Papiertaschentücher pl tissues
Pappe f cardboard
Paprikaschote f pepper (vegetable)
Parfüm nt perfume
Parfümerie f perfumery
Park m park
parken to park
  Parken verboten no parking
Parkett nt stalls (in theatre)
Parkhaus nt multi-storey car park
Parkkralle f wheel clamp
Parkplatz m car park
Parkscheibe f parking disk
Parkschein m parking ticket (to display)
Parkuhr f parking meter
Parkverbot nt no parking zone
Partei f political party
Partner(in) m/f partner (boy/girlfriend)
Party f party (celebration)
Pass m passport ; pass (in mountains)
  Pass geschlossen pass closed
Passagier m passenger
passen to fit
passieren to happen

Passkontrolle f passport control
Passnummer f passport number
Patient(in) m/f patient (in hospital)
Pauschalreise f package tour
Pauschaltarif m flat-rate tariff
Pause f pause ; interval
  keine Pausen no intervals
Pelz m fur
Pelzmantel m fur coat
Pendelverkehr m shuttle (service)
Penis m penis
Penizillin nt penicillin
Pension f boarding house
pensioniert retired
per via ; by
  per Express by express mail
  per Post by post
perfekt perfect
Periode f period (menstruation)
Perlen pl pearls
perlend sparkling
Person f person
Personal nt staff
Personalausweis m identity card
Personalien pl particulars
persönlich personal(ly)
Perücke f wig
Pessar nt cap (diaphragm)
Petersilie f parsley
Pfalz f Palatinate
Pfannkuchen m pancake
Pfarrer(in) m/f church minister
Pfeffer m pepper (spice)
Pfefferkuchen m gingerbread
Pfefferminzbonbon nt mint (sweet)
Pfefferminztee m mint tea
Pfeife f pipe (smoker's)
Pferd nt horse
Pferderennen nt horse-racing
Pfirsich(e) m peach(es)
Pflanze f plant (green)
Pflaster nt plaster (for cut)
Pflaume(n) f plum(s)
Pforte f gate
Pfund nt pound
Pfund Sterling nt sterling (pound)
Picknick nt picnic
Picknickdecke f picnic rug
Pier m jetty ; pier
pikant savoury

Pille f pill
Pilot(in) m/f pilot
Pils/Pilsner nt lager
Pilz(e) m mushroom(s)
Pilzkrankheit f thrush (candida)
Pinzette f tweezers
Pistazie f pistachio
Piste f runway ; ski run
Pizza f pizza
planmäßig scheduled
Planschbecken nt paddling pool
Plastik- plastic (made of)
Plastikbeutel m plastic bag
Platte f plate ; dish ; record
Platz m seat ; space ; square (in town) ; court
Plätzchen nt biscuit(s)
Platzkarte f seat reservation (ticket)
Plombe f filling (in tooth)
plötzlich suddenly
pochiert poached (egg, fish)
Polen nt Poland
Polizei f police
Polizeirevier nt police station
Polizeiwache f police station
Polizist(in) m/f policeman/woman
Pommes frites pl chips (french fries)
Pony nt pony
Ponyreiten nt pony trekking
Porree m leek
Portier m porter (for door)
Portion f portion
Portrait nt portrait
Portugal nt Portugal
Portugiese/Portugiesin m/f Portuguese
portugiesisch adj Portuguese
Post f post ; post office
Post- postal
Postamt nt post office
Postanweisung f money order
Poster nt poster
Postkarte f postcard
postlagernd poste restante
Postleitzahl f postcode
praktisch handy ; practical
Pralinen pl chocolates
Präservativ nt condom
Praxis f doctor's surgery
Preis m prize ; price

Preisliste f price list
Priester m priest
Prinz m prince
Prinzessin f princess
privat private
Privatstrand m private beach
Privatweg m private road
pro per
  pro Stunde per hour
  pro Kopf per person
  pro Jahr per annum
probieren to taste ; to sample
Problem nt problem
Programm nt programme
Programmierer(in) m/f computer programmer
prost! cheers!
protestantisch Protestant
provisorisch temporary
Prozent nt per cent
prüfen to check (oil, water, etc)
Prüfung f exam (school, university)
Publikum nt audience
Puderzucker m icing sugar
Pullover m sweater ; jumper
Pulver nt powder
pulverförmig in powder form
Pulverkaffee m instant coffee
pünktlich on schedule ; punctual
Puppe f doll ; puppet
Puppenspiel nt puppet show
pur straight (drink)
Pute f turkey
Pyjama m pyjamas

Q

Qualität f quality
Qualitätswein m good quality wine
Qualle f jellyfish
Quantität f quantity
Quarantäne f quarantine
Quelle f spring (of water) ; source
quetschen to squeeze
Quetschung f bruise
Quittung f receipt
Quiz nt quiz show

R

Rabatt m discount
Rad nt wheel ; bicycle
Rad fahren to cycle
Radfahrer(in) m/f cyclist

Radiergummi m rubber (eraser)
Radieschen pl radishes
Radio nt radio
Radweg m cycle track
Rahmen m frame (picture)
Rand m verge ; border ; edge
Randstein m kerb
Rang m circle (in theatre) ; rank
Rasen m lawn
Rasierapparat m shaver ; razor
Rasiercreme f shaving cream
rasieren to shave
Rasierklinge f razor blade
Rasierschaum m shaving foam
Rasierwasser nt aftershave (lotion)
Rasthof m service area; travel inn
Rastplatz m picnic area
Raststätte f service area
raten to advise
Rathaus nt town hall
rau rough
Rauch m smoke
rauchen to smoke
  Rauchen verboten no smoking
Raucher(in) m/f smoker (person)
Raum m space (room)
rechnen to calculate
Rechnung f bill (account) ; invoice
rechte(r/s) right (not left)
rechts to the right ; on the right
Rechtsanwalt m lawyer ; solicitor
Rechtsanwältin f lawyer ; solicitor
reden to speak
reduzieren to reduce
Reformhaus nt health food shop
Regal nt shelf
Regen m rain
Regenmantel m raincoat
Regenschirm m umbrella
regnen to rain
Reibe f grater (for cheese, etc)
reich rich (person)
Reich nt empire
reichhaltig rich (food)
reif ripe ; mature (cheese)
Reifen m tyre
Reifendruck m tyre pressure
Reifenpanne f flat tyre
Reihe f row (line) ; tier
rein pure
reinigen to clean
Reinigung f dry-cleaner's
Reis m rice

Reise f trip (journey)
  gute Reise! have a good trip!
Reisebüro nt travel agency
Reiseführer m guidebook
Reiseführer(in) m/f tour guide
Reisegruppe f party (of tourists)
Reisekrankheit f travel sickness
reisen to travel
Reisepapiere pl travel documents
Reisepass m passport
Reisescheck m traveller's cheque
Reiseveranstalter m tour operator
Reiseziel nt destination
Reißverschluss m zip
reiten to ride (horse)
Reiten nt riding
Rennbahn f racecourse
rennen to run
Rennen nt race (sport)
Rentner(in) m/f pensioner ; senior citizen
Reparatur f repair
Reparaturwerkstatt f car repairs
reparieren to repair ; to mend
reservieren to book ; to reserve
reserviert reserved
Reservierung f booking (in hotel)
Reservierungen pl reservations
Restaurant nt restaurant
Restgeld nt change (money)
retten to rescue ; to save (person)
Rettungsboot nt lifeboat
Rettungsinsel f life raft
Rettungsring m lifebelt
Rettungsschwimmer(in) m/f lifeguard
Rezept nt prescription ; recipe
R-Gespräch nt reverse charge call
Rhein m Rhine
Rheinfahrten pl Rhine cruises
Rheumatismus m rheumatism
Richter(in) m/f judge
richtig correct ; right ; proper
Richtung f direction
riechen to smell
Rinderbraten m roast beef
Rindfleisch nt beef
Ring m ring
Ringstraße f ring road
Riss m tear (in material)
Rock m skirt
Roggenbrot nt rye bread

roh raw
Rohr nt pipe (drain, etc)
Rollo nt blind (for window)
Rollschuhe pl roller skates
Rollstuhl m wheelchair
Rolltreppe f escalator
Roman m novel
romanisch Romanesque
Röntgenaufnahme f X-ray
rosa pink
Rose f rose (flower)
Rosenkohl m Brussels sprouts
Rosenmontag m carnival (Monday before Shrove Tuesday)
Roséwein m rosé wine
Rosine(n) f raisin(s)
Rost m rust ; grill
Rost- roast
Rostbraten m roast
rosten to rust
rostfreier Stahl m stainless steel
rostig rusty
Röstkartoffeln pl sautéed potatoes
rot red
Rote Bete f beetroot
Röteln pl German measles ; rubella
rote Johannisbeeren pl redcurrants
Rotwein m red wine
Rücken m back (of body, hand)
Rückerstattung f refund
Rückfahrkarte f return ticket
Rückfahrt f return journey
Rückflugticket nt return airticket
Rückgrat nt spine
Rücklicht nt rear light
Rucksack m rucksack
Rückspiegel m rearview mirror
rückwärts backwards
rückwärts fahren to reverse (car)
Rückwärtsgang m reverse (gear)
Ruder nt rudder ; oar
Ruderboot nt rowing boat
rudern to row (boat)
rufen to shout
Rufnummer f telephone number
Ruhe f rest (repose) ; peace (calm)
  Ruhe! be quiet!
ruhen to rest
ruhig calm ; quiet(ly) ; peaceful
Rührei nt scrambled egg

Ruine f ruin (castle, etc)
rund round
Rundfahrt f tour ; round trip
Rundreise f round trip
Rundwanderweg m circular trail for ramblers
Rutschbahn f slide (chute)
rutschen to slip
rutschig slippery

S

Saal m hall (room)
Sache f thing
Sachen pl stuff (things) ; belongings
Sachsen nt Saxony
Sackgasse f cul-de-sac
Safe m safe (for valuables)
Saft m juice
sagen to say ; to tell (fact, news)
Sahne f cream (dairy)
  mit Sahne with whipped cream
Saison f season
Salat m salad
Salatsoße f salad dressing
Salbe f ointment
Salz nt salt
Salzkartoffeln pl boiled potatoes
Salzwasser nt salt water
Samstag m Saturday
Sand m sand
Sandalen pl sandals
Sandstrand m sandy beach
Satellitenfernsehen nt satellite TV
satt full
Sattel m saddle
Satteltaschen pl panniers (for bike)
Satz m set (collection) ; sentence
sauber clean
säubern to clean
sauer sour
Sauerkraut nt sauerkraut
Sauerstoff m oxygen
Sauger m teat (on bottle)
Säule f petrol pump
Saum m hem
Sauna f sauna
Säure f acid
saure Sahne f soured cream
S-Bahn f suburban railway
Schach nt chess
Schaden m damage
schädlich harmful

Schaf nt sheep
Schaffner(in) m/f conductor (bus, train) ; guard
Schale f shell (egg, nut) ; dish
schälen to peel (fruit)
Schallplatte f record (music)
Schalter m switch
Schaltgetriebe nt manual (gear change)
Schaltknüppel m gear lever ; gearshift
Schaltuhr f timer
scharf hot (spicy) ; sharp
Schatten m shade
schätzen to value ; to estimate
Schauer m rain shower
Schaufel und Handfeger dustpan and brush
Schaufenster nt shop window
Schaukel f swing (for children)
Schaum m foam
Schaumbad nt bubble bath
Schaumfestiger m hair mousse
Schaumwein m sparkling wine
Schauspiel nt play
Schauspieler(in) m/f actor/actress
Scheck m cheque
Scheckbuch nt cheque book
Scheckkarte f cheque card
Scheibe f slice
Scheibenputzmittel nt screenwash
Scheibenwischer pl windscreen wipers
Schein(e) m banknote(s) ; certificate(s)
scheinen to shine (sun, etc) ; to seem
Scheinwerfer m headlight ; floodlight ; spotlight
   Scheinwerfer anschalten switch on headlights
Schere f scissors (pair of)
scherzen to joke
Scheuerlappen m floorcloth
Scheune f barn
Schi- see Ski-
schicken to send
schießen to shoot
Schiff nt ship
Schild nt sign (notice) ; label
Schinken m ham
Schirm m umbrella ; screen
Schlachterei f butcher's
schlafen to sleep
Schlafsack m sleeping bag
Schlaftablette f sleeping pill
Schlafwagen m sleeping car (on train)
Schlafzimmer nt bedroom
Schlag m shock (electric)

german-eng   s

Schlaganfall m stroke (medical)
schlagen to hit
Schläger m racket (tennis, etc)
Schlagloch nt pothole
Schlagsahne f whipped cream
Schlange f queue ; snake
Schlangenbiss m snake bite
Schlauch m hosepipe ; inner tube
Schlauchboot nt dinghy (rubber)
schlecht bad ; badly
Schlepplift m ski tow
schließen to shut ; to close
Schließfach nt locker (luggage)
schlimm serious
Schlitten m sleigh ; sledge
Schlittschuh laufen to ice skate
Schlittschuh(e) m ice skate(s)
Schlittschuhbahn f ice rink
Schloss nt castle ; lock (on door, etc)
Schluss m end
Schlüssel m key
Schlüsselbein nt collar bone
Schlüsselkarte f cardkey (for hotel)
Schlüsselring m keyring
Schlusslichter pl rear lights
Schlussverkauf m sale
schmecken to taste
schmelzen to melt
Schmerz m pain ; ache
schmerzhaft painful
Schmerzmittel nt painkiller
Schmerztablette f painkiller
Schmuck m jewellery ; decorations
schmutzig dirty
Schnaps m schnapps ; spirit
schnarchen to snore
Schnee m snow
Schneebrille f snow goggles
Schneeketten pl snow chains
Schneepflug m snowplough
schneiden to cut
schnell fast ; quick
Schnellboot nt speedboat
Schnellimbiss m snack bar
Schnellzug m express (train)
Schnittbohnen pl green beans
Schnittlauch m chives
Schnittwunde f cut
Schnorchel m snorkel
Schnuller m dummy (for baby)

Schnur f string
Schnurrbart m moustache
Schnürschuhe pl boots (ankle)
Schnürsenkel pl shoelaces
Schokolade f chocolate
schön lovely ; fine ; beautiful ; good (pleasant)
Schornstein m chimney
Schotte (Schottin) m/f Scot
schottisch Scottish
Schottland nt Scotland
Schrank m cupboard
Schraube f screw
Schraubenmutter f nut (for bolt)
Schraubenschlüssel m spanner
Schraubenzieher m screwdriver
schrecklich awful
schreiben to write
Schreibmaschine f typewriter
Schreibtisch m desk
Schreibwarenhandlung f stationer's
schriftlich in writing
Schritt m pace ; step
  Schritt fahren! dead slow
Schublade f drawer
Schuh(e) m shoe(s)
Schuhcreme f shoe polish
Schuhgeschäft nt shoe shop
Schuhputzmittel nt shoe polish
schulden to owe
Schulden pl debts
Schule f school
Schulter f shoulder
Schuppen pl scales (of fish) ; dandruff
Schürze f apron
Schüssel f bowl (for soup, etc)
Schuster m shoe mender's
Schutzhelm m helmet (for bike)
Schutzimpfung f vaccination
schwach weak
Schwager m brother-in-law
Schwägerin f sister-in-law
Schwamm m sponge
schwanger pregnant
schwarz black
Schwarzbrot nt brown bread
schwarze Johannisbeeren pl blackcurrants
Schwarzweißfilm m black and white film
Schwein nt pig

Schweinefleisch nt pork
Schweiß m sweat
Schweiz f Switzerland
Schweizer(in) m/f Swiss
schweizerisch adj Swiss
Schwellung f swelling
schwer heavy
Schwester f sister ; nurse ; nun
Schwiegermutter f mother-in-law
Schwiegersohn m son-in-law
Schwiegertochter f daughter-in-law
Schwiegervater m father-in-law
schwierig hard (difficult)
Schwimmbad nt swimming pool
schwimmen to swim
Schwimmflossen pl flippers
Schwimmweste f life jacket
schwindelig dizzy
schwitzen to sweat
See f sea
See m lake
seekrank seasick
Segel nt sail
Segelboot nt sailing boat
segeln to sail
sehen to see
Sehenswürdigkeit f sight
Sehne f tendon
sehr very
seicht shallow (water)
Seide f silk
Seife f soap
Seil nt rope
Seilbahn f cable railway ; funicular
sein(e) his
sein to be
seit since
Seite f page ; side
Seitenspiegel m wing mirror
Seitenstraße f side street
Seitenstreifen m hard shoulder
Sekretär(in) m/f secretary
Sekt m sparkling wine
Sekunde f second (time)
Selbstbedienung f self-service
selten rare (unique)
seltsam strange (odd)
Senf m mustard
September m September
servieren to serve (food)
Serviette f napkin
Servolenkung f power steering
Sessel m armchair

179 **Sessellift** *m* chairlift

setzen to place ; to put
  sich setzen to sit down
  setzen Sie sich bitte please take a seat
Sex *m* sex *(intercourse)*
Shampoo *nt* shampoo
Shorts *pl* shorts
sicher sure ; safe ; definite
Sicherheit *f* safety
Sicherheitsgurt *m* seatbelt ;
  safety belt
Sicherheitsnadel *f* safety pin
Sicherung *f* fuse
Sicherungskasten *m* fuse box
sie she ; they
Sie you *(polite singular and plural)*
Sieb *nt* sieve ; colander
Silber *nt* silver
Silvester *m* New Year's Eve
singen to sing
Sitz *m* seat
sitzen to sit
Ski(er) *m* ski(s)
  Ski fahren to ski
Skianzug *m* ski suit
Skihose *f* ski pants
Skijacke *f* ski jacket
Skilanglauf *m* cross-country skiing
Skilaufen *nt* skiing
Skilehrer(in) *m/f* ski instructor
Skilift *m* ski lift
Skipass *m* ski pass
Skipiste *f* ski run
Skistiefel *pl* ski boots
Skistock *m* ski stick/pole
Skiverleih *m* ski hire
Slip *m* knickers ; underpants
Slipeinlage *f* panty liner
Snack *m* snack
Snowboard *nt* snow board
Socken *pl* socks
Soda *nt* soda water
Sodbrennen *nt* heartburn
Sofa *nt* sofa
Sofabett *nt* sofa bed
sofort at once ; immediately
Software *f* computer software
Sohle *f* sole *(of shoe)*
Sohn *m* son
Sojabohnen *pl* soya beans
Sojamilch *f* soya milk
Sommer *m* summer
Sommerfahrplan *m* summer railway
  timetable

german-eng **s**

Sommerferien *pl* summer holidays
Sonder- special
sonn- und feiertags on Sundays and
  public holidays
Sonnabend *m* Saturday
Sonne *f* sun
Sonnenaufgang *m* sunrise
sonnenbaden to sunbathe
Sonnenbrand *m* sunburn *(painful)*
Sonnenbräune *f* suntan
Sonnenbrille *f* sunglasses
Sonnencreme *f* sunblock
Sonnendach *nt* sunroof *(car)*
Sonnenöl *nt* suntan oil
Sonnenschirm *m* sun umbrella ; sun-
  shade
Sonnenstich *m* sunstroke
Sonnenuntergang *m* sunset
sonnig sunny
Sonntag *m* Sunday
Sonntagsdienst *m* Sunday duty *(chemist,
  doctor, etc)*
sorgen für to look after ; to take care of
Soße *f* dressing *(salad)* ; sauce
Souterrain *nt* basement
Souvenir *nt* souvenir
Spanien *nt* Spain
Spanier(in) *m/f* Spaniard
spanisch *adj* Spanish
Spannung *f* voltage
sparen to save *(money)*
Spargel *m* asparagus
Sparpreis *m* economy fare
Spaß *m* fun ; joke
spät late
Spaten *m* spade
Spätvorstellung *f* late show
Spaziergang *m* stroll ; walk
Speck *m* bacon
Speise *f* dish ; food
Speiseeis *nt* ice cream
Speisekarte *f* menu
Speisewagen *m* dining car
Spesen *pl* expenses
Spezialität *f* speciality
Spiegel *m* mirror
Spiegelei *nt* fried egg
Spiel *nt* game ; pack *(of cards)*
Spielbank *f* casino
spielen to gamble ; to play

Spielkarte f card (playing)
Spielplatz m playground
Spielzeug nt toy
Spielzeugladen m toy shop
Spielzimmer nt playroom
Spinat m spinach
Spirale f coil (IUD) ; spiral
Spirituosen pl spirits (alcohol)
Spitze f lace ; point (tip)
Splitter m splinter
Sportartikel pl sports equipment
Sportgeschäft nt sports shop
Sporttauchen nt scuba diving
Sprache f speech ; language
Sprachführer m phrase book
Spraydose f aerosol
sprechen to speak
  sprechen mit to talk to
springen to jump
Spritze f injection ; hypodermic needle
sprudelnd fizzy
Sprudelwasser nt sparkling water
Sprungschanze f ski jump
Spülbecken nt sink (kitchen)
spülen to flush toilet ; to rinse
Spülkasten m cistern (of toilet)
Spülmittel nt washing-up liquid
Spur f lane (of motorway/main road)
Staatsangehörigkeit f nationality
Stachel m sting
Stadion nt stadium
Stadt f town ; city
Stadtführung f guided tour of the town
Stadtmitte f city centre
Stadtplan m map (of town)
Stadtzentrum nt town/city centre
Stahl m steel
Stand m stall ; taxi rank
ständig permanent(ly) ; continuous(ly)
Standlicht nt sidelight
stark strong
Starthilfekabel nt jump leads
Station f station ; stop ; hospital ward
statt instead of
stattfinden to take place
Statue f statue
Stau m traffic jam
Staub m dust
Staubsauger m vacuum cleaner
Staubtuch nt duster

stechen to bite (insect)
Stechmücke f mosquito ; gnat
Steckdose f socket (electrical)
Stecker m plug (electric)
stehen to stand
stehlen to steal
steil steep
Stein m stone
Stelle f job ; place ; point (in space)
stellen to set (alarm) ; to put
stempeln to stamp (visa)
Steppdecke f quilt
sterben to die
Stereoanlage f stereo
Stern m star
Steuer f tax
Steuerung f controls
Steward (Stewardess) m/f steward/
stewardess
Stich m bite (by insect) ; stitch (sewing) ;
sting
Stiefel pl boots (long)
Stiefmutter f stepmother
Stiefvater m stepfather
Stil m style
still still (motionless)
stilles Wasser nt still water
Stimme f voice
stimmt so! keep the change!
Stirn f forehead
Stock m cane (walking stick) ; stick ;
floor
Stockwerk nt storey
Stoff m cloth (fabric)
Stoppschild nt stop (sign)
Stöpsel m plug (in sink)
stören to disturb (interrupt)
  bitte nicht stören do not disturb
stornieren to cancel
Stornierung f cancellation
Störung f hold-up ; fault ; medical
disorder
Stoßdämpfer m shock absorber
stoßen to knock ; to push
Stoßstange f bumper (on car)
Stoßzeit f rush hour
Strafe f punishment ; fine
Strafzettel m parking ticket (fine)
Strand m beach
Strandkorb m wicker beach chair with
a hood ; beach hut
Straße f road ; street
  Straße gesperrt road closed
Straßenarbeiten pl roadworks

Straßenbahn f tram
Straßenkarte f road map
Streichhölzer pl matches
Streifenkarte f multiple journey travelcard
Streik m strike (industrial)
streiten to quarrel
Stress m stress
stricken to knit
Strickjacke f cardigan
Stricknadel f knitting needle
Strohhalm m straw (for drinking)
Strom m current ; electricity
Stromanschluss m electric point
Strömung f current (water)
Stromzähler m electricity meter
Strümpfe pl stockings
Strumpfhose f tights
Stück nt bit ; piece ; cut of meat ; play (theatre)
Student(in) m/f student m/f
Studentenermäßigung f student discount
Stufe f step (stair)
Stuhl m chair
stumpf blunt (knife, blade)
Stunde f hour ; lesson
Sturm m storm
Sturzhelm m crash helmet
suchen to look for
Süden m south
südlich southern
Summe f sum (total amount)
Sumpf m marsh
Super(benzin) nt four-star petrol
Supermarkt m supermarket
Suppe f soup
Surfbrett nt surfboard
surfen to surf
süß sweet
Süßigkeiten pl sweets
Süßstoff m sweetener ; saccharin
Süßwaren pl confectionery
Synagoge f synagogue
Szene f scene

T

Tabak m tobacco
Tabakwarenhandlung f tobacconist's
Tablett nt tray
Tablette(n) f tablet(s) ; pill(s)
Tachometer nt speedometer
Tafel f table ; board ; bar of chocolate

german-eng s/t

Tafelwein m table wine
Tag m day
  jeden Tag every day
Tageskarte f day ticket ; menu of the day
Tagespauschale f daily unlimited rate
Tagessuppe f soup of the day
täglich daily
Taille f waist
Tal nt valley
Tampons pl tampons
Tank m fuel/petrol tank
Tankanzeige f fuel gauge
Tankdeckel m petrol cap
Tanksäule f petrol pump
Tankstelle f petrol station
Tanne f fir
Tante f aunt
Tanz m dance
tanzen to dance
Tarif m rate ; tariff
Tasche f pocket ; bag
Taschenbuch nt paperback
Taschendieb m pickpocket
Taschenlampe f torch ; flashlight
Taschenmesser nt penknife
Taschenrechner m calculator
Taschentuch nt handkerchief
Tasse f cup
Taste f button ; key (on keyboard)
  Taste drücken push button
taub deaf
Taube f pigeon
tauchen to dive
Tauchen nt diving
Taucheranzug m wetsuit
Taucherbrille f goggles (swimming)
tauschen to exchange
tausend thousand
Taxi nt taxi ; cab
Taxifahrer(in) m/f taxi driver
Taxistand m taxi rank
Tee m tea
Teebeutel m tea bag
Teekanne f teapot
Teelöffel m teaspoon
Teig m pastry
Teil nt part
teilen to divide ; to share
Teilkaskoversicherung f third party, fire and theft insurance

Telefon *nt* telephone
Telefonauskunft *f* directory enquiries
Telefonbuch *nt* phone directory
telefonieren to telephone
Telefonkarte *f* phonecard
Telefonnummer *f* phone number
Telefonzelle *f* phonebox
Telegramm *nt* telegram
Teller *m* plate
Tempel *m* temple
Temperatur *f* temperature
Tennis *nt* tennis
Tennisplatz *m* tennis court
Tennisschläger *m* tennis racket
Teppich *m* rug
Teppichboden *m* fitted carpet
Termin *m* date ; deadline ; appointment
Terminal *m* terminal *(airport)*
Terminkalender *m* diary ; Filofax®
Terminplaner *m* personal organizer
Terrasse *f* patio ; terrace *(of café)*
Terrorist(in) *m/f* terrorist
Tesafilm® *m* Sellotape®
teuer dear *(expensive)*
Theater *nt* theatre
Theke *f* counter *(in shop, bar, etc)*
Thermometer *nt* thermometer
Thermosflasche *f* flask *(thermos)*
Thunfisch *m* tuna
Thüringen *nt* Thuringia
Thymian *m* thyme
tief deep ; low *(in pitch)*
Tiefkühltruhe *f* deep freeze ; freezer
Tier *nt* animal
Tierarzt (Tierärztin) *m/f* vet
Tinte *f* ink
Tintenfisch *m* octopus ; squid
Tisch *m* table
Tischdecke *f* tablecloth
Tischler(in) *m/f* carpenter
Tischtennis *nt* table tennis
Tischwein *m* table wine
Toastbrot *nt* sliced white bread for toasting
Tochter *f* daughter
Toilette *f* toilet ; lavatory
Toilettenartikel *pl* toiletries
Toilettenbürste *f* toilet brush
Toilettenpapier *nt* toilet paper
Tollwut *f* rabies

Tomate *f* tomato
Tomatenpüree *nt* tomato purée
Tomatensaft *m* tomato juice
Tomatensoße *f* tomato sauce
Ton *m* sound ; tone ; clay
Tönung *f* hair dye
Töpferwaren *pl* pottery
Tor *nt* gate ; goal *(sport)*
Törtchen *nt* cake *(small)*
Torte *f* gâteau ; tart
tot dead
töten to kill
Tourist(in) *m/f* tourist
Touristen-Information *f* tourist information
Touristenkarte *f* tourist ticket
Touristenklasse *f* economy class
Touristenroute *f* tourist route
Touristenticket *nt* tourist ticket
tragbar portable
tragen to carry ; to wear
Tragflügelboot *nt* hydrofoil
Trainingsschuhe *pl* trainers
trampen to hitchhike
Trauben *pl* grapes
traurig sad
Treffen *nt* meeting
treffen to meet *(by chance)*
Treppe *f* stairs
Tresor *m* safe
Tretboot *nt* pedalo
trinken to drink
Trinkgeld *nt* tip *(for waiter, etc)*
Trinkwasser *nt* drinking water
trocken dry ; stale *(bread)*
Trockenmilch *f* powdered milk
Trockenobst *nt* dried fruit
trocknen to dry
Truthahn *m* turkey
Tschechien *nt* Czech Republic
tschüs cheerio ; bye
T-shirt *nt* T-shirt
Tuch *nt* cloth ; scarf ; towel ; shawl
tun to do ; to put
   das tut nichts that doesn't matter
Tunnel *m* tunnel
Tür *f* door
türkis turquoise *(colour)*
Turm *m* tower
Turnschuhe *pl* gym shoes
typisch typical

u.A.w.g. RSVP
U-Bahn f metro ; underground
übel sick *(nauseous)* ; bad
über over ; above ; about ; via
überall everywhere
überbuchen to overbook
Überfahrt f crossing *(sea)*
Überfall m mugging
überfällig overdue
überfüllt crowded *(train, shop, etc)*
übergeben to hand over ; to present *(give)*
  sich übergeben to vomit
Übergewicht nt excess baggage
überhitzen to overheat
überholen to overtake
Überholverbot nt no overtaking
Übernachtung mit Frühstück bed and breakfast
überprüfen to check *(to examine)*
Überschwemmung f flash flood
übersetzen to translate
Übersetzung f translation
überweisen to transfer *(money)*
Überzelt nt fly sheet
Überzieher m overcoat
übrig left over ; extra *(spare)*
Ufer nt bank *(of river)* ; shore
Uhr f clock ; watch
Uhrarmband nt watch strap
Uhrmacher m watchmaker's
um around
  um 4 Uhr at 4 o'clock
umdrehen to turn around
umgeben von surrounded by
Umgehungsstraße f ring road ; bypass *(road)*
Umkleidekabine f changing room *(at swimming pool, in shop)*
Umleitung f diversion
Umschlag m envelope
umsonst free *(costing nothing)*
umsteigen to change
umstoßen to knock over *(object)*
Umweg m detour
Umwelt f environment
unbefugt unauthorized
  Unbefugten Zutritt verboten no entry to unauthorized persons
unbegrenzt unlimited
und and
Unfall m accident

Unfallstation nt casualty department
ungefähr approximately
ungefährlich safe *(not dangerous)*
ungerade odd *(number)*
ungewöhnlich unusual
Unglück nt accident
ungültig invalid
ungültig werden to expire *(ticket, passport)*
Universität f university
unmöglich impossible ; unsafe
uns us
unser(e) our
unsicher uncertain *(fact)*
unten downstairs ; below
  nach unten downward(s) ; downstairs
unter under(neath)
unter Wasser underwater
unterbrechen to interrupt
Unterbrecher m circuit breaker
Unterbrecherkontakte pl points *(in car)*
untere(r/s) lower ; bottom
Unterführung f subway ; underpass *(for pedestrians)*
Unterhemd nt vest
Unterhose f underpants
Unterkunft f accommodation
unterrichten to teach
Unterrichtsstunde f lesson
unterschreiben to sign
Unterschrift f signature
Untersuchung f test ; medical examination
Untertasse f saucer
Untertitel pl subtitles
Unterwäsche f underwear ; lingerie
unwohl unwell
Urin m urine
Urlaub m leave ; holiday
  auf Urlaub on holiday ; on leave
Urlaubsgebiet nt resort *(holiday)*
Ursprungsland nt country of origin
USA pl USA

V

Vagina f vagina
Vanille f vanilla
Vanilleeis nt vanilla ice cream
Vanillesoße f custard
Vase f vase

Vater m father
Vegetarier(in) m/f vegetarian
vegetarisch vegetarian
Veilchen nt violet (flower)
Ventil nt valve
Ventilator m fan (electric) ; ventilator
Verband m bandage
Verbandskasten m first aid kit
verbinden to connect (join)
Verbindung f connection (train, etc) ;
  service (bus, etc) ; line (phone)
verbleit leaded
verboten forbidden
Verbrechen nt crime
verbrennen to burn
Verbrennung f burn
verbringen to spend (time)
verderben to go bad (food) ; to spoil
verdienen to deserve ; to earn
verdorben bad (fruit, vegetables)
Verein m society (club)
vereinbaren to agree upon ; to arrange
Vereinbarung f agreement
Vereinigtes Königreich nt United
  Kingdom
Vereinigte Staaten (von Amerika) pl
  United States (of America)
Verfallsdatum nt expiry date ; eat-by date
verfault rotten (fruit, etc)
Vergangenheit f past
Vergaser m carburettor
vergeben to forgive
vergessen to forget
vergewaltigen to rape
Vergewaltigung f rape
Vergnügen nt enjoyment ; pleasure
  viel Vergnügen! have a good time!
Vergnügungspark m amusement park
vergoldet gold-plated
Vergrößerung f enlargement
verhaften to arrest
verheiratet married
verhindern to prevent
Verhütungsmittel nt contraceptive
Verkauf m sale
verkaufen to sell
Verkäufer(in) m/f salesman/woman
Verkehr m traffic
Verkehrsbüro nt tourist information
Verkehrspolizist(in) m/f traffic warden

Verkehrszeichen nt road sign
verkehrt wrong
verkehrt herum upside down
Verlängerungskabel nt extension cable
Verleih m rental company ; hire company
verletzen to injure
verletzt injured (person)
Verletzung f injury
verlieren to lose
verlobt engaged (to be married)
Verlobte(r) m/f fiancé(e)
verloren lost (object)
vermeiden to avoid
vermieten to rent ; to let (room, house)
Vermieter(in) m/f landlord/lady
Vermietung f hire
vermisst missing (person)
Vermittlung f telephone exchange ;
  operator
verpassen to miss (plane, train, etc)
Verrenkung f sprain
verschieben to postpone
verschieden different
verschiedene several ; different
verschlucken to swallow
verschmutzt polluted
verschreiben to prescribe
verschwinden to disappear
verschwunden missing
versichern to insure
versichert sein to be insured
Versicherung f insurance
Versicherungsbescheinigung f insurance
  certificate
versilbert silver-plated
verspätet delayed
Verspätung f delay
versprechen to promise
Verstauchung f sprain
verstecken to hide
verstehen to understand
verstopft blocked (pipe) ; blocked
  (road) ; constipated
versuchen to try
Vertrag m contract
Vertreter(in) m/f sales rep
Verwandte(r) m/f relative
verwenden to use
verwirrt confused
Verzeihung! sorry ; excuse me
verzollen to declare (customs)
Video nt video
Videokamera f video camera

Videokassette f video cassette/tape
viel much
viele many
vielleicht perhaps
Viertel nt quarter
Viertelstunde f quarter of an hour
vierzehn Tage fortnight
Villa f villa
violett purple
Virus nt virus
Visitenkarte f business card
Visum nt visa
Vitamin nt vitamin
Vogel m bird
Volkslied nt folk song
Volkstanz m folk dance
voll full
Volleyball m volleyball
Vollkornbrot nt dark rye bread; whole-meal bread
Vollmilchschokolade f milk chocolate
Vollnarkose f general anaesthetic
Vollpension f full board
vollständig whole
voll tanken to fill tank (petrol)
von from ; of
vor before ; in front of
 vor 4 Jahren 4 years ago
voraus ahead
 im Voraus in advance
vorbei past
vorbereiten to prepare
Vorbestellung f reservation
Vorder- front
Vorderradantrieb m front-wheel drive
Vorfahrt f right of way (on road)
 Vorfahrt beachten give way
vorgekocht ready-cooked
Vorhang m curtain
Vorhängeschloss nt padlock
Vorname m first name
vorne einsteigen enter by front door
Vorschrift f regulation (rule)
Vorsicht f caution
Vorspeise f starter (in meal) ; hors d'œuvre
Vorstellung f performance
Vor- und Zuname m first name and surname
Vorverkauf m advance booking
Vorwahl(nummer) f dialling code
vorziehen to prefer
Vulkan m volcano

W

Waage f scales (weighing)
wach awake
Wache f security guard
Wachsbehandlung f waxing
Waffe f gun
Wagen m car ; carriage (railway)
Wagenheber m jack (for car)
Wahl f choice ; election
wählen to dial (number) ; to choose
Wählton m dialling tone
während while ; during
Währung f currency
Wald m wood ; forest
Waldlehrpfad m nature trail
Wales nt Wales
Waliser(in) m/f Welshman/woman
walisisch Welsh
Walnuss(-nüsse) f walnut(s)
wandern to hike
Wanderschuhe pl walking boots
Wanderstock m walking stick
Wanderung f hike
Wanderweg m trail for ramblers
Wange f cheek
wann? when?
Waren pl goods
warm warm
Wärmflasche f hot-water bottle
Warmwasser nt hot water
Warnblinkanlage f hazard warning lights
Warndreieck nt warning triangle
Warnung f warning
Wartehalle f lounge (at airport)
warten (auf) to wait (for)
Wartesaal m waiting room
warum? why?
was? what?
waschbar washable
Waschbecken nt washbasin
Wäsche f linen ; washing (clothes)
Wäscheklammer f clothes peg
Wäscheleine f clothes line
waschen to wash
Waschen und Föhnen wash and blow dry
Wäscheraum m laundry room
Wäscherei f laundry

w   german-eng

Wäschereiservice m laundry service
Wäschetrockner m tumble dryer
Waschmaschine f washing machine
Waschmittel nt detergent
Waschpulver nt washing powder
Waschsalon m launderette
Wasser nt water
wasserdicht waterproof
Wasserfall m waterfall
Wasserhahn m tap
Wassermelone f water melon
Wassermotorrad nt jet ski
Wasserski fahren to water ski
Wassertreter m pedal boat/pedalo
Watte f cotton wool
Wattebausch m cotton bud
Wechsel m change
Wechselgeld nt change (small coins)
Wechselkurs m exchange rate
wechseln to change (money) ; to give change
Wechselstube f bureau de change
Weckdienst m early morning call
Wecker m alarm clock
Weckruf m alarm call
weder ... noch neither ... nor
Weg m path ; way ; country lane
wegfahren to leave in vehicle
weggehen to leave on foot
Wegweiser m signpost
Wegwerfwindeln pl disposable nappies
weh tun to ache ; to hurt (be painful)
weiblich female ; feminine
weich soft
weich gekochtes Ei nt soft-boiled egg
Weihnachten nt Christmas
Weihnachtsgeschenk nt Christmas present
Weihnachtskarte f Christmas card
weil because
Wein m wine
Weinberg m vineyard
Weinbrand m brandy
weinen to cry (weep)
Weinhandlung f wine shop
Weinkarte f wine list
Weinkeller m wine cellar
Weinprobe f wine-tasting
Weinstube f wine bar
Weintrauben pl grapes

weiß white
Weißbrot nt white bread
Weißwein m white wine
weit far ; loose (clothing)
weiter farther ; further on
weitermachen to continue
weitsichtig long sighted
Weizen m wheat
welche(r/s) which ; what ; which one
Wellen pl waves (on sea)
Welt f world
Wende f U-turn (in car)
wenden to turn
wenig little
weniger less
wenn if ; when (with present tense)
wer? who?
Werbespot m advert (on TV)
werden to become
Werk nt plant (factory) ; work (of art)
Werkstatt f garage (for repairs)
Werktag m weekday
Werkzeug nt tool
Werkzeugkasten m toolkit
Wert m value
Wertbrief m registered letter
Wertsachen pl valuables
wertvoll valuable
wesentlich essential
Wespe f wasp
wessen? whose?
Weste f waistcoat
Westen m west
westlich western
Wetter nt weather
Wetterbericht m weather forecast
Wettervorhersage f weather forecast
Wettkampf m match (sport)
Whirlpool m jacuzzi
wichtig important
wie like ; how
  wie viel? how much?
  wie viele? how many?
wieder again
wiederaufladen to recharge (battery)
wiederholen to repeat
wiegen to weigh
Wien Vienna
Wiese f lawn ; meadow
Wild nt game (hunting, meat)
Wildleder nt suede
Wildschwein nt boar
willkommen welcome

Wimpern *pl* eyelashes
Wimperntusche *f* mascara
Wind *m* wind
Windeln *pl* nappies ; diapers
windig windy
Windmühle *f* windmill
Windpocken *pl* chickenpox
Windschutz *m* windbreak *(camping)*
Windschutzscheibe *f* windscreen
windstill calm *(weather)*
Winter *m* winter
Winterreifen *pl* snow tyres
wir we
wirksam effective *(remedy, etc)*
Wirt(in) *m(f)* landlord (landlady)
Wirtschaft *f* pub ; inn ; economy
wissen to know *(facts)*
Witwe(r) *f(m)* widow(er)
Witz *m* joke
wo? where?
Woche *f* week
Wochenende *nt* weekend
Wochentag *m* weekday
wöchentlich weekly
woher? where from?
wohin? where to?
Wohnadresse *f* home address
wohnen to stay ; to live *(reside)*
Wohnheim *nt* hostel
Wohnmobil *nt* dormobile
Wohnort *m* home address
Wohnung *f* flat *(apartment)*
Wohnwagen *m* caravan
Wohnzimmer *nt* living room ; lounge *(in house)*
wolkig cloudy
Woll- woollen
Wolldecke *f* blanket
Wolle *f* wool
wollen to want *(wish for)*
Wort *nt* word
   in Worten in words *(on cheques)*
Wörterbuch *nt* dictionary
Wunde *f* wound *(injury)*
Würfel *m* dice
Wurst *f* sausage
Würstchenbude *f* hot-dog stand
würzig spicy
Würzmischung *f* seasoning

Y

Yachthafen *m* marina

Z

zäh tough *(meat)*
Zahl *f* number *(figure)*
zahlen to pay
Zähler *m* meter
Zahn *m* tooth
Zahnarzt (Zahnärztin) *m/f* dentist
Zahnbürste *f* toothbrush
Zahncreme *f* toothpaste
Zähne *pl* teeth
Zahnpasta *f* toothpaste
Zahnschmerzen *pl* toothache
Zahnseide *f* dental floss
Zahnstocher *m* toothpick
Zange *f* pliers
Zäpfchen *nt* suppository
z.B. e.g.
Zebrastreifen *m* zebra crossing
Zehe *f* toe
Zeichentrickfilm *m* cartoon
Zeichnung *f* drawing
zeigen to show
Zeit *f* time *(of day)*
Zeitkarte *f* season ticket
Zeitschrift *f* magazine
Zeitung *f* newspaper
Zeitungskiosk *m* newsstand
Zelt *nt* tent
Zeltboden *m* groundsheet
zelten to camp
Zentimeter *m* centimetre
zentral central
Zentralheizung *f* central heating
Zentralverriegelung *f* central locking *(car)*
Zentrum *nt* centre
zerbrechlich fragile ; breakable
zerrissen torn
Ziege *f* goat
Ziegel *m* brick
ziehen pull
Ziel *nt* destination ; goal ; target
ziemlich quite *(rather)*
Zigarette(n) *f* cigarette(s)
Zigarettenpapier *nt* cigarette papers
Zigarre(n) *f* cigar(s)
Zimmer *nt* room *(in house, hotel)*
   Zimmer frei vacancies
Zimmermädchen *nt* chambermaid

Zimmernachweis *m* accommodation information
Zimmernummer *f* room number
Zimmerservice *m* room service
Zirkus *m* circus
Zitrone *f* lemon
Zitronentee *m* lemon tea
Zoll *m* customs/toll
zollfrei duty-free
Zone *f* zone
Zoo *m* zoo
Zopf *m* plait
zornig angry
zu to ; off *(water supply)* ; too ; at
 zu Hause at home
 zu mieten for hire
 zu verkaufen for sale
 zu viel too much
 zu viel berechnen to overcharge
zubereiten to prepare
Zucchini *pl* courgettes
Zucker *m* sugar
zuckerfrei sugar-free
Zuckerkrankheit *f* diabetes
zudrehen to turn off *(tap)*
Zug *m* train
Zuhause *nt* home
zuhören to listen
Zukunft *f* future
Zulassung *f* log book *(car)*
Zuname *m* surname
Zündkerzen *pl* spark plugs
Zündschlüssel *m* ignition key
Zündung *f* ignition
Zunge *f* tongue
zurück back
zurückfahren to go back *(by car)*
zurückgeben to give back
zurückgehen to go back *(on foot)*
zurückkommen to come back
zurücklassen to leave behind
zusammen together
Zusammenstoß *m* crash *(collision)*
zusätzlich extra ; additional
zuschauen to watch
Zuschlag *m* surcharge ; supplement
zuschließen to lock
Zustellung *f* delivery *(of mail)*
Zutaten *pl* ingredients
Zutritt *m* entry ; admission
 Zutritt verboten no entry

zu viel too much
 zu viel berechnen to overcharge
zuzüglich extra
zwanglose Kleidung *f* informal dress
zwei two
Zweigstelle *f* branch *(office)*
zweimal twice
zweite(r/s) second
zweite Klasse *f* second class
Zwiebel *f* bulb ; onion
Zwillinge *pl* twins
zwischen between
Zwischenstecker *m* adaptor
Zyste *f* cyst

HOW GERMAN WORKS

NOUNS

*A **noun** is word such as **car**, **horse** or **Mary** which is used to refer to
a person or thing.*

Unlike English, German nouns have a gender: they are either masculine (**der**),
feminine (**die**) or neuter (**das**). Therefore words for *the* and *a(n)* must agree
with the noun they accompany whether masculine, feminine, neuter or plural.
Note that in German all nouns begin with a capital letter.

	masculine	*feminine*	*neuter*
the	**der Mann**	**die Frau**	**das Licht**
a, **an**	**ein Mann**	**eine Frau**	**ein Licht**

The plural forms vary from noun to noun – there is no universal plural as in
English (cat – cats, dog – dogs):

singular	*plural*
Mann	**Männer**
Frau	**Frauen**
Tisch	**Tische**

The plural for **the** for all forms is **die**:

die Männer   **die Frauen**   **die Lichter**

There's no plural for the **ein** form. The plural noun is used on its own.

From the phrases in this book you'll see that the endings for the word for **the**
vary according to what part the noun plays in the sentence:

If the noun is the subject of the sentence, i.e. carrying out the action, then it is
in the *nominative* case (the one found in dictionaries), e.g. **der Mann steht
auf** (**the man stands up**). The subject **der Mann** comes before the verb.

If the noun is the direct object of the sentence, i.e. the action of the verb is
being carried out on the noun, then the noun is in the *accusative* case, e.g.
ich sehe den Mann (**I see the man**). Note how **der** has changed to **den**. The
same applies to **ein**,
e.g. **ich sehe einen Mann** (**I see a man**).

If you see in front of the English noun **of**, or **'s** or **s'** at the end of the noun,
then the noun is in the *genitive* case (i.e. it belongs to someone or something),
e.g. **das Haus der Frau** (**the woman's house**). Note how **die** has changed to
der. The same applies to **ein**,
e.g. **das Haus einer Frau** (**a woman's house**).

If you see **to the** or **to a** in front of the English noun, then the noun is in the
dative case, e.g. **ich gebe es der Frau** (**I give it to the woman**). Note how
die has changed to **der**. The same applies to **ein**,
e.g. **ich gebe es einer Frau** (**I give it to a woman**).

Other words used before nouns have similar endings to **der** and **ein**.

Those like **der** are:
dieser (**this**) ; **jener** (**that**) ; **jeder** (**each**) ; **welcher** (**which**)

Those like **ein** are:
mein (**my**) ; **dein** (**your** – familiar singular) ; **Ihr** (**your** – polite singular and
plural) ; **sein** (**this**) ; **ihr** (**her**) ; **unser** (**our**) ; **euer** (**your** – familiar plural) ; **ihr**
(**their**)

Below are the cases for **der**:

	masculine	feminine	neuter	plural
Nominative	**der Mann**	**die Frau**	**das Licht**	**die Frauen**
Accusative	**den Mann**	**die Frau**	**das Licht**	**die Frauen**
Genitive	**des Mannes**	**der Frau**	**des Lichtes**	**der Frauen**
Dative	**dem Mann**	**der Frau**	**dem Licht**	**den Frauen**

Here are the cases for **ein**:

	masculine	feminine	neuter
Nominative	**ein Mann**	**eine Frau**	**ein Licht**
Accusative	**einen Mann**	**eine Frau**	**ein Licht**
Genitive	**eines Mannes**	**einer Frau**	**eines Lichtes**
Dative	**einem Mann**	**einer Frau**	**einem Licht**

The word **kein** (**no**, **not any**) also has the same endings as for **ein**, except that it can be used in the plural:

Nominative	**keine Männer**	Genitive	**keiner Männer**
Accusative	**keine Männer**	Dative	**keinen Männern**

MY, YOUR, HIS, HER, OUR, ITS, THEIR

These words all take the same endings as for **ein** and agree with the noun they accompany, i.e. whether *masculine*, *feminine*, etc and according to the noun's function (*nominative*, *accusative*, etc):

mein Mann kommt (**my husband is coming**) *(nominative)*

ich liebe meinen Mann (**I love my husband**) *(accusative)*

das Auto meines Mannes (**my husband's car**) *(genitive)*

ich gebe es meinem Mann (**I give it to my husband**) *(dative)*

meine Kinder kommen (**my children are coming**) *(nominative plural)*

ich liebe meine Kinder (**I love my children**) *(accusative plural)*

die Spielsachen meiner (**Kinder my children's toys**) *(genitive plural)*

ich gebe es meinen (**Kindern I give it to my children**) *(dative plural)*

Other words which take these endings are:
dein (**your** – familiar singular) ; **sein** (**his**) ; **ihr** (**her**) ; **unser** (**our**) ; **euer** (**your** – familiar plural) ; **Ihr** (**your** – polite singular and plural) ; **ihr** (**their**)

ADJECTIVES

*An **adjective** is a word such as **small**, **pretty** or **practical** that describes a person or thing, or gives extra information about them.*

When adjectives are used before a noun, their endings vary like the words for **der** and **ein**, depending on the gender (*masculine*, *feminine* or *neuter*) and whether the noun is plural, and how the noun is used in the sentence (whether it is the subject, object, etc). Here are examples using the adjective **klug – clever**

	masculine	feminine
Nominative	**der kluge Mann**	**die kluge Frau**
	ein kluger Mann	**eine kluge Frau**
Accusative	**den klugen Mann**	**die kluge Frau**
	einen klugen Mann	**eine kluge Frau**
Genitive	**des klugen Mannes**	**der klugen Frau**
	eines klugen Mannes	**einer klugen Frau**
Dative	**dem klugen Mann**	**der klugen Frau**
	einem klugen Mann	**einer klugen Frau**

	neuter	plural
Nominative	**das kluge Kind**	**die klugen Männer**
	ein kluges Kind	**kluge Frauen**
Accusative	**das kluge Kind**	**die klugen Männer**
	ein kluges Kind	**kluge Frauen**
Genitive	**des klugen Kindes**	**der klugen Männer**
	eines klugen Kindes	**kluger Frauen**
Dative	**dem klugen Kind**	**den klugen Männern**
	einem klugen Kind	**klugen Frauen**

When the adjective follows the verb, then there is no agreement:
der Mann ist klug / die Frau ist klug / das Kind ist klug

PRONOUNS

*A **pronoun** is a word that you use to refer to someone or something when you do not need to use a noun, often because the person or thing has been mentioned earlier. Examples are **it**, **she**, **something** and **myself**.*

subject		direct object	
I	ich	**me**	mich
you *(familiar singular)*	du	**you** *(familiar singular)*	dich
he/it *(masculine)*	er	**him/it** *(masculine)*	ihn
she/it *(feminine)*	sie	**her/it** *(feminine)*	sie
it *(neuter)*	es	**it** *(neuter)*	es
we	wir	**us**	uns
you *(familiar plural)*	ihr	**you** *(familiar plural)*	euch
you *(polite singular & plural)*	**Sie**	**you** *(polite singular & plural)*	**Sie**
they *(all genders)*	sie	**them** *(all genders)*	sie

Indirect object pronouns are:

mir (**to me**) ; **dir** (**to you**) *(familiar singular)* ; **ihm** (**to him/it**) ; **ihr** (**to her/it**) ; **ihm** (**to it**) *(neuter)* ; **uns** (**to us**) ; **euch** (**to you**) *(familiar plural)* ; **Ihnen** (**to you**) *(polite singular and plural)* ; **ihnen** (**to them**)

In German there are two ways of addressing people: the familiar form – **du** (when talking to just one person you know well), **ihr** (when talking to more than one person you know well), and the polite form – **Sie** (always written with a capital letter), which can be used for one or more people.

VERBS

19

*A **verb** is a word such as **sing**, **walk** or **cry** which is used with a subject to say what someone or something does or what happens to them. **Regular verbs** (weak verbs in German) follow the same pattern of endings. **Irregular verbs** (strong verbs in German) do not follow a regular pattern so you need to learn the different endings.*

There are two main types of verb in German – **weak** verbs (which are regular) and **strong** verbs (which are irregular).

	weak	*strong*
	SPIELEN (TO PLAY)	HELFEN (TO HELP)
ich	spiele	helfe
du	spielst	hilfst
er/sie/es	spielt	hilft
wir	spielen	helfen
ihr	spielt	helft
Sie	spielen	helfen
sie	spielen	helfen

Other examples of **strong** verbs are:

	SEIN (TO BE)	HABEN (TO HAVE)
ich	bin	habe
du	bist	hast
er/sie/es	ist	hat
wir	sind	haben
ihr	seid	habt
Sie	sind	haben
sie	sind	haben

To make a verb negative, add **nicht**:

ich verstehe nicht	*I don't understand*
das funktioniert nicht	*it doesn't work*

PAST TENSE

Here are a number of useful past tenses:

ich war	*I was*
wir waren	*we were*
Sie waren	*you were (polite)*
ich hatte	*I had*
wir hatten	*we had*
Sie hatten	*you had (polite)*
ich/er/sie/es spielte	*I/he/she/it played*
Sie/wir/sie spielten	*you/we/they played*
ich/er/sie/es half	*I/he/she/it helped*
Sie/wir/sie halfen	*you/we/they helped*

Another past form corresponds to the English **have ...ed** and uses the verb **haben** (**to have**):

ich habe gespielt	*I have played*
wir haben geholfen	*we have helped*

In German the present tense is very often used where we would use the future tense in English:

ich schicke ein Fax	*I will send a fax*
ich schreibe einen Brief	*I will write a letter*